DEVELOPMENT OF THE EMERGING COUNTRIES

Paper $2.75   Library edition in cloth $3.75

Development of the Emerging Countries

An Agenda for Research

ROBERT E. ASHER
EVERETT E. HAGEN
ALBERT O. HIRSCHMAN
GERHARD COLM
THEODORE GEIGER

ARTHUR T. MOSHER
R. S. ECKAUS
MARY JEAN BOWMAN
C. ARNOLD ANDERSON
HOWARD WRIGGINS

1962

THE BROOKINGS INSTITUTION · WASHINGTON, D.C.

© 1962 by

THE BROOKINGS INSTITUTION

Published February 1962

Library of Congress Catalog Card Number 62-12716

Foreword

THE PROMOTION OF GROWTH AND ORDERLY CHANGE in the less developed nations of the world has become, unlike the weather, a problem about which everyone not only talks—but almost everyone is now doing something. Nevertheless, our present knowledge of the economics, politics, sociology, and psychology of development is gravely deficient.

The essays which follow suggest research that might contribute in some measure to remedying the present deficiency. They were prepared for the Brookings Institution early in 1961. They were not commissioned with a view to providing a comprehensive catalog of research needs, but with the more modest objective of singling out a few problems expected to be of particular concern to American policy makers during the 1960's—problems on which additional research might be especially necessary and timely.

The essays were prepared in the first instance as papers or statements for a conference of some 75 specialists from universities, government agencies, foundations, and research institutions. The conference was held at the Brookings Institution May 25-27, 1961. The papers and statements were then revised in the light of the discussions at the conference and reproduced in multilithed form in limited quantity under the title *Research Needs for Development Assistance Programs*. The present volume is issued in order to make certain of those essays available in a more permanent form to a wider audience.

The authors are indebted to the conference participants for many stimulating, constructive suggestions. The essays, however, express their personal views and should not be interpreted as necessarily reflecting the views of other conference participants or of the trustees, the officers, or other staff members of the Brookings Institution.

The Institution is grateful not only to the authors—C. Arnold Anderson, Robert E. Asher (who assumed primary responsibility for organizing the Brookings conference and for bringing out this volume), Mary Jean Bowman, Gerhard Colm, Richard S. Eckaus, Theodore

Geiger, Everett E. Hagen, Albert O. Hirschman, Arthur T. Mosher, and Howard Wriggins—but also to the Advisory Committee whose active interest and wise counsel have been immensely helpful since the inception of the project. The members of the Advisory Committee are: Robert E. Asher, Stephen Bailey, Vincent M. Barnett, Jr., William C. Foster, Theodore Geiger, James P. Grant, Everett E. Hagen, Samuel P. Hayes, Bert F. Hoselitz, John B. Howard, Edward S. Mason, Walsh McDermott, Henry Owen, James Quillen, Joseph E. Slater, Donald C. Stone, and Kenneth Thompson.

The project has been executed under the general supervision of H. Field Haviland, Jr., Director of Foreign Policy Studies. The manuscript has been ably edited by A. Evelyn Breck and the index prepared by Pauline Manning.

Financing has been provided jointly by the Ford Foundation and the International Cooperation Administration (ICA). References in the text to the ICA have for the most part been left unchanged but may be regarded as applicable also to the Agency for International Development (AID), which succeeded the ICA in November 1961. The full and friendly cooperation received by the Brookings Institution at every stage of the undertaking from the staffs of the Ford Foundation, the ICA, and the AID has been even more important than the financial support of these organizations.

Robert D. Calkins
President

January 2, 1962

Contents

ix

1

A Framework for Analyzing Economic and Political Change

EVERETT E. HAGEN*

THE RESULTS OF ECONOMIC AND TECHNICAL AID to low-income countries have sometimes been gratifying, but at other times they have been disappointing. The assistance sometimes seems to make no impact, and some projects that seem technically and economically sound to Americans simply do not work well.

The reasons for these disappointing results often given by frustrated technical advisers and aid administrators are in the general vein that the recipients were venal or nepotistic, careless or thoughtless, or just do not want to change or have "no head for business." But, since the people of the low-income countries obviously are intelligent and obviously do want economic progress, these reasons do not get very far into the matter. It is useful to ask: If individuals are careless or thoughtless, or do not want to change, why is this true? Why do they permit nepotism or venality to interfere with economic efficiency? The history of virtually every country indicates administrative feats (in war, empire-building, or engineering, for example) far exceeding in complexity the operation of business enterprises. Why, then, are they inept at business operations at this moment in their histories?

Obviously, the difficulties rest deep in the culture and social structure of a society, but this observation is of little value unless something useful can be said concerning their roots. Obviously, too, some of the attitudes mentioned must change if economic development is to pro-

* Professor of Economics, Center for International Studies, Massachusetts Institute of Technology.

1

ceed, or if democratic government is to emerge. Do we have any systematic analytical knowledge concerning the causes and course of social and cultural change and its relationship to technical, economic, and political change?

The purpose of this essay is to discuss four questions: (1) Is technical-economic change necessarily interwoven with social-political change? (2) Do we have enough knowledge of the forces at work so that we can understand some of the interrelationships? (3) Do we know enough to say anything to administrators of economic and technical aid that will aid them in their operations? (4) What further research is pertinent?

The answer given to each of the first three questions is "yes," though it is spoken in a rather low voice concerning the third.

TABLE 1.1

Classification of Asian and African Countries by Type of Political Structure and Rank in Economic Development

RANK IN ECONOMIC DEVELOPMENT	COMPETITIVENESS OF POLITICAL STRUCTURE		
	COMPETITIVE	SEMICOMPETITIVE	AUTHORITARIAN
1	Lebanon		
2	Malaya		
3			United Arab Republic
4	Philippines		
5	Turkey		
6			Iraq
7	Ceylon		
8		Morocco	
9		Jordan	
10		Tunisia	
11			Libya
12		Ghana	
13			Iran
14		Thailand	
15		Indonesia	
16	India		
17		Malagasy Republic	
18			Saudi Arabia
19		Burma	
20		Cambodia	
21		Cameroons	
22		South Vietnam	
23		Nigeria	
24			Pakistan
25			Laos
26			Liberia
27			Sudan
28		Togoland	
29			Ethiopia
30			Afghanistan

Source: See footnote 2, p. 5.

THE INTERRELATEDNESS OF SOCIAL, CULTURAL, POLITICAL, AND TECHNICAL-ECONOMIC CHANGE

In fully traditional societies, the political structure is hierarchical and authoritarian, methods of production continue unchanged or little changed from generation to generation, and the level of income is constant. When technical and economic changes have occurred in such societies, they have been concomitant with far-reaching changes in attitudes toward life, social structure, and political organization. These changes are not merely results of economic change; often they have occurred first. The interrelatedness in time is so striking that it suggests important questions about the causal relationships, and about the nature and degree of social and cultural change that must occur if technical and economic change is to proceed.[1]

Political Structure and Economic Development

Impressive evidence of the interrelations lies in the correlation between the nature of the political structure in the countries of Asia, Africa, and Latin America and the level of economic development. In Table 1.1 forty countries or colonies of Asia and Africa have been arranged in three columns, according to whether their political processes were judged to be authoritarian, semicompetitive, or competitive, and have been ranked vertically according to their position on an index of economic development derived by averaging eleven separate economic indexes. In Table 1.2, the same has been done for twenty countries of Latin America. All independent countries for which data were availa-

[1] Among the major contributions to the literature examining the relationships among the various dimensions of change within a society are the following: G. A. Almond, J. S. Coleman *et al.*, *The Politics of the Developing Areas* (Princeton University Press, 1960); K. Davis and H. H. Golden, "Urbanization and the Development of Pre-Industrial Areas," *Economic Development and Cultural Change*, Vol. 3 (October 1954); H. H. Golden, "Literacy and Social Change in Underdeveloped Countries," *Rural Sociology*, Vol. 20 (March 1955); D. Lerner, "Communications Systems and Social Systems: Statistical Exploration in History and Policy," *Behavioral Science*, Vol. 2 (October 1957); Lerner with L. W. Pevsner, *The Passing of Traditional Society* (Free Press, 1958); S. Lipset, "Some Social Requisites of Democracy: Economic Development and Political Legitimacy," *American Political Science Review*, Vol. 53 (March 1959); L. W. Shannon, *Underdeveloped Areas* (Harper, 1957); Shannon, "Is Level of Development Related to Capacity for Self-Government?" *American Journal of Economics and Sociology*, Vol. 17 (July 1958); Shannon, "Socio-Economic Development and Political Status," *Social Problems*, Vol. 7 (Fall 1959); C. Wolf, Jr., *Foreign Aid: Theory and Practice in Southern Asia* (Princeton University Press, 1960).

ble except the Union of South Africa and a few odd cases such as Kuwait and Qatar have been included.

A competitive social structure is one in which the interests of different groups in the society obtain a voice in political decisions, the decision being a compromise or a victory for some group or groups over others; a semicompetitive structure is one in which among a sector of the population there is competitive political activity, but another important sector has no voice; and an authoritarian structure is one in which there is a hierarchy of power, with political decisions coming from the top. It should be noted that the former two categories are not equivalent to semidemocratic and democratic, though there is a relationship. In the semicompetitive and competitive structures, the interests of each group, which compete for satisfaction, may be those of traditional or otherwise authoritative leaders, not a democratic expression of desires. The classification is admittedly rough and subjective, but political systems do differ in their degrees of competitiveness, and it is justifiable to attempt to classify them according to this difference. Ideally, there should be more than three classes, but information available does not permit a finer classification. Even concerning the group-

TABLE 1.2

Classification of Latin American Countries by Type of Political Structure and Rank in Economic Development

RANK IN ECONOMIC DEVELOPMENT	COMPETITIVENESS OF POLITICAL STRUCTURE		
	COMPETITIVE	SEMICOMPETITIVE	AUTHORITARIAN
1	Argentina		
2	Uruguay		
3	Venezuela		
4			Cuba
5	Chile		
6		Panama	
7		Mexico	
8	Costa Rica		
9		Colombia	
10	Brazil		
11			Paraguay
12		Peru	
13		Ecuador	
14			Dominican Republic
15			Nicaragua
16			El Salvador
17			Bolivia
18		Guatemala	
19			Honduras
20			Haiti

Source: See footnote 2, p. 5.

ing into three categories, the reader will probably disagree in individual cases, but his disagreements will probably not greatly alter the groupings or the degree of correlation shown in Tables 1.1 and 1.2.

The eleven indexes of economic development reflected in the vertical position of the countries are the following:[2]

Welfare:
  1. GNP per person in 1957.
  2. Doctors per 1,000 persons in about 1956.
Communications:
  3. Vehicles per 10,000 persons in about 1958.
  4. Telephones per 10,000 persons in about 1958.
  5. Radios per 1,000 persons in about 1957.
  6. Newspaper circulation per 1,000 persons in about 1956.
Industrialization:
  7. Energy consumption per person in about 1958.
  8. Per cent of labor force employed outside agriculture and service sectors, latest census year.
Urbanization:
  9. Per cent of population in cities over 100,000 population in about 1955.
Education:
  10. Per cent of population literate at a date within or close to 1950-1960.
  11. Ratio of enrollment in primary schools to population of school age.

[2] An exercise similar to this one is presented by James S. Coleman in the concluding chapter of *The Politics of the Developing Areas*, and acknowledgment is due to Coleman for the idea and procedure of the correlation. The analysis presented here, however, was done at the Center for International Studies, Massachusetts Institute of Technology, and subsequently adapted slightly by this author. It differs from Coleman's in certain respects, of which the most important are the omission of colonies, substitution of one new index of economic modernization, and giving equal weight in the combined index to each of the five groups rather than to each of the eleven indexes.

Before Coleman, S. Lipset had suggested the relationship and performed a similar exercise.

For Coleman's category *Per cent of population in labor unions,* that of *Per cent of labor force outside agriculture and service sector* was substituted. The data were gathered independently and no doubt differ from Coleman's in detail. Coleman ranked his countries according to each of the eleven indexes, then took a simple average of the rankings for each country and derived his composite ranking from it. Various alternative methods of averaging were used in the M.I.T. research, to determine whether the method of weighting materially affects the results. As among the different methods of weighting tested, it does not. Before weighting, the magnitudes (not indexes) in each of the eleven categories were first reduced to an index whose lowest value is zero by reducing the magnitude for each country by the amount of the minimum one (thereby reducing that one to zero), then dividing each either by (a) the maximum or (b) the mean of the resulting magnitudes. The methods of weighting tested then were: equal weighting for each of the five groups indicated in the text, using variant (a); the same, using variant (b); and each of these two variants, using only four groups, consisting of categories 1 and 7; 5 and 6; 9; and 10. Tables 1.1 and 1.2 are the first variant. I have altered Coleman's classification of the following countries according to their political structure: Coleman classed Cambodia, Venezuela, and Guatemala as authoritarian, and Iran as semicompetitive. Like the tables, the textual discussion reflects suggestions by Coleman, but it does not rest on his material to the degree that the basic idea of the exercise and the preparation of the rankings does.

Latin America versus Asia-Africa

Politically, socially, culturally, and technically, the situation in Latin America and that in Asia and Africa are so different that separate treatment seems appropriate. In the independent countries of Asia and Africa, with the exception of the Union of South Africa, the problem is one of change in an indigenous society, whereas in Latin America Europeans conquered the countries and continued to rule them after gaining independence from their motherlands, so that the problem is one of adaptation of European culture to a new situation by a conquering group. The Spanish and Portuguese came to sparsely populated Latin America in numbers and strength great enough so that they settled down, remained the national elite even after the various countries attained independence between 1810 and 1825, and, with much intermarriage with the Indian populations, remain the national elites today. Economic growth therefore did not have to be implanted into a non-European culture. Personality traits and social practices moderately favorable to it were brought over by the continuing stream of immigrants. Even though these immigrants were largely from southern Europe, where growth has been slower than in northwestern Europe, still they were European in their culture and technical background, and this fact probably explains the greater degree of economic development of Latin America.

But independence was not independence of indigenous populations from Europeans, but only of colonial Europeans from continental Europeans. The colonial Europeans continued to dominate their countries in the authoritarian manner of colonial administrations. The colonial relationship was domesticated. A voice in the government for the majorities of the populations was denied in every Latin American country until the twentieth century, and in some up to the present time. As might be supposed, Latin American countries as a group are relatively advanced economically, relatively authoritarian or noncompetitive politically.

Exceptions: Reactive Authoritarian Reformers

It is obvious from Tables 1.1 and 1.2 that there is a high degree of correlation between degree of political competitiveness and degree of economic development. By and large, the array of countries sweeps downward to the right. Higher degrees of economic modernization are associated with greater competitiveness of political structure.

The correlation would be even higher except for the presence in the authoritarian category of three countries that are not traditional authoritarian cases. These three are Cuba, the United Arab Republic, and Iraq. In these cases, the country was ruled by force for a substantial period by repressive governments which, while permitting extensive foreign activities and while tolerating or even encouraging certain kinds of modernization, based their domestic power on landowners and other conservative groups linked to the traditional society. These governments and groups indicated not only lack of sympathy but contempt for the persons and purposes of the lower classes of the people; treated them indeed, like cattle, or as tools to satisfy their own interests. Ultimately, revolution resulted.

Over a considerable period of time the old regimes had harshly suppressed moderate reform movements, killing their leaders or driving them into hiding, exile, or passivity. Such a situation has two important results that are pertinent here.

First, it tends to breed a revolutionary movement with an authoritarian dynamic of its own. If the revolutionary movement is to succeed in such conspiratorial circumstances, it must develop a highly disciplined and hierarchical style of organization which may have important implications for the structure of its rule over the country once the revolution has taken place. In addition, a repressive framework of political activity tends to draw into underground revolutionary activity individuals who themselves are authoritarian, individuals who feel anxiety when any rival power exists and feel safe only when possessing undisputed supreme power themselves, or when following the leadership of a fellow rebel who possesses such power.[3] The government that such

---

[3] This may seem like retrospective definition; a person is said to have such a personality if he is seen to act in this way. In fact, however, the personality type involved is one that in clear cases can be identified in childhood, before any action is manifest. The psychologist Erik H. Erikson has suggested that some individuals develop these personality traits because in infancy and childhood they faced tyranny by arbitrary fathers, but whose childhood was such that they dared to dream of attacking authority rather than submitting supinely. When the emotional pattern thus learned in childhood fits the facts of later public life, their childhood emotional patterns are reinforced and dominate their life histories. See Erikson, *Childhood and Society* (W. W. Norton, 1950), chapter on "Hitler's Childhood," and his *Young Man Luther* (W. W. Norton, 1958). Such individuals, it may be added, tend to occur in considerable numbers when the customary authoritarian patterns of child care in a traditional society are carried over into transitional circumstances. In the traditional society, they bred individuals who simply submitted to authority, but in the less rigid circumstances of transitional society, they may breed individuals who dream of revolt and of supreme authority for themselves.

individuals set up in the name of liberty is, by a familiar historical pattern, an authoritarian one.

Secondly, the political repression gradually convinces the mass of the people, increasingly bitter under their frustration and humiliation, that they can find no relief in moderate movements for reform, and it gradually breeds in them bitterness and rage that are satisfied only by the harsh suppression of the old tyrants, the class that supported them, and all who are thought to have been associated with them. Violence and extremism are demanded. Those demands may continue until the bitter generation dies, by which time a new authoritarian government may be firmly established in power and may for the time being satisfy the people so long as it meets their emotional needs.

For these and related reasons, movements that overthrew despotisms often have themselves been authoritarian. The more despotic the old regime, the more likely this result. Thus Nasser, Kassem, and Castro, and before them Lenin and Mao, and before them the leaders of the French Revolution and many other revolutionaries, substituted one authoritarian regime for another, finding their support in the peasants, workers, and intellectuals whose interests had been underrepresented in the previous authoritarian regimes. If the three conspicuous cases noted above are removed from the classifications in Tables 1.1 and 1.2, the correlations, as has been suggested, are appreciably increased. There are other countries in all three continents where the presence of repressive regimes poses the threat of authoritarian revolt, but they need not concern us here.[4]

Apart from these cases of authoritarian rebellion against despotism, there are other countries which lie at one side of a perfect line of relationship between degree of political competitiveness and of economic development. In spite of these complicating factors, Tables 1.1 and 1.2 present impressive evidence of the relationship between political and economic change.

[4] As of mid-1961, Iran in Asia and the Dominican Republic in Latin America appear to be examples of nations standing in some danger of a revolutionary upheaval which might lead to such a new authoritarianism. Yet the turmoil in May 1961 which led Shah Pahlevi Reza of Iran to install a prime minister who sincerely desires reform and will act to get it may avert the revolution there if the Shah continues to support him. As this is written in June 1961, the superficial evidence of political change in the Dominican Republic is less impressive. Only the dominating physical power of the non-native elite, which for the time being is unassailable, prevents revolution in the Union of South Africa, and one may suppose that the incredibly bloody result would be either tribal chaos or government far more extreme in its authoritarianism than that in Cuba. One wonders, also, about one or two other examples in Latin America (e.g., Paraguay), in Africa (e.g., Angola), and in Asia (e.g., Thailand), which on the surface are currently more quiet.

The Evidence of Historical Records

The histories of individual countries that are no longer traditional provide further evidence.

In Britain, the industrial revolution which gathered force gradually in the eighteenth century followed more than two centuries of social and religious tensions. During this period there occurred the adoption of Calvinism by the Scots and the emergence of strong Protestant dissent in England. And the dissenters and lowland Scots were present among the economic innovators in numbers out of all proportion to their numbers in the population at large.

In the countries of Western Europe, the industrial revolution got under way during or shortly after the series of upheavals in government and the social order which stretched from the French Revolution to the revolutions of the mid-nineteenth century. It is associated in time with the abolition of most elements of serfdom, with marked change in the accepted concepts of appropriate relationships among social classes, with extensions of representative government.

In Japan, in about 1600, after a period of disturbance and confusion, the Tokugawa and associated clans established an hegemony over the nation that was to last for more than 250 years. After their ascendancy to national power, the Tokugawa enforced regulations whose purpose was to freeze the social order and perpetuate the Tokugawa rule. Their result in fact was to create tensions that, economically, caused great pressure for expansion of income, and, socially, inexorably undermined the traditional structure. During the seventeenth and eighteenth centuries, discontented and frustrated social groups, after casting about elsewhere for satisfaction, turned gradually to study of the "barbarian books" of the West, which told how Westerners had become powerful. Early in the nineteenth century, individuals of these groups began to build pilot plants using Western methods, and before the Meiji Restoration, these economic shoots that had rooted in social discontent were flourishing. The discontent led to overthrow of the Tokugawa in 1868 and establishment of a centralized national government with radically new goals. When that government took steps to remove the institutional barriers to economic innovation, the economic shoots burst into flower.

In Russia, in 1667, the patriarch of Moscow, for the sake of diplomatic advantage, revised the Orthodox Church ritual and liturgical books to bring them into agreement with Greek practice. To many lower class members of the church, the change seemed sacrilegious and a threat to their bond with God. These Old Believers were condemned as schismatics, and were persecuted with varying vigor and harshness from the latter part of the seventeenth century until the early years of the twentieth. It surely is not coincidence that the Old Believers were prominent in the economic innovation which began to change the face of Russia in the nineteenth century.

In Turkey, economic growth began within a generation after Ataturk had seized the social order by the scruff of the neck and shaken it vigorously. Throughout Latin America, political tension and the transition to economic growth are intertwined. In China, the political upheaval associated with growth was as radical as in Russia.

It is contrary to the customary view of the world of most of us to think of these social and political changes as necessarily related to economic growth. We keep social history and economic history in different compartments in our minds. But can anyone who clears his mind of our assumptions and takes a fresh look at this evidence doubt that there are causal connections between social, cultural, political, and technical-economic change which have been little explored, and which need to be understood by aid administrators?

The Significance of the Correlation

The correlation between technical-economic and social-political change of course gives no indication of the direction of causation. It is rather obvious that economic change breeds social and political change. Increased productivity of the land gives new hope, or if the fruits are all taken from them, new frustrations, to peasants. The expansion of industrial activity, even if it is a gradual growth of small enterprises rather than a spectacular change, creates a middle class with interests opposed to those of a traditional ruling landed group. Increased industrialization, urbanization, and geographic movement widen horizons and create new ambitions. All of these changes breed political change.

But it would be reckless to neglect the possible flow of causation in the opposite direction, a recklessness in which many persons indulge. Without the breakdown of traditional social structure and, more important, traditional attitudes, economic and technical aid may produce little economic change. And perhaps the breakdown of tradition may not occur simply because traditional people see Western methods. Perhaps it has independent causes without understanding of which aid administrators are beating their heads rather naively against a stone wall. The sections to follow will suggest that is true.

SOCIAL AND CULTURAL BARRIERS TO ECONOMIC PROGRESS

What, then, are the social and cultural barriers which prevent individuals in traditional societies from acting effectively to obtain the economic progress whose fruits they desire?

Barriers in the Social Structure

Some aspects of the social structure that may be barriers to economic change are obvious. The members of a ruling landed class may be slow to consent to measures for transportation facilities, irrigation, or other projects to open up new land which its members do not own, especially if the results will be to create alternative opportunities for the agricultural laboring class which they now employ at subsistence wages. They may be slow to approve measures for communication and urban facilities which will have the same effect. They may be actively engaged in promoting measures that will siphon government revenues or economic aid funds into their pockets.

To some degree, these attitudes are apt to exist in any traditional society. Active opposition to a development program because it would disturb vested interests is the extreme case and not common, but it must be expected that the members of traditional influential groups will at best be indifferent to development and may attempt to divert development measures for their benefit. But it would be wrong to assume that if such individuals can be pushed aside, development will proceed. The more pervasive barriers are attitudes within most individuals in all groups of the society which constrain their own actions— make it impossible for them to visualize the possibility of change, make the activities necessary for economic change uninteresting or repugnant to them, or limit their creativity so that they cannot effectively carry out the necessary activities.

The Traditional View of the World as a Barrier

The simple folk of traditional society (the peasants, the menials, and the craftsmen) are impotent in the face of overwhelming forces around them. The peasant is a wise and skillful craftsman in the planting and cultivation of his crops, but drought or excessive rainfall may bring disaster, or the loss of an ox by disease may be a financial burden so insupportable that he is reduced from the status of cultivator to agricultural laborer. Through forces over which he has no control, and which he must assume to be the will of unseen powers, for he has no other explanation, half of the children he begets may die before the age of one year, and more before ten. His helplessness gives him a sense of impotence that makes it extremely difficult for him really to believe and act on the notion that by changing his method of doing things he can affect his destiny. It is dangerous to experiment, and that sense of danger often makes his mind reject suggestions of changes in methods that he is fully capable of understanding and applying.

Further, this sense of impotence and of danger in the environment around him makes him prefer to rely on others for decisions. It relieves his anxiety if the elders and persons in positions of authority make the decisions. But he does not merely wish to be dependent and submissive; it is always a component of such a personality that even the lowliest person expects in turn to exercise authority over his subordinates. The peasant will become an authority in the village when he becomes an elder. He will then share in the decision of village problems, but he will avoid the anxiety that being bold would create by making the decisions on the basis of tradition.

He will also be authoritarian in his parenthood. He feels that his children cannot cope with life out of their own resources, since he could not. Hence, after indulgence during their first few years of life, he expects them mainly to obey. His alarm and rebuke at independent initiative by them creates alarm and anxiety in them, and thus his sense of impotence, dependence, and anxiety at experimenting is bred into the next generation. These attitudes are not changeable by mere verbal logic; they are bred deep into the unconscious processes of personality.

As an extension of this sense that he is controlled by his father's will, he assumes that the major phenomena of life are caused by the wills of forces superior to him, namely, unseen spirits. On this assumption, the way to control events is to appeal to the spirits—by magic, by religious observances, by carefully following the ways of behavior that tradition has indicated seem acceptable to the spiritual powers. Since the spirits might disapprove of unconventional activity (as his father did), there are powerful inhibitions on him not to be a deviant—an innovator—in his behavior. These inhibitions may control his judgment. Moreover, by being a deviant, and offending the powers, he may endanger his community. Hence there are also strong social sanctions against unconventional experimentation in methods of production or other aspects of behavior.

It is often supposed that these personality factors influence the simple folk of traditional societies, but not the upper classes, who have more knowledge and wider contacts. However, the elite individual is in fact almost as impotent in the face of physical forces as is the peasant. Though he has more medical protection than does the peasant, his children too die from diseases he is largely helpless to fend off. Far more deaths in traditional societies are from lack of community sanitation and from mosquito-carried malaria than from causes associated with poverty. Even the medical care available to the rich is far from the equivalent of modern Western preventive and curative medicine. Moreover, the personalities of the upper classes are influenced by the fact that their childhood experiences are as authoritarian as are the childhood experiences of the children of the poor. The same sense of impotence and anxiety at depending on their own judgment is bred into them as is bred into the simple folk. This is why, under a verbal veneer of modern knowledge, members of the upper classes of traditional societies have the same deeply built-in sense of impotence as the poor, which inhibits their ability truly to believe that they can influence the course of events of the physical world, and to act on that belief.[5]

Traditional Values as Barriers

More important among the members of the elite may be their sense of the necessity of having an identity that distinguishes them from the simple folk. In any society, every man must have some sense of the justi-

[5] If the reader thinks that knowledge is a preventive of such an attitude, let him reflect that in the United States, in 1906, when mature, responsible, experienced newspaper and magazine reporters saw the Wrights fly their aeroplane at Kitty Hawk, and wired reports to their editors, the editors rejected the reports out of the desire not to be made to look foolish. Their assumption that the law of gravity prevents man from flying made them reject the evidence of unimpeachable witnesses.

fication of his being what he is. In a modern society, the individual can believe that he got ahead in life because of his own endeavors; this gives him a justification for having a position superior to that of someone else. In traditional society, however, with few exceptions the individual has his position in life through inheritance. He inherits his landed status, or his position as a member of the professional classes that the landed families spawn. He gets his governmental position, his scholarship to study abroad, virtually all of his advantages in life, in the same way.

For an individual so favored by virtue of simply who he is to be able to live with himself, it is necessary for him to believe that of his essence, not by virtue of what he does, he is superior to the simple folk. The most conspicuous characteristic of the simple folk is that they work with their hands, with tools, at jobs related to the physical world, jobs that get them dirty. Hence it is necessary for the upper class individual to believe that he is sufficiently refined so that such activity is uninteresting or repugnant to him. He learns this "with his guts," that is, in his unconscious processes, while a child, and not as a conscious mental conclusion—just as an American woman learns to fear a mouse or to be repelled by a snake. He can no more get over his attitude, and use his talents in technology or in managing a business enterprise than the American woman can overcome her aversion to mice. He will seek and accept a prestige-bearing position as head of a government enterprise, because such positions of authority are the due of his class, but his inhibitions make him incapable of performing effectively the functions needed to make the enterprise operate well.

Authority has a significance to elite individuals in a traditional society different from its significance to a person from a culture in which technical progress is going on. The typical elite official received his authority, not because of his demonstrated capability in the field, but because he has the proper family background and has been educated at the proper schools. His authority is a symbol of his eliteness, his superior identity as an individual. To delegate part of his authority to subordinates is to give up part of his eliteness. To ask subordinates for their judgment before making a decision is to suggest that they are as worthy of elite status as he. Even to ask them for factual information as a basis for decision may imply that he is not really worthy enough to bear the authority, since he must depend on subordinates. Doing so threatens the difference in identity between him and the subordinate. Hence he will cling to his authority, not deliberately but unconsciously. He will not be able effectively to manage an enterprise except one in which he can depend on traditional rules. His decisions concerning new functions will be authoritarian and often not responsive to the purposes to be served, objectively viewed. Technical and scientific education or formal training in administration will have almost no impact on these inhibitions, just as learning in a biology class that snakes are clean creatures and perform useful functions does not make them attractive to a person who is repelled by them.

Moreover, in an uncertain and somewhat hazardous world, the security offered by an individual's position within his family or clan or other primary group is of especial importance, and to protect his family and advance its interests is a moral duty that takes primacy over any more general obligations to the society. In pursuing this moral duty, the individual will often be, in Western terms, corrupt, insensitive to the public interest, and nepotistic. But only to a person who has acquired modern values does this conduct seem immoral.

Such factors as these, I suggest, explain why technical advice is sometimes disregarded; why intelligent men fail grossly to run productive government enterprises effectively; why, in spite of agreeing with the principle of delegation, they turn out in fact to be incapable of delegating to inferiors the authority necessary to make modern business enterprises work or to carry out a government economic development program effectively.

These are not the only factors that inhibit change. It seems probable that the conditions of life and of childhood environment sketched above make traditional individuals less creative than they would have become in other circumstances. This is certainly an important deterrent to economic growth, for economic growth requires a high degree of creativity.

Creativity Necessary in the Transition to Economic Growth

Advance in scientific and technical knowledge beyond present frontiers obviously requires creativity. But, it is sometimes suggested, the advances that have occurred in the West are here for all the world to learn. Since underdeveloped countries can draw on them, technical and economic advance in these countries requires not creativity, but mainly imitation.

This, however, turns out not to be true. Previous technological advance abroad of course makes technological progress in a low-income society easier than otherwise. Nevertheless, a tremendous degree of creative innovation is required for technological progress in any traditional society, even with the techniques of the West available for the asking.

This is true for several reasons. First, Western methods use elaborate facilities and much productive equipment per worker. Every worker in every industry directly and indirectly has available a tremendous amount of equipment. In the West, this mass of equipment exists because for 150 years the West has been accumulating it. Underdeveloped societies, on the other hand, have little capital per worker. The amount of equipment they can add per year in the country as a whole, even with generous aid from the West, is small by Western standards, even though it may be a 2 or 3 per cent increase in their stock of equipment. Insofar as their method of attempting to increase productivity is to import (or construct) productive apparatus of the type used in the West, the equipment obtained each year will be sufficient for only a tiny fraction of their workers—typically fewer, indeed, than the annual increase in their labor force. There will be no increase whatever in the equipment available to the labor force in general.

And while the increase in productivity per worker in the production affected will be great (if the Western methods work well, a point considered in the following paragraph), the increase in aggregate production in the economic system will not be great. The spectacular few large Western projects in a development program are often a necessary part of it, but they are not the main source of a continuing rise in per capita income. The simple importation of Western methods is never the main source of progress. The main source is more widespread improvements in methods, which use more equipment or more expensive materials (seed, fertilizer, etc.) than has been traditional, but far less than is the practice in the West. These methods are not simply the importation of selected portions of Western practice. Rather, a great deal of adaptation is an essential ingredient. Creativity is necessary to devise such adaptations.

An experienced technical assistance worker may suggest that in agricultural production there are a number of advances that do not require much added equipment. This of course is correct. The traditional attitudes mentioned above, rather than the cost, are barriers to some of these.

Creativity is necessary, in the second place, because the simple imitation of Western methods is typically impossible. Perhaps the most obvious problem is that the available labor force differs greatly. In the West, the mass of men are literate and able to read instructions and information. Moreover, they have an understanding of the functioning of machinery, and thereby of its care and handling, which they have absorbed through their pores, so to speak, as they grew up in a mechanized civilization. Among them are many with varying degrees of training in engineering, scientific, financial, accounting, and managerial knowledge and techniques—and the elements of this knowledge, acquired unconsciously from the entire world around one, are as important as the elements learned in formal education. It is impossible to man an enterprise in an underdeveloped economy with corresponding individuals. Men anywhere can be trained rapidly in skills, for men everywhere are intelligent, but the broad background of other individual characteristics cannot be duplicated. A Western-type enterprise must be adapted to the human differences, and indeed a perceptive observer of an efficient industrial enterprise in a low-income society will note in how many ways both conspicuous and seemingly insignificant its operation differs from that of an enterprise in the West.

Equally important, every Western industry depends for its efficiency on other industries. It assumes the ready availability of materials, components, and tools. It depends also on auxiliary enterprises that can provide technical, financial, and managerial services on demand; on a complex network of communication and transportation facilities; and an intricate system of business practices. A Western economy is a technical (and cultural) complex, not a set of isolated pieces of technology. In an underdeveloped society the auxiliary industries are missing, and the framework of business practices is different. One piece cannot be detached from the complex and used efficiently elsewhere without skillful adaptation.[6]

[6] In another place, I have illustrated this fact by citing the difficulty even of substituting the spade for the digging hoe, in a traditional society. "Economics and Economic Development," *Economics and the Policy Maker, Brookings Lectures, 1958-1959* (The Brookings Institution, 1959).

Moreover, the difficulty runs deeper than these technical problems. It is perhaps not an exaggeration to state that solving the technical problems is the easy aspect of technological progress for present-day low-income countries. Technological advance also requires the creation of new economic and other organizations and relationships, or the adaptation of old types and principles of organization to new functions. For example, the moral obligations of traditional society may require an enterpriser to employ his relatives or the social inferiors who depend on him, whether or not they have appropriate skills and capacities, and to employ them in excess of his needs. These ethical obligations may also require him to lend his money to them, if their needs require this, whether or not he needs it in his business. Moreover, the principle that authority is the prerogative of the individual at the top of the hierarchy prevents the delegation of authority.

It is of no use to say that these are outmoded attitudes that must be discarded. These are ethical imperatives. Where social tensions and the slow course of social change have not yet eroded these attitudes, progress in techniques will be greatly impeded unless someone is creative enough to adapt organizations so that they can accommodate these ethical imperatives and still be effective in new economic tasks.

Another example: traders often have the liquid capital that might finance economic change, but the "trading mentality" prevents them from using it for this purpose. By the trading mentality I refer to the attitude of trusting no one and of regarding each transaction as a separate act in which the maximum immediate gain should be made. These attitudes are not illogical. For social and historical reasons, trader financiers are a class apart in every traditional society, distrusted by the society as a whole. (The distrust is often justified.) In self-defense, they will do well to keep their assets in hidden and liquid form, which cannot be so easily levied on, rather than to put them into large recognizable productive plants which might be confiscated or taxed heavily. The devising of social institutions to overcome this barrier is not a technique that can be borrowed from the West.

Absence of Creativity

In short, creativity as real as that in the original industrial revolution is required for technical and economic progress in traditional societies, and in the main it will have to be creativity by the members of the society, for outsiders are peculiarly ill-suited to solve some of these problems, even if they were creative enough to do so. It is pertinent, therefore, that creativity seems to be in shorter supply in traditional societies than in socially and economically changing ones. Creativity involves, in addition to intelligence and energy, such characteristics as pleasure in facing and attacking new problems, absence of any sense that one must seek someone else's judgment before judging what will work, and a knack of seeing that familiar elements mean new things, lead to new conclusions, and can be organized in new ways.[7]

From the discussion of elite values and attitudes above, it is fairly clear that such creative individuals as appear among the middle and upper classes of traditional societies are apt to channel their energies into some field other than technological progress—war, politics, or philosophy. There is an added difficulty. The dependence on tradition, custom, and a hierarchy of authority that are characteristic of traditional societies are not conducive to creativity, and the environment in which the members of traditional societies grow up tends to inculcate uncreative personalities in them. While the relevant evidence is qualitative and subject to some controversy, there is a fairly impressive body of theory and empirical evidence to suggest that the incidence of creativity in fully traditional societies is much less than where cultural conditions are different.

This is not an unalterable situation. Where social tensions appear in traditional societies and make the social structure of the traditional society seem undesirable and inequitable to some groups, these tensions seem not only to create new values in individuals from generation to generation but also to raise the level of creativity.

This circumstance is not one on which the administrator of economic or technical aid can have a rapid impact; the passage of time is a necessary ingredient in such personality changes. However, economic growth can go forward at some pace within any social-political-cultural milieu, and by being aware of the causes and nature of social and personality change, the aid administrator can act more intelligently within the situation he finds and can thus make the pace faster than it would otherwise be.

[7] "Scientific genius is the capacity to be surprised," Raymond Poincaré, quoted in *Creativity and Its Cultivation*, Harold H. Anderson, ed. (Harper, 1959), p. 48. Creativity involves "openness to experience," Carl R. Rogers, quoted in *ibid.*, p. 75.

HOW TRADITIONAL SOCIETIES CHANGE

It hardly needs argument that the most powerful instrument for change which has operated on traditional societies has been contact with the West and specifically the disruption of the traditional social order of almost all of these societies by Western intrusion, conquest, and administration.

Contact With the West

Knowledge of Western techniques obviously greatly increases the possible speed of technical progress. For even though adaptation of Western methods is necessary, the fact that they exist to be adapted makes possible far faster material advance than if the traditional societies were isolated from the West and had to go independently through a process of technical invention parallel to that which the West has already gone through. This is true even though the traditional societies will also invent methods of their own, as Japan has done repeatedly.

For this reason, it seems certain that intrusion by the West has accelerated technical progress. Colonial rule disrupted the traditional social order and culture so basically that Humpty Dumpty can never be put together again. Social incoherence and chaos result in the revolt against colonial rule, from the frustrations and hatreds caused by that rule, and there are some tendencies inimical to economic growth in that social incoherence and chaos; yet in their search for power and thereby dignity the former colonial peoples are apt to move toward technological progress more rapidly than if their traditional societies had never come in contact with the West.

But that intrusion by the West, and an attempt to impose Western values, knowledge, and social forms on the non-Western societies by force, has brought or will bring technological progress more rapidly than mere contact with the West without intrusion is much more doubtful. In fact, the contrary seems to be the case.

The evidence that can be adduced most simply and briefly is that of the four largest Asian nations, Indonesia, India, China, and Japan. Indonesia and India, which were conquered, have had the longest and most intensive contact with the West. China, which was forced to submit to the establishment of Western beachheads along the coast and to accept trade between the interior and the West, has had the next longest and most intensive contact, while since 1600 the rulers of Japan effectively prevented almost all contact with the West. Further, most Western capital, and over the longest period, has been invested in Indonesia and India, next most, over a shorter period but still a century or more, in China, but literally none in Japan until her economic modernization was well under way. But the order of entry on economic growth has been, first Japan; next, seventy or eighty years later, China and India, with the growth in China (in spite of her current serious difficulties in agriculture) more vigorous than that in India; and, last of the four, Indonesia, which indeed shows no evidence of growth at present.

As between India and Indonesia, the difference may be due to the less advanced state of the Indonesian material culture before the European intrusion—the lesser base from which to start in Indonesia, but as between India, China, and Japan, the difference must be due either to the deterrent effects of intrusion by the West, pre-existing differences among the cultures of the three societies, or to other differences in their histories. I shall suggest both that intrusion has had deterrent effects, and that Japan's relationship to the West was singularly conducive to economic growth.

The Importance of Selected Groups Within the Society

The sketches of the transition to economic growth in several countries presented early in this essay suggest that economic growth has been led, not by individuals distributed at random throughout the society, but disproportionately by individuals from some distinctive social group or groups. Consider this fact for a moment further.

In the last half of the eighteenth century, nonconformists formed only about 7 per cent of the population of England and Wales. The Scottish dissenters from the established Presbyterian Church hardly formed a higher percentage of the population of Scotland. It is a fact of significance for the study of economic growth, that, judging by a sample study that I made of British entrepreneurs these groups provided one half of the innovating entrepreneurs in Britain in the eighteenth and nineteenth centuries. In proportion to their number in the population as a whole, these dissenting groups provided more than ten times as many innovators as did the rest of the society.

Consider next the case of Colombia. The Spanish conquistadores came to Colombia during the 1530's. They readily conquered the Indians and occupied the high plateau around the present Bogotá (the Sabana), the valley of the upper Cauca river (known simply as the Valle), and the valley of Antioquia. They were in search of gold and adventure. They found little gold or silver on the Sabana or in the Valle, but they did find healthful fertile lands, and set themselves up as gentry on large estates or ranches. The Indians, whom they took under their guardianship to save their souls, performed the manual labor. In Antioquia they found some gold and silver, and thereafter the continued quest for this received much greater relative economic emphasis in Antioquia than on the Sabana or in the Valle. They found it impossible to keep their small mines manned with Indians and with the Negro slaves they brought from Africa, and, presently, increasingly they became mine workers themselves.

The conquistadores in all three areas were predominantly from the lower socio-economic classes of Spain, not the higher. When the occupants of the other two areas became landed gentry or cattle ranchers, with the fervor of new insecure elite they felt and expressed contempt for their grubby neighbors in Antioquia, who labored with their own hands, a feeling manifest in the literature and historical writings of the eighteenth and nineteenth centuries. The Antioqueños, on the other hand, conscious of their equal claim to Spanish blood and culture, felt resentment at the attitudes of superiority.

During Colombia's colonial period, the central colonial city was Bogotá, and after independence Bogotá was the national capital. The Bogotanos had far greater contact with the various countries of Western Europe than did the Antioqueños. Further, access from Cali, the main city of the Valle, both to Bogotá and to the Pacific was somewhat better than that from Antioquia and its main city, Medellín. Of the three areas, Antioquia was the most isolated. Yet as economic growth has proceeded in Colombia, it has turned out that, out of all proportion to their numbers, the Antioqueños are the innovating entrepreneurs.

Research I now have under way suggests that in Japan, while the innovating entrepreneurs came more widely from various groups of the population, here too they probably came disproportionately from certain groups that under the social and political rules laid down by the

Tokugawa had, from 1600 on, steadily lost their previous social status. This statement must, however, remain tentative until the research is completed.

No study available to me indicates clearly whether the Old Believers were active in nineteenth century economic innovation in Russia in numbers greater than in proportion to their number in the population. The historical research necessary to answer this question has not been done. However, in view of the historical references to their activity, it is probable that they were.

The essential characteristic of the innovating groups is not religious dissidence or adherence or nonadherence to any given religious creed. In England they were Protestant dissenters; in Russia (if the Old Believers were indeed the most innovational group) adherents to traditional aspects of the Orthodox creed; in Colombia, like the rest of the population, fervent Catholics; in Japan, presumably Shintoists and Buddhists. What seems of central importance is that they were a group that had had a secure place in the traditional society, and then in new circumstances found that place spurned, derogated, or taken away by other social groups. That is, what seems conducive to the changes in personality (in creativity, values, and view of the world) which stimulate innovation is that the group shall, so to speak, be ejected from its erstwhile place in the traditional society, and feel impelled therefore to find some new field in which to prove its worth (old avenues to accepted social status having been closed to it). Men seem to be as much pushed as pulled into economic advance.

I suggest therefore that one of the differences among societies that is important in explaining the appearance of noneconomic growth is whether internal social tensions of this sort developed, which served to push some group to new fields of endeavor.

Japan

In the case of Japan, not only did severe internal tensions develop. In addition, all Japan felt threatened by the West, for the Japanese knew well that Western powers had gobbled up South and Southeast Asia, Indonesia, and the Philippines, and had humiliated China. Japan felt its dignity threatened by the West. All of Japan, that is, felt the same relationship to the West that derogated social groups in Britain, Russia, and Colombia did to the country as a whole. This dual set of pressures in Japan may explain Japan's very rapid growth.

The Impact of Colonial Rule

While colonial rule brought contact with Western ideas and disrupted traditional social order and culture, it had one effect inimical to economic advance. Colonial administrators and businessmen (in part inadvertently) hacked up and cast aside as though they were dung the economic, social, political, and religious institutions of the governed peoples. For example, by introducing the ownership of land in fee simple they swept away systems of land use on which the family's economic security and its right to a place in the community depended. They humiliated the leaders on whom the people depended for guidance and for contact with the spiritual powers. They committed sacrilege on sacred temple grounds. They did these things in the name of progress, which is to say, because of their contempt for the indigenous religion and the wishes and purposes in life of the indigenous peoples. More important, they typically treated the people of the conquered nation as inferiors, who by virtue of their skin color were unworthy and might appropriately be humbled. The emotional impact of all this cut deep.

These are relationships of the immediate past and the present, not of history. They were characteristic of colonial rule by the British as well as by the French, the Dutch, the Belgians, the Spanish, the Portuguese. There were differences in the degree of harshness of administration, but little in the fundamental impressions conveyed to the conquered peoples.

Two results of this relationship are pertinent.

One is that if members of the colonial society accepted the Western ways of life and the Western view of life, in doing so they were implicitly agreeing with the Western evaluation that they themselves in their previous culture were worthless. Indeed, the matter went further than this, for they found out that no matter how Western they became the colonial administrators and businessmen still treated them as inferiors. Thus if they accepted Western culture they were admitting that of their essence they were inferior. I suggest that this situation has created emotional blocks that have made it difficult for indigenous individuals to perform effectively functions of the sort they associate with their colonial rulers, no matter how much they want the result.

The other is that they suspect the motives of Westerners in offering them technical advice. Throughout a long colonial history, Westerners had shown contempt for the purposes and values of the indigenous people, and had used them for their own purposes. Why should it now be supposed that Westerners are doing anything different? Anthropologists cite numerous cases in which attempts by employees of the central government in low-income societies to introduce improvements in methods and practices into the villages have failed. New wells have not been used; new seeds used as feed; and methods of improving sanitation disregarded. Anthropological studies have shown that the reason has often been that the chief contacts of the central government with the villagers for decades or generations had been to collect taxes, to enforce landlords' demands, or to collect a levy of men for the army. Automatically, unconsciously, the villagers assume that no good for them can be intended by the central government, and these gut reactions make them unable to consider with their minds the possible benefits of what the governmental agents now offer. Similarly, colonial peoples have breathed in with their mothers' milk the perception that Westerners wish merely to *use* them. As a result, technical advice provided by Westerners may be shed as an oilskin sheds water—and all this in spite of desire to gain the productivity and power of the West.

The Value Placed on Power

To avoid misunderstanding in this summary statement, let it be noted as it was noted concerning a previous point that these tendencies are not absolutes. In any society there are deviants—individuals who because of the idiosyncracies of their individual lives have partly rejected the traditional culture or are ready to do so. And this is no doubt true in some degree, even though a small one, of virtually every individual. The barriers created by colonialism are important ones, but there are contrary tendencies. One of the contrary factors is that in every culture of any historical importance that anthropologists have studied, high value is placed on power. The characteristic which Westerners manifested in supreme degree in traditional societies was power. This attracts indigenous peoples to Western ways of life, and this attraction counteracts at least to some degree the considerations that make Western ways of life repugnant. This attraction no doubt differs among individuals, being greatest, as has been noted, among individuals and groups who for some reason are unhappy with their position in the traditional society.

Culture May Change Rapidly

Moreover, there is evidence that culture can change with great rapidity. The most spectacular evidence is provided by Margaret Mead in *New Lives for Old* (1956). After World War II, revisiting the Manus on a small island in the Admiralties whom she had visited two decades or so earlier, she found that their culture and social structure was undergoing drastic change year by year. The immediate cause was that in World War II they had seen the might of United States armies and decided to westernize. This is an extreme case. The Manus had been exposed to the presence of American soldiers in numbers perhaps one hundred times as great as their total population, and using lavishly the seemingly inexhaustible and incredibly impressive equipment of modern war. Moreover, the changes that Dr. Mead observed may be more superficial, and less eradicative of the basic culture, than appears on the surface. One would like to wait another two decades, and see whether basic traditional features had reasserted themselves. But with all the qualifications one can conjure up out of caution, the speed of change is impressive. And even though this is an extreme case, it illustrates the principle that even radical social-cultural change may occur rapidly.

MORALS FOR UNITED STATES POLICY AND OPERATIONS

The tenor of the discussion above may be discouraging to practitioners of the giving of aid to development. For the typical case seems to be that economic growth gained momentum only after a process of social and cultural change of many generations. If so, it may seem of little use to extend economic and technical aid if conditions in the society are not conducive to economic growth, and hardly necessary if they are.

However, the bare statement of these extremes may suggest the fallacy of the viewpoint stated. Almost all underdeveloped countries are somewhere between the extremes. Conditions are somewhat conducive to growth, and somewhat deterrent. The differences are matters of degree. The number of rather creative individuals varies, but everywhere there are some. Within a fairly wide range of the available amount of economic and technical aid, economic growth will proceed faster in almost all underdeveloped countries, if more aid is given than if less is given, provided that the aid is extended in an effective manner. Awareness of the interrelations between social-cultural conditions and technical and economic progress should make the practitioner of aid less facile in his approach to the problem, less inclined to assume that a goodly amount of aid should accomplish the desired result in a few years if the recipients are sensible. It should make him more appreciative of the creativity that he and his colleagues need to manifest if their help is to be effective. Various suggestions for United States policy and operations in economic and technical aid suggest themselves, some narrow in scope, some broad, some simple, some complex.

Effect of the United States Policy Stance

Since World War II, the United States has conveyed the impression to the low-income countries that it does not respect their purposes in life, but rather wishes to use them for its purposes. The United States has conveyed this impression partly because in the low-income countries small incidents loom large, but perhaps mainly because, unfortunately, it has been true. The American government has made military alliances and encouraged rulers to muster up large armies for its purposes, not purposes which the peoples felt were theirs—purposes which might have plunged them into a war which they felt was not their concern. (After their colonial experience, that they should be neutralist rather than pro-Western is not surprising.) The United States has associated itself with repressive rulers, who used its arms to maintain their power. It is commonly thought in Latin America that the American government intervened in Guatemala to obtain the overthrow of a duly elected president, Arbenz—a president, moreover, who was thought to be moving forward rapidly with plans for land reform, while under his successors, Castillo Armas and Ydigoras, action stopped. The United States has in the past refused aid to Brazil to develop a national petroleum enterprise, and Brazilians and other Latin Americans believe the reason is that it would compete with American private oil companies.

I suggest that reversing this image of the United States is not only in the national interest on broader grounds, but would probably make American development assistance more effective. The United States has now voted in the United Nations in favor of an investigation of Portuguese administration in Angola, and seems to have taken a stance in favor of neutralism in Laos, abandoning its support by arms of a prince for whom there is no evidence of great popular support. A few dozen other similar reversals in policy may have as much effect in making the work of technical advisers in say India, Nigeria, or Colombia effective as the technical competence of the advisers. Unconscious attitudes inculcated over a lifetime cannot be wiped out rapidly, but the image cast currently certainly has, as an important by-product, some effect on the degree to which American technical advice takes hold.

Specific Suggestions Concerning Technical Assistance

1. *Do not feel superior.* A matter related to that discussed above is the impression cast by the individual technical assistance expert concerning his own relationship to the persons he is advising. Insofar as the indigenous individuals receive the perception that the adviser feels that in essence he is superior, unconscious barriers rise; the gut assumption of the indigenous individual that the adviser is interested in his own purposes comes into play; and the technical advice tends not to take. In an orientation talk by a friend at the time I was entering a low-income country, I was advised not to let the people feel that I thought I was superior. Clearly, the implication was that I was superior, but should not show it. Where that attitude prevails, indigenous individuals will not be deceived, and a block to effective technical assistance will be created. Technical assistance experts should be people who understand that they are not superior, but merely happen to have some knowledge and skills that can be of use.

This understanding can be inculcated only in small degree by orientation programs. The view of the world that includes "cultural arrogance" is deeply built into personality, just as the attitudes of individuals in traditional societies are. The American who is culturally arrogant when he accepts a position in an American foreign assistance agency will still be culturally arrogant after an orientation course. I suggest therefore that a selection procedure that employs sophisticated examination of prospective aid officials would be a useful addition to the personnel procedures of the agency.

2. *Start from their viewpoint.* It is an important principle of administration as well as of education that an individual will not learn effectively unless he is being helped to do something he wants to do.[8] The principle is of great importance in technical assistance. The technical adviser must try to understand the complicated set of goals of the recipient of technical assistance and must help him attain what he wants, not what the American thinks he ought to want.

The importance of the ethical values of the indigenous culture, the appropriate relationships between inferior and superior, the need for appropriate relationships to one's community and to the spiritual powers, and other cultural factors, have been suggested above. The indigenous individual probably wants increased efficiency, but not at the cost of other goals that are important to him and alien to the American. If he is to attain increased efficiency, he must do so within the framework of relationships dictated by *his* moral values, sense of identity, and obligations to his fellows and the spiritual powers. The American who feels that his technical method of doing a job, and of organizing the enterprise for its doing, is the most efficient way, and that his job is to show the indigenous individual the efficient Western way has partly failed in his job before he starts. The adviser's job is to learn the context within which the indigenous individual operates and to be creative in adapting advanced techniques so that they will function within that relationship. For example, the adviser who tries to organize a factory as it is organized in the United States, or who suggests that authority must be delegated in a governmental ministry as it is in the West, because that is the way it works well in the West, or who suggests that the procedure of economic programing should embody relationships between ministries and planners parallel to those by which the United States Bureau of the Budget operates, has largely defeated himself before he starts to advise. Creativity is necessary among advisers, as well as within the indigenous culture.

If feasible, every technical aid mission should have one member

[8] For a discussion of this principle in industry, see Douglas McGregor, *The Human Side of Enterprise* (McGraw-Hill, 1960). (Reprinted from "Adventure in Thought and Action," proceedings of the Fifth Anniversary Convocation of the School of Industrial Management.)

who is sensitive to cultural determinants of behavior and can give advice concerning values and relationships and unconscious attitudes governing behavior that would not occur to other mission members. He will also need to advise the other mission members about their unconscious attitudes and motivations, for many of their difficulties will arise from attempting, consciously or unconsciously, to impose values that they regard as laws of the universe, but which in fact are elements of Western but not of traditional culture. Ideally, every mission should have an anthropologist-psychologist, and one who is acquainted with the culture, or with related cultures, when he begins his job. This, of course, is a counsel of the ideal. Moreover, often a professional anthropologist who is available for such a position may be an individual who has learned the verbalisms of his craft, but nevertheless does not understand either himself or the functioning of culture. Here, as in some other circumstances, a little learning is a dangerous thing.

If, as I believe, there are so few persons qualified for this function by training and capability that a competent individual cannot be obtained for each mission, then a more feasible substitute is to have a small group of such individuals operating in a staff capacity out of the Washington office. They may be able to do field studies, to analyze difficulties, and to elaborate in a perceptive, practical, specific manner the observations which have been summarized imperfectly here in general terms.

These comments should not be taken to imply that Western techniques must always be carried on within a traditional frame of values. On the contrary, once Western techniques have infiltrated into the traditional framework, and the degree to which they can further some of the aims of indigenous individuals is appreciated in practice, further pursuit of them will inexorably alter traditional values. But this alteration occurs in the process of living and from one generation to the next. It cannot be brought about by verbal exhortation by an adviser, which usually has an effect contrary to its purpose.

3. *Be their creature.* As one technique to lessen the barrier created by the unconscious assumption that the Westerner is serving his own interests, it seems useful to create a relationship by which as many technical advisers as possible are not members of a United States technical aid mission in the country, but rather are creatures of a governmental agency of the country. One technique is creation of a trust fund out of which the host government employs the men, so that they

do not report to someone in the United States Embassy. Whatever the devices necessary, achieving this relationship is useful.

4. *Find the individual.* In some contexts, technical advisers have the opportunity to select individuals or groups with whom to operate. An adviser assigned to a Ministry may be free to operate with any of a number of officials within the Ministry. An adviser who is to train a group of young people may have some discretion in selecting members of the group. In the first case, it is only sensible to work with the official who is most amenable to being helped, assuming that his post is important enough to make helping him sufficiently useful. In the second case, more delicate problems arise.

The comments above about the tendency of innovators to appear in a socially rebellious group might suggest looking for such a group. This, however, is dangerous procedure. Indigenous peoples may remember a colonial policy of divide and rule; even if they do not, they are as acutely aware as a visitor could be of the tensions within their society. Any overt tendency to select for attention one group that is somewhat at odds with the rest of the society, may create antipathies that may destroy the program. Moreover, while a disproportionate number of innovators may come from some socially rebellious group, such individuals are also found scattered throughout the population. Even in the extreme case in England, in which the dissenters provided half of the entrepreneurs, the rest of the population provided the other half. The safest advice for intruders from the outside is: if you have freedom of choice, select individuals who seem most capable and most receptive to advice, but only within the rules of behavior of the society. Here, as elsewhere, creatively adapt to the situation you find; use only rules of selection that you are willing to discuss quite openly with the authorities of the country. These rules, of course, may involve rejection of nepotism and other "favoritism," but only insofar as you are able frankly though discreetly to discuss this situation.

5. *First convince the "reference group."* Each of us carries around in his head a sense that the good opinion of certain individuals is more important than that of others. Many of our actions are guided or greatly influenced by the awareness that individuals or groups whose approval we desire would or would not approve of what we are contemplating doing. Thus a young boy may be conscious of the attitudes of his parents, or his boy playmates, or (at a certain age) the girls he knows, or, in various compartments of his behavior, of all three. A scholar may work primarily for the approval of other scholars in his

field. A professional or technical man in a ministry may value professional approval. A peasant may be guided by the values of his fellow villagers and especially of the village priest or monk. A government official of an underdeveloped country may be conscious most of all of the attitudes of European elites (though if he is, he is somewhat isolated from his own culture and may lose his influence there).

The individual or group whose approval each person consciously or unconsciously seeks is termed his "reference group." The work of an adviser will benefit if he is able to discover the reference group of the person he is advising. If the reference group is a local individual or group, and if that person or those persons can be shown the advantages of a method or course of action, the person being advised will sense that he will have the approval of his reference group if he adopts it, and it will have become something he wants to do. In short, approach the influential individual first, if the situation permits.

6. *Do not expect to change the culture.* A layman, impressed with the importance of culture and assuming that the way to bring about changes in attitudes is by education, might think that the key to progress lies in inducing the host government to introduce a school system in which the virtues of thrift, the laws of science, the dignity of manual labor, the fascinating character of the physical world, and the equality of all men, would be taught.

However, the expectation that such education will change basic attitudes arises in large part from a misunderstanding of how the basic attitudes of personality are inculcated. They are inculcated only in small degree by the conscious mental learning of school. In the main, they are inculcated by conclusions about the best way to meet the problems of life that the child unconsciously draws between the ages of zero and say six or eight, and perhaps especially before the age of five. There are generalizations about the nature of the environment in which he lives and the best way of defending himself from its dangers and taking advantage of its opportunities. Few things impress modern social and clinical psychologists more than the powerful ability of even the youngest children to generalize from the clues of their immediate environment and the strength and persistence of the behavior patterns they thereby build into their unconscious processes.

The aspects of that environment that are most influential in forming the child's personality are the personality and behavior of his father and mother and other persons equally close to him—not what they consciously do with respect to him, but what unconsciously they do and are and how satisfactory all this seems to the child. While every event throughout life makes its impression on the individual, these early years are extremely important. Even in later years, general interpersonal relationships and ways of behavior in the society are much more important in confirming or altering earlier attitudes than are mental acquisitions during the process of education. The influence of school in building on basic attitudes and in providing facts and tools is tremendous, but it should not be assumed to be the major culture-molding institution.

The technical adviser must realize that in the main he can not mold the culture, but must creatively adapt himself to make new techniques work within it. If he possesses enough genius to do this, he may be amazed at his effectiveness. And each of us has a tiny bit of genius; each of us may perceive some bit of the reason why our technical advice fails, and by perceiving that bit of the truth become more effective than otherwise.

7. *Be aware of the values and purposes of the people.* Finally, I would suggest that in evaluating projects for economic aid (as distinguished from technical aid) the interrelationships between social-cultural and technical-economic change must also be considered. At times, projects are proposed and intensely desired by the government of the underdeveloped country that as analyzed by technical and economic experts of the United States are poor projects—or worse. For example, economic advisers are often baffled by the attractiveness of steel mills to countries that have no economic sources of iron ore or coking coal.

These projects satisfy emotional needs. These needs cause the officials of the country to persuade themselves that the projects are good, almost regardless of the economic and technical considerations presented to them. Since rejection of requests for aid for such proposals is apt to arouse the old suspicion that the United States does not want the country to become strong, but wants to keep it in an inferior status, a problem is created.

I suggest that if in many other ways the United States and its employees in the country have created the perception that they do respect the purposes and values of the indigenous people, it will be easier to reject such proposals without damage, for the individuals of the country will be the more able to perceive that the United States has reasons which do not imply contempt for the purposes and values of the country.

On the other hand, the United States should be slow to reject projects merely because they seem to be less advantageous than some others. The fact that a project is desired (by representative officials who reflect public attitudes, and not by an eccentric individual or for personal or class gain) is in itself a consideration of some importance in favor of the project. If a project will raise material income somewhat less than would another project, but will raise psychic income more, the latter should not be ignored. Of course, the situation may be more difficult than this. Projects which are desired because they satisfy needs for dignity, prestige, etc., may not produce any economic benefit; they may be economic burdens. What is desired may be the symbol, not the function. The questions involved are complex; all that I am suggesting is that a purely economic and technical analysis is inadequate.

SOME OBSERVATIONS ON POLITICAL STABILITY AND CHANGE

The discussion so far has, in appearance at least, dealt with technical-economic rather than political change. It has done so for three reasons. One is that I feel more competent to discuss economic than political change. A second is that whereas the United States is as interested in political development as in economic development in the economically underdeveloped societies that it is aiding, its aid is specifically aimed at promoting economic growth. It does not purport to intervene in the process of political change. The third is that, after all, the neglect of political change is in part a mirage. Most of the generalizations concerning economic change stated above apply also to any other type of basic change in a social system, and specifically are as pertinent to political as to economic change.

Political Stability in a Traditional Society

Specifically, then, in a fully traditional society, the sense of impotence in the face of their physical environment that is felt by individuals in the society, the relief from anxiety they feel at being able to depend on the judgment of a superior, the satisfaction they feel at being able in turn to dominate inferiors, and their lack of creativity, all cause the hierarchical and authoritarian structure of traditional society to be satisfying to them. If, in addition, each class in the society—peasants, craftsmen, lords, warriors, the learned—feels that its place in the society is understood and respected by the other classes, there is little tendency toward either political or economic change. Strange though it may seem to us today, this was true in almost all peasant-based societies until two or three hundred years ago.

Social Tensions as a Cause of Change

To the members of such societies, the way of life of other societies did not seem attractive and did not exert any considerable stimulus toward change. Even the perception that the members of other societies enjoyed a higher level of living did not have a strong disrupting effect, since the means by which they attained it seemed demeaning and repugnant to traditional individuals. In Benjamin Franklin's phrase, the whistle was not worth the penny. (When Europeans with their un-Japanese and un-Burmese ways of behavior first appeared in Japan and Burma, the Japanese and the Burmese both referred to them as barbarians, with precisely the connotation with which the term barbarian is used by Europeans with reference to other people.)

However, through some historical change the function in life and the desires and purposes of one or more classes in a traditional society may no longer be respected by the classes above them or by their fellows of equal social status. Instead, they may merely be used as tools to serve upper-class purposes or may be derogated by their fellows. Examples from England, Russia, Japan, and Colombia were cited earlier in this essay. If these tensions continue for some generations so that changes in personality occur, the cement that held the society together is replaced by forces that tend to break it apart.

The old social structure is then preserved only by the power in the hands of the upper classes. The discontented groups will look where they can, including outside the society, for new ways of living in which they can prove their worth, force others to respect them, and perhaps satisfy the rage that has built up in them. If the winds of history carry to the discontented groups of such a society the perception that they no longer have to submit to their social lot, that they can take matters into their own hands, sooner or later there will be a social and political revolution, gradual or abrupt, peaceful or by force.

This is the change that has occurred in the world between the seventeenth and twentieth centuries. In almost all of the economically underdeveloped societies of the world, during the past several hundred years the sense that their place in society is respected was lost by most classes. It was largely destroyed in every colonial society, where as I have noted above, the colonial administrators, no matter how kindly their rule, made abundantly clear that they had little but contempt for the indigenous culture and the social, political, and religious beliefs and desires of all of the groups of the indigenous society. Independence does not resolve the problem, for the traditional social system is disrupted beyond restoration, and the people, still aware of the derogation of their ex-masters, still seek for dignity, proof of their worth, and perhaps revenge. Even in low-income societies that were never fully colonial—for example, Thailand and some societies of the Middle East—through circumstances of history too complex to sketch here, the upper classes no longer serve as the religious and social leaders of the simple folk and provide meaning to their lives. Rather, the upper classes in the main have contempt for the function in the society of the simple folk, and use them so far as they can merely as tools to serve upper class purposes. This had happened before the twentieth century. Then in the twentieth century came the perception by the common people of these societies that they can do something about the lack of respect accorded them, that they do not need to remain in roles in which they are not treated with dignity.

This situation need not result in revolutionary political change. If the political repression is not too severe, and if discontented individuals who no longer hold traditional values see ways in which they can individually prove their worth, they may pursue them, and the tensions may never rise to the level necessary for political revolution. The individuals may, for example, become economic innovators, and the growing commercial and industrial middle class may accomplish basic social and political change gradually. But if the political repression is great, or if the upper classes are especially self-centered even at the cost of the general welfare, tensions will build up leading to political revolution, probably extremist. This, with qualifications which brevity prevents stating here, was the cause of Communist revolt in Russia, and a main reason why communism was attractive in China. It explains also the Castro-led revolution in Cuba and the more moderate ones in Egypt and Iraq. It may easily happen elsewhere.

Comments on "A Framework for Analyzing Economic and Political Change"

ALBERT O. HIRSCHMAN*

I HAVE A GREAT DEAL OF SYMPATHY with Everett Hagen's stress on the need to understand better why some things are so uncommonly difficult in the less developed countries; with his emphasis on the distance that separates most of us in the industrial countries, not only from the rural masses, but also from the ruling groups in the less industrialized nations; and I find many things he says about the "gut assumptions" of colonial or semicolonial people quite illuminating.

I do have a quibble or two with his basic hypothesis about the relationship between the "ejected groups" and the beginning of economic growth. A few years ago I wrote a comment on a paper entitled "Non-economic Factors in Economic Development" in which Bert Hoselitz laid much stress on the importance of minorities and other deviants for the emergence of able and vigorous entrepreneurs. My criticism which, I believe, is also applicable to the interesting turn Hagen has given to this idea took the form of two questions: First, is the relationship reliable? In other words, aren't there some deviants, for example, homosexuals or ex-convicts, who have not shown particularly strong entrepreneurial inclinations? Must social scientists perhaps entertain the Toynbee-type hypothesis of "optimum deviancy," with all the attendant conceptual difficulties of defining the optimal point?

My other question relates to the direction of the causal nexus. Hoselitz' deviants or Hagen's ejected groups may well make for economic development, but development in turn creates an *esprit de*

---

* Professor of International Economic Relations, Columbia University.

corps among its principal agents and welds them into an identifiable group, with a personality and perhaps an ideology of its own. *Ex post,* it may look therefore as though the separateness of the group was a cause of development when in actual fact it was its result. Historical examples of this type of relationship can easily be given.

I am glad, in any event, that Hagen specifically warns against taking lantern in hand and looking for the deviants and putting them in charge. Yet the logic of his argument certainly implies that the transfer of capital alone would not work unless the ground is prepared through the presence of some such group. In this sense, then, Hagen's analysis is an extension of W. W. Rostow's preconditions. He does not say whether he proposes to substitute his set of preconditions for Rostow's or whether he considers his set as pre-preconditions to Rostow's preconditions. I am anxious and, what is more, I am worried. For when one adds to the number of preconditions, one lengthens, by the same token, the list of potential obstacles to development. The discovery of such obstacles comes in waves, usually after something has gone wrong. It is not surprising that after the Congo, Cuba, and Laos, all three recipients of large amounts of public or private capital in the past, the United States should be riding the crest of such a wave.

The most articulate reflection of a new mood of disillusion with past reliance on capital plus technical assistance is the recent article in *Foreign Affairs* by Ambassador John Kenneth Galbraith.[1] Readers are told that the development process can hardly be expected to be brought under way and that an infusion of financial aid and experts will be useless unless there be present in the to-be-aided society (1) "a substantial degree of literacy" and an "educated elite of substantial size"; (2) "a substantial measure of social justice"; (3) "a reliable apparatus of government and public administration"; and (4) "a clear and purposeful view of what development involves."

This is a counsel of perfection. In no advanced industrial country were these four conditions realized *prior* to industrialization. Moreover, if these four conditions were found to be present in any country today, that country could easily dispense with foreign financial and technical assistance; in fact, it should probably be an exporter of such assistance, with the United States as a recipient!

The Galbraithian conditions should supply, therefore, a final *reductio ad absurdum* of one approach to foreign aid that has domi-

[1] Vol. 39 (April 1961), pp. 445-46.

nated American thinking during the whole postwar period: the "will to believe"—rooted perhaps in the need to so persuade the Congress— that foreign aid is the "missing component," the "catalyst" whose addition will surely bring the alchemy of the development process to its climactic reaction: self support, "take-off," or bliss in general. The search for the components that have to be in place so that foreign capital and technical assistance from abroad can play this sure-fire role has focused successively on monetary stability, on a "favorable investment climate," on "integrated development programs," and lately on land and tax reforms. The diagnosis of "the experts" has thus fluctuated wildly, in line with the ideological preferences of the moment and with the lessons of the latest disaster.

If only as much attention had been devoted to the successes as to the failures, we should have noticed that whenever development occurs, it does so invariably in the absence of one or several of these "required" components or preconditions. In nineteenth century Germany, it occurred without much primitive accumulation of capital and in Italy without the Protestant ethic, to mention some of the earlier theories on prerequisites; and during the postwar period, Brazil experienced development in the absence of monetary stability, and Colombia even in the absence of public order, not to speak of land reform.

These experiences cast great doubt on the whole notion of preconditions or prerequisites. In fact, I believe with Gerschenkron that the only generalization one can make about the development of late comers is that they will not follow the sequence of their predecessors, but will insist on changing it around or on skipping entirely some stages as well as some "preconditions." Therefore, I continue to advocate that in their research, the experts pay special attention to the emergence and possible rationality of new or inverted sequences. When they discover an "obstacle," such as poor public administration or uneconomic land use, their job does not consist in merely advising its removal; they ought to explore also how, by moving the economy forward elsewhere, additional pressure (economic and political) could be brought on the obstacle to give way. The analysis of sequences I have in mind should be as comprehensive as possible and describe the interplay of economic, political, and cultural factors.

I am at present engaged, with the support of the Twentieth Century Fund, in the detailed analysis of sequences in economic policy-making around particular problems such as land reform or inflation or regional imbalance in five Latin American countries. In each case I am seeking answers to the question: At what particular point, under what combination of pressures, after what kind of learning process, are new insights about the nature of the problem acquired? When and why does it suddenly become possible to take effective action after decades of ineffective legislation and tinkering? I would be very interested to find out if similar efforts have been or are being undertaken by other social scientists.

But let me return to my theme. The American people might as well reconcile themselves to the fact that they will never be called on to give aid to a country unless it is afflicted with many, more or less loosely interrelated, facets of backwardness or obstacles to development. In this view, aid is a way of getting involved in the recipient country's battle against these obstacles. At first, the best the United States can do when joining the battle is often to follow Napoleon's maxim *"on s'engage; puis on voit."* Little by little, after getting committed and "seeing," that is, learning about the country's problems, some hypotheses should emerge about the sequence in which a country is likely to attack successfully the multifarious obstacles. In the search for the best hypothesis, those who administer aid programs should use what Dr. Carl Rogers, already aptly quoted by Hagen, calls "client-centered therapy." The well-known similarity in characteristics exhibited by underdeveloped countries at any one stage of development is matched only by the far less noticed variety of sequences and processes through which they move from one stage to the next. For example, the wide range of means by which one particular obstacle can be overcome was strikingly if somewhat inadvertently illustrated by Frank Tannenbaum when he wrote recently that Mexico acquired a feeling of pride in its own identity and achievements through its protracted revolution, whereas Brazil achieved similar confidence in its own destiny through the publication of a book, namely, Freyre's classic *Masters and Slaves*.

But there remains a serious question that is really the basic one to which Ambassador Galbraith was addressing himself. What if we have acquired the conviction that no further progress is possible unless a corrupt government gets ousted or a thorough-going land reform is instituted? Far be it from me to say that such situations are inconceivable. But perhaps Americans today are a little too ready to jump to this kind of conclusion. In reaction to the Cuban events they wish to rid themselves in a hurry of what Robert Heilbroner has recently called "American ostrichism," by which he means the earlier lack of attention to the social struggles and tensions that have so important a bearing on the course of development. At last, Americans have become painfully aware that it may be impossible to effect significant economic progress as long as aid actually strengthens those who are opposed to the social changes without which economic advance is impossible or meaningless.

Naturally, if the situation is the one depicted in the Communist textbook where the government is entirely the expression of one homogeneously reactionary and parasitic ruling clique while the country's popular energies and developmental resources wait to be unshackled through revolution, little can be said in favor of making aid available until the revolution has taken over. If this is the situation, the best thing for the United States Operations Mission to do is to join the rioting students or the backbush guerillas. But ordinarily reality is not that simple: the government in question may be unwilling to decree (or its parliament may be unwilling to vote) certain reforms that the United States Mission thinks are desirable; at the same time it may be anxious to undertake a variety of unexceptionable tasks of economic development. If the reforms are as central to further progress as the American experts think they are, these other tasks will either be impossible to carry out in the absence of the reforms, or they will make the need for the reforms even more compelling than before. Both eventualities bring the reforms closer, for they either force the hand of the government or hasten its downfall.

In this perspective, financial or technical help is justified, provided we Americans realize the kind of difficult game in which we are involved and are not caught unaware by the outbreak of crisis. By helping in peripheral tasks of economic development or by proving that such ventures are bound to fail within the existing socio-economic framework, one is waging a kind of guerilla warfare against the holdouts of reaction and backwardness at the center. From this point of view even the failure of a technical assistance mission can have its uses: nothing demonstrates as clearly the need to undertake thoroughgoing land reform as the failure of an attempt to establish an equitable land tax system.

Foreign aid does not necessarily always work to the benefit of the group that happens to be in power. It is desired by governments to enhance their prestige, but may turn out to undermine it. Frequently, foreign aid is requested to stave off reforms, but it may be made to accelerate them. The exploration and utilization of such disruptive and subversive potentialities of aid is perhaps particularly important for the United States as long as it is neither much given to guerilla warfare proper nor apparently very good at it. In order to be able to use aid in this fashion and not to be unduly surprised by the explosive consequences, the United States should devise ways of giving aid in a fashion that does not imply a wholesale endorsement of the programs, objectives, and values of the recipient government. It should learn—it has already done so in some cases, but is rather shamefaced about it— to cooperate with other governments in a variety of tasks, fully aware that the governments giving and receiving aid are pursuing objectives that overlap initially only to a very small extent. This way of using financial and technical assistance implies techniques quite different from those toward which the United States is now gravitating. To underwrite a development program—which appears to be the new formula, to be applied the world over—may be the appropriate technique when there is a rather complete meeting of minds. But not to underwrite a development program may be just as important at times; and it need not mean the absence of an over-all design on the part of the United States, or resignation to having just a collection of random projects. It may be a deliberate choice to remain aloof from full cooperation while giving support to certain aspirations. Perhaps research can help identify different types of aid policies appropriate to different constellations so that we will stop looking for the one best policy applicable to all possible circumstances.

2

Country Programing as a Guide to Development

GERHARD COLM AND THEODORE GEIGER*

THE RECENT REAPPRAISAL and reorganization of the United States foreign aid effort have given increased importance to long-range planning for development. Both the *Alianza para el Progreso* for Latin America and President Kennedy's 1961 messages to the Congress on foreign aid are explicitly based on the premise that American assistance of all types should be provided within the context of "carefully thought through programs tailored to meet the needs and resource potential of each individual country." (Special Message of March 22, 1961.) In the same document, the President stresses the principle that "long-term planning and financing is the only way to make meaningful and economical commitments." Thus, the United States government seems committed to a policy of using long-range development planning as a major essential component of its foreign aid strategy.

Well-conceived planning and programing can be of great usefulness in the process of economic and social development, and the current emphasis on them is a welcome change from the previous attitude of the United States government agencies concerned. After its successful use in the European Recovery Program (1948-1952), planning fell into disfavor in the government, and during the 1950's it was not encouraged in the underdeveloped countries receiving American aid. In contrast, the danger today is that the current enthusiasm for

---

* Gerhard Colm is Chief Economist and Theodore Geiger is Chief of International Studies, National Planning Association.

planning may inadvertently produce undesirable results at the opposite extreme. Too much reliance may be placed on plans and programs that have been hastily prepared, on the basis of little or no data, and which the governments involved may not have either the intention or the ability to implement. Planning may be regarded as the panacea to all development problems, with inevitable disappointment when it fails—as it must—to fulfill this unrealistic expectation. Plans will be of little use if they are presented in unnecessarily technical forms; in addition to their possible lack of realism, such esoteric documents may be ignored or resented by the administrators on whose cooperation their implementation depends. Government planning will also fail if the development plan or its constituent programs are too rigidly enforced without regard to changing circumstances or are not adequately related to private, decentralized, economic decision-making and activity. If the high hopes currently placed in planning are unfulfilled, a reaction may occur that could result in the loss of much of the progress currently being made in improving development methods.

These dangers would be lessened by a better understanding of the proper role of planning and of the nature and applications of effective planning techniques, including implementation of the plan. This essay is an attempt to outline the kinds of planning that are useful in the process of economic development and to suggest some of the main problems related to planning and planning techniques on which research is needed.

DEFINITIONS

In this paper, the terms "country programing" and "development planning" are used synonymously. They refer to deliberate, rational, continuous efforts by governments to accelerate the process of development and to channel it into desired directions by means of the comprehensive and detailed choice of objectives and the determination and allocation of the resources necessary for their achievement. Such a general definition of planning would cover a wide variety of specific types. In the Communist states, for example, the government's economic plan is centrally prepared and administered, covers virtually all sectors and activities, and its specific goals and resource allocations are enforced as law both by the government and by the ruling political party. In systems in which most of the economic decisions are made by private producers, consumers, and investors, it is usually only the government sectors that are planned in detail, while for key private sectors or industries general targets may be identified as guidelines for private activity. We deal specifically in this paper with planning techniques that are suitable for the economic development of countries in which public and private decision-making and activity are maintained side by side.

The term "development" is not used synonymously with "growth." In the underdeveloped countries of Asia, Africa, and Latin America, development requires social and cultural change as well as economic growth; that is, qualitative transformations must occur concurrently with quantitative increases. There is, in fact, a reciprocal relation between the two, and neither process is likely to continue for long or go very far without the other. Hence, development means change plus growth.

The terms "plans," "programs," and "projects" are used to refer to three different levels or degrees of specificity in the planning process. A *plan* relates to the economy as a whole, divided into major sectors and, perhaps, regions within the country. A *program* is the more detailed determination of the specific objectives to be achieved within each sector and region in accordance with a specified time schedule. *Projects* are the individual components of programs.

Another distinction employed in this paper is that between mathematical decision planning (use of decision models) and pragmatic development planning. The first relates to plans that are logically deduced from a model by mathematical methods; the second makes allowance for qualitative judgments in real-life situations. The distinction is by no means a clear-cut one, and, as will be indicated, pragmatic planning often makes use of mathematical models. The respective contributions and applicability of both aspects of planning are discussed below.[1]

Certain specific fields of development planning are not treated in this chapter because they are the assigned subjects of other authors

---

[1] It would have been desirable had it been possible to make a comprehensive and detailed analysis of the experience with mathematical decision planning and pragmatic planning, particularly of the efforts to use mathematical methods in the planning process with full allowance for policy judgments. Such an appraisal of the experiences of various countries would be one of the most useful research undertakings in this field.

(agriculture, rural community planning, the planning of education, and that aspect of economic planning called the choice of technologies) or are outside the scope of the series (project design and analysis). Although there is, in consequence, no discussion of project analysis per se in this essay, the authors fully recognize that it is an essential part of the total planning process.

PURPOSES OF DEVELOPMENT PLANNING

Contemporary decisions to use planning techniques reflect twentieth century unwillingness to leave to uncontrolled market forces the determination of a country's rate of growth, division of income, allocation of investment resources, and other variables affecting its economic condition and prospects. In contrast, the nineteenth century believed that such determinations could and should be made only by the free market mechanism, which was supposed automatically to bring about the greatest good for the greatest number by means of the most economical use of resources. Today, the purpose of planning is to enable governments deliberately to influence economic processes in order to supplement, reinforce, support, and guide the market process of private decision-making and activity.

More specifically, planning seeks directly or indirectly to influence those factors believed to determine the rate and direction of development. Hence, every development plan either consciously or unconsciously implies some particular theory of development and some notion of the specific ways in which the factors considered relevant can be stimulated to produce their effects. Development planning is, explicitly or implicitly, a strategy for development.

The development theories or strategies implied by development plans may be classified into three general types in accordance with their major—though not necessarily their exclusive—emphasis.[2] In the first category are quantitative economic theories, most of which stress the amount of saving and capital investment as the determining element in development. The second type may be called qualitative economic theories because they emphasize the generative role of specific economic activities or sectors: growth industry and leading sector

[2] See footnotes 14, 15, and 16 for the names of scholars identified with each type of theory.

theories, balanced or unbalanced growth theories, theories based on the dynamic role of particular economic groups, theories recognizing the function of "intangible" investments, and so forth. The third category comprises theories emphasizing noneconomic factors: the effects of changes in social values and attitudes, challenge and response, disaffected social classes, or deviant individuals.

However development theories may be classified, most scholars today recognize that no single factor can adequately account for a process as complex as development. Nor has empirical research as yet been thorough enough to enable us to identify all of the significant factors, and their specific modes of operation, that have been involved in the development experience of an actual country. Hence, quantitative theories—whose usefulness will be discussed in a later section—cannot normally reveal the intricacies of the development process because many of the relevant factors cannot be quantified either by their nature or in consequence of inadequate knowledge about them.

In the broadest sense, development is a social process that produces results that can be described and measured in economic terms. In the advanced industrialized societies, it is possible to assume as given the multitude of noneconomic factors that underlie and interpenetrate economic phenomena. Growth in these economies refers to economic expansion within a given social and cultural structure. Economic analysis need explicitly concern itself only with economic manifestations, which already embody the resultants of the operation of complex social, political, psychological, and other noneconomic factors. In contrast, economic analysis in the underdeveloped countries cannot do so because the noneconomic factors do not express themselves in the kind of economic behavior which conforms to the conventional assumptions of Western economic theory. Hirschman's distinction between the economics of growth and the economics of development is a useful one.[3] Our own definition of development as change plus growth is only another way of stressing the fact that, in the underdeveloped countries, noneconomic factors affecting development cannot be assumed as given, and therefore, discounted. Rather, they must be explicitly taken into account in the economic analysis of development.

It is for this reason that we use the general term "development" and not the more restrictive term "economic development." A devel-

[3] Albert O. Hirschman, *The Strategy of Economic Development* (Yale University Press, 1958), p. 29.

opment plan that is not consciously related to the major noneconomic factors operating in the country concerned—even if they are not formally incorporated into the plan itself—would be only a theoretical exercise.

THE COMPONENTS OF DEVELOPMENT PLANNING

A number of components or elements can be distinguished on logical grounds in the process of development planning. These are not necessarily carried on in chronological order: indeed, as will be indicated below, better planning probably results if they are not.

Logically, the first component of a development plan is the definition of the purposes for which development is being undertaken. Three levels of specificity in national purposes may be distinguished. The first relates to the general *objectives* of the plan. For example, the purpose of the plan may be to raise living standards, or to improve defense capabilities, or to increase the nation's prestige and influence abroad, or some combination of these or other purposes. In turn, these objectives must be broken down into more specific *goals,* for example, the increases in production, savings, investment, consumption, foreign trade, and other aggregative variables needed to accomplish the objectives of the plan. Finally, *targets* need to be distinguished—the specific quantitative increases that must be achieved in particular economic sectors, for example, rice production, miles of railroads to be built, or number of schools to be constructed. All three levels must also be related to specific time periods within which they are to be accomplished.

The second logical element is determination of the resources actually and potentially available for achieving the specific goals and targets of the development plan. Resources include not only the necessary production inputs but also the capital required both to utilize existing material and human resources and to develop additional ones.

The third logical component is selection of the means whereby resources can be mobilized to achieve the specified goals and targets. A government has at its disposal various types of policies and measures for directly or indirectly bringing about the desired development. These include direct public investment; making public funds available in various ways to the private sector; aid of different kinds obtained from foreign governments and international organizations; encouragement of private foreign investment; fiscal and monetary policies to limit consumption, augment savings, and stimulate and channel indigenous private investment; and other instruments at the disposal of the national government. The particular combination of means that the government selects depends on the particular needs, administrative capabilities and limitations, and past experiences of the country concerned. There is, of course, a reciprocal relationship between ends and means. The economic institutions and values of the society will play a major role in predetermining the specific kinds of means believed appropriate, while the means employed will inevitably modify to some degree the pre-existing institutions and values and hence the goals of the development effort. Moreover, means may also be ends in certain respects. Better health and education and improved working conditions are not only means to higher productivity; they are also desirable ends in themselves.

The fourth logical component of the development planning process is the formulation of specific programs within the general plan. Programs embody the decisions about targets, priorities, and timing within particular agricultural and industrial sectors; specific regions within the country; functional activities (distribution, foreign trade); educational, health, and social service fields. Each program includes not only a description of the specific targets to be achieved, but also an inventory of the material and financial resources required, and the phasing of the program over time. In addition, the program specifies the means whereby the resources are to be mobilized for achieving the program goals. Ideally, each program should be refined to the point where it lists the individual projects which must be undertaken to achieve it.

The final element of a well-conceived development plan is the provision for its implementation. This includes the organization of the planning function and its administrative relationships with the chief executive, the policy-making and operating departments of the government, and the legislature; the assignment of responsibilities for carrying out its component programs; the relationship of the plan to the national budget; the roles of the fiscal and monetary authorities; the provisions for progress reporting and evaluation; and the selection and training of planning personnel. The arrangements for implementation of the plan are too often neglected entirely or are inadequate in development planning today.

PLANNING IN MIXED ECONOMIES

A plan for a country in which public and private decisions are expected to contribute to economic development will normally consist of two parts. One presents guides for government decisions. If the plan is formally adopted, this part has an obligatory character. The other presents estimates of the effects of voluntary decisions of private individuals and organizations as they are likely to be made under the conditions induced by the government measures posited in the plan.

Depending on the economic structure of a country, the obligatory and voluntary parts of the plan will have different relative importance. Even in the plans of Communist countries, voluntary decisions of individuals to buy consumer goods under the terms prescribed by the government are at least implied. At the other extreme, even in a completely free enterprise system, investment, production, and consumption would be influenced by the public facilities provided by the government, by its tax and credit policies, and by such regulatory measures as it might enforce. In countries in which private and public enterprises exist side by side, the government additionally influences private decisions in consequence of its role as a supplement to, or competitor of, private activities, which it may support, stimulate, or restrict.

Moreover, while the plan itself may involve forecasts of voluntary private activities, it may also, by its very existence, exert a significant influence on private decisions. Private enterprises may use the plan as a guide in determining their own voluntary actions. Business decision makers plan their investments in plant and equipment in the light of expected future markets for their products. If they have confidence in the planners and in the government's determination to play the role specified for it in the plan, they may use the plan as a guide for estimating their own future markets and make their decisions accordingly. In mixed economies, the confidence of private decision makers in the realism of the plan adds to the likelihood that it will be realized. This is the announcement effect of the plan, and it can be either positive or negative.

For the success of any development planning effort consistent with democratic institutions or goals, it is important that arrangements be made for the effective participation of private producers, consumers, and investors in the planning process at some stage prior to the final adoption of the plan. This participation not only is relevant to the preparation of estimates for the private sectors, as explained in a later section, but should also include opportunities for the major private organizations and groups to express their views on the plan as a whole, and on its policy implications for them, before it is finalized. For a variety of reasons, such participation is difficult to organize effectively, especially in underdeveloped countries where the necessary degree of education and experience may be lacking. This is one of the major problems on which research is needed.

In the highly industrialized Western countries, various methods have been evolved for the participation of the private sectors in national planning. Particularly in the United States, many large business firms do their own long-range investment, production, and market planning. Information about these individual company plans is available to government agencies and private research organizations. In turn, business enterprises use both official and other long-range economic projections as frameworks within which their own plans can be reviewed and appraised.

There are some countries in Asia and Latin America (India, Argentina, Brazil, Mexico) in which private enterprises are already large and experienced enough to engage in similar long-range planning of their own. This is not the case, however, in most underdeveloped countries. There, the government planning authority will usually have to take the initiative in encouraging business firms, cooperatives, and other private enterprises—or at least the larger ones—to formulate individual plans for additional investment and production for the specified planning period.[4] As the number, size, and self-confidence of private enterprises increase, they are likely of their own accord to adopt more effective methods of private planning.

We do not mean to imply that the private sector in underdeveloped countries will or should necessarily consist predominantly of large corporate enterprises like those that characterize the advanced Western economies. In addition to the corporate type, there are other pos-

[4] Such information from individual private firms and enterprises should be held in strict confidence by the data collecting agency.

sible forms of private or quasi-private, decentralized decision-making and activity that may be equally—or even more—congenial and appropriate to the limitations and potentialities of underdeveloped countries, for example, individual and family enterprises, agricultural and industrial producers' and marketing cooperatives of various kinds, and rural community organizations. These should participate in the planning process along with indigenous private business corporations. Foreign-owned firms operating in the country, especially when their activities have a significant influence on the rate and direction of development, should also be consulted at appropriate stages in the planning process.

THE THEORETICAL BASIS OF PRAGMATIC PLANNING

It would be desirable if pragmatic planning consisted only of applying a theoretical decision model, which in turn was based on a generally accepted theory of development. This ideal situation has not been attained and, as already indicated, we doubt whether it is possible of achievement. Nonetheless, we do not question the value of theoretical work for development planning; nor that the collection of empirical data for the past and their analysis and explanation in the light of theory are prerequisites for planning of every type.

Here, we are concerned only with some of the claims made regarding the direct application to development planning of mathematical formulations of growth models. Outstanding examples of such models are the Cobb-Douglas production function and the Harrod-Domar theory of growth. These and similar theories have the value of compelling analysts to identify many of the economic variables which contribute to—or, more precisely, condition—economic growth. Later in this chapter, the use of mathematical models to test the internal consistency of plans derived in a pragmatic manner will also be emphasized. However, their direct use as practical decision models is, in our opinion, very limited, particularly in the conditions of the underdeveloped countries.

The production function type of analysis (for example, in the Cobb-Douglas form) can help in understanding the relationship between increases in production and increases in labor, capital, and other factors. While one can obtain fairly good data on the input of labor, it is difficult to obtain and interpret empirical data for capital input. But, the greatest difficulty is with the "other factors," which include improvements in education and health, technological and managerial advances, effect of size of markets, direct and indirect impact of government actions, and other, less tangible changes in the social environment and culture. These other factors are difficult enough to appraise with the data available in highly developed economies; they usually defy measurement in the underdeveloped countries. We have already emphasized that these other factors are essential elements in development. Decision models and mathematical planning embodying in their equations only the quantifiable elements can be very misleading.

Or, take as another example the very elegant Harrod-Domar equation: rate of growth equals rate of saving over capital-output ratio. The capital-output ratio is estimated for various countries—usually with some apology for using the average instead of the marginal ratio—and treated as a constant. Then, a computation is made of the rate of savings (personal, corporate, and government savings) needed to accomplish a desired rate of growth. In consequence of the practical limits in low income countries on increasing the rate of savings by such measures as tax and credit policies, a savings gap results; and the rate of growth then becomes to a considerable extent a function of the new capital import.

It is obvious that a decision model based on this theory would give little guidance on the *domestic* policies needed to support economic growth in underdeveloped countries. The possible contribution of many of these policies would be hidden in the "constant" capital-output ratio.

Not all who advocate the direct use of mathematical decision planning overlook this difficulty. Thus, the experts of the Economic Commission for Asia and the Far East[5] made a special effort to introduce education as one type of investment. However, their proposal to use aggregate marks in examinations as a means of quantifying the social benefits of education demonstrates, on the contrary, the impossibility of building such factors into a quantitative model.

[5] U. N. Economic Commission for Asia and the Far East, *Programming Techniques for Economic Development,* Bangkok (1960).

In a valuable United Nations survey "Use of Models in Programing,"[6] it is claimed that the use of decision models has great advantages over more intuitive or qualitative methods. Though quantitative studies of the contributions of various factors to economic growth are an indispensable basis for rational decision-making, it is also clear that the importance of some—possibly the most significant—factors in the process of economic development can be appraised only with a considerable element of intuition or qualitative judgment. Even for the United States, the National Planning Association has characterized the estimates used in its long-term projections and targets as a "judgment model." By advocating the use of judgment models, which admittedly do not have the rigor of mathematical deductions, we do not deny at all the usefulness of the latter. Pragmatic planning, as we use the term, is not anti-mathematical. It recognizes both the limits of mathematical methods and the role that qualitative judgment— and also trial and error—must play in planning. Particularly in conditions of "growth plus change" and under the limitation of available data, it is not possible to derive appropriate policy conclusions by methods of mathematical rigor which exclude the "subjectivity" of intuition and judgment.

THE PROCESS OF PRAGMATIC PLANNING AND PROGRAMING

All planning—both by use of mathematical deductions and by pragmatic methods—depends on reliable data or estimates for a base period of the recent past (and, where obtainable, on historical series going further back into the past) from which trends can be extrapolated.[7] These past data should, of course, not be used for a mere mechanical projection because one of the major purposes of planning is to help formulate policies that would bring about desirable changes in trends.

Long-range perspective planning (ten years or longer) must be distinguished from intermediate and short-range operational planning (usually two to five years). Perspective planning sets goals in

---

[6] U. N. Department of Economic and Social Affairs, *Industrialization and Productivity*, Bulletin No. 4 (1961), p. 8.
[7] The types of data needed are discussed in the next section.

terms of total production, employment, income, consumption, foreign trade, and possibly prices, with a breakdown only by major component sectors. It is used as a perspective in preparing the more detailed operational plan.

Operational planning consists essentially of two processes: from the top down and from the bottom up.

From the Top Down

The from-the-top-down process starts by setting tentative quantitative goals for the planning period. These are derived from the long-term perspective plan in order to make sure that a long step in the desired direction is taken. Whether directly or via the long-term perspective plan, the goals are ultimately based on as detailed an analysis as possible of the country's developed and undeveloped material and human resources. Such resource surveys indicate each country's specific potentials for development.

The formulation of goals also depends on the existing character and structure of the country's economy. Goals will differ for countries where the factors limiting growth are in the labor supply (in size or skills), in capital supply, in export opportunities, in management talent, in cultural conditions, or in a combination of these and many other factors.

Goals should be established not only for countries as a whole but also for various regions within the country. In this connection, it is especially important for the planners not to concentrate only on the metropolitan areas, for which the best data are usually available and where government influence may be strongest. The planners must be aware of the "centralizing pull" (to use a phrase of John P. Lewis) that is implicit in the planning process. It may be harder, but it is equally important to work on the development of the hinterland and to stimulate industries in suitable locations outside the metropolitan areas.

The second step consists of estimating the expansion in various sectors of final demand which would be in accordance with the goals. Estimates are needed of investment in agriculture and in public and private nonagricultural enterprises; of possible increases of output in agriculture and other sectors due to productivity gains or labor force increases; of corresponding increases in goods and services available for public administration and public services (including education); of consumer supplies of housing, durables, and other goods and services. How far aggregates are broken down into component parts depends, of course, on the data available for the base period.

Next, an estimate is needed of the imports required for the projected increase in production, divided into raw materials, capital equipment, and consumer goods. Also, exports have to be estimated, as one of the demand factors, in the light of the probable development of world markets and of possible changes in international competitive conditions.

Once estimates for the major categories of final demand and their component parts have been obtained, it is possible to estimate production by finer subclassifications. If it can possibly be prepared, an input-output table will be of great assistance in this part of the work.

In addition to the plan expressed in physical units of production or in values of constant general purchasing power (although with modified price relations), a financial plan should also be prepared. It should spell out the tax revenues, borrowing, and other financial resources required by the government, and also the financial resources required by privately and publicly financed enterprises. At the same time, estimates should be prepared of the generation of financial resources by individuals, enterprises, government, and—when appropriate—by the central bank. Any gap between the financial requirements and the estimated indigenous financial resources would be one of the factors indicating the need to obtain loans or grants from abroad.[8]

There should also be a specific projection of the international balance of payments, incorporating the import and export projections already described. The balance-of-payments estimate should be consistent with the projected increase in domestic production and income and with the needs for capital equipment and raw materials. Anticipated payments of interest and principal would reflect the existing foreign debt and the expected increase in external indebtedness. The balance-of-payments projections would have to take account of proposed changes in policies, for example, intended diversification of exports, stimulation of domestic production of goods wholly imported in the past, and encouragement of private foreign investment. If the balance of payments still shows a residual future gap, alternative policies to close the gap would have to be considered, and their effects es-

[8] The domestic financial gap is usually not the same as the foreign exchange gap, nor does external assistance for the latter automatically take care of the former.

timated. Should the gap between the need for and the availability of capital, or that between payments to and receipts from abroad, be larger than could be closed with feasible policies, the goals of the development plan obviously have to be reconsidered.

From the Bottom Up

While the planning authorities are engaged in the from-the-top-down process, they should also initiate a from-the-bottom-up procedure. This consists of asking the individual units of government (central government departments or ministries, and public corporations, as well as regional and local bodies) for information about the changes in plans and policies they contemplate or recommend for the ensuing planning period. Similar information should also be obtained from private enterprises of all types, and they should be encouraged to prepare their own individual plans for additional investments and production for the specified period.

Agencies concerned with special projects of substantial size (such as hydroelectric power or transportation facilities) would be asked to submit their plans in detail, including expected benefits, costs, required imports, and possible alternatives. The planning agency would evaluate all of these projects in terms of the general objectives and goals of the plan.[9]

The government ministries concerned with the labor market and the educational system would contribute their estimates of the probable changes in the labor supply due to demographic causes, the expected migration among the various regions, the availability of trained labor, and so forth. The appropriate private and public agencies would also submit estimates about the foreign capital resources likely to become available.

Testing and Adoption of a Final Plan

The next step in the planning process consists of matching the from-the-top-down and the from-the-bottom-up estimates. The infor-

---

[9] As already noted, this paper does not discuss the various methods proposed, and in part used, for the evaluation of individual projects. For a survey of methods see Hollis B. Chenery, "Comparative Advantage and Development Policy," *American Economic Review*, Vol. 51 (March 1961), pp. 18-51. It is interesting to note that, according to Eckstein, some "social judgment" is also needed for integrating the appraisal of investment projects into the planning process.

mation about the investment and production plans of public agencies and private enterprises obtained under the latter procedure can be used to help appraise the feasibility of the general estimates which were calculated as needed for reaching the goals tentatively derived in the from-the-top-down procedure. This comparison, as well as the other checks used at this stage of the planning process, will inevitably reveal discrepancies, but will also yield tentative indications of how they might be resolved. Decisions now have to be made concerning the adjustments in the goals required to make them feasible; the shifts in programs needed to provide the necessary social overhead capital (in the broadest sense); and the policy changes requisite to stimulating public and private enterprises to undertake actions consistent with fulfillment of the plan.

It is at this stage of the planning process that the internal consistency of the plan should be tested before final decisions are made and the plan is officially approved. For example, projected advances in manufacturing industry must be in accordance with the projected supply of raw materials either from domestic production or imports; requisite capital formation should be checked against the expected savings of individuals, enterprises, or the government, with any excess of planned capital outlays limited by realistic expectations of private capital imports and foreign financial assistance; and other variables matched with one another.

Mathematical techniques can be useful in checking the internal consistency of the plan, for this testing process is essentially a quantitative operation. However, it must be stressed that, particularly in the underdeveloped countries, mathematical methods need to be used with realism and restraint. The availability and quality of statistical information will largely determine the choice of techniques to be used. Data may not be available for quantifying enough of the component terms of mathematical models to produce useful, or even meaningful, results. Hence, simple algebraic procedures are more likely to be appropriate for the rather rough and sketchy data with which many underdeveloped countries must work. As their statistical information becomes comprehensive and detailed, more sophisticated mathematical techniques and high-speed computers will become useful.

The discrepancies affecting the activities of public and private enterprises should not be arbitrarily eliminated by the planning authority. Their nature and implications should be explained to the public and private organizations and groups concerned (or their representatives), and efforts should be made to reach agreements with them on the changes in individual private plans—or perhaps in the conflicting government programs—which might be needed to resolve, or at least minimize, serious discrepancies. However, care should be taken that such agreements are not used by the public and private enterprises involved to protect their market positions rather than to help them undertake expansion and modernization consistent with the goals of the plan.

When a final plan has been developed by reconciliation of the two types of estimates, a list can be compiled of those policy changes and government measures that are required for reaching the revised goals. These programs should then be formally submitted for approval to the executive and legislative authorities. To the extent applicable, the development plan should be incorporated into the budget plans of the central and local governments. It is essential that the development planning process not be carried on independently of, or isolated from, the ordinary budgetary planning operations of the government. To be successfully implemented, development planning must be fully integrated into the government machinery as a whole.

On the basis of the final plan, the production and investment targets for specific industries should also be revised (again, if possible, by use of input-output techniques). There is, however, a question about the amount of detail that should be incorporated into the government plan when it is published as an official document. It may be preferable to include in the official publication only aggregates by major economic sectors and regions, while issuing the corresponding projections (targets) for specific industries as unofficial studies. Alternatively, they could be published by a separate national research institute, or by an appropriate private research organization. The argument against including the specific projections in the official plan is that private enterprises, which take these targets into account but get into trouble, may claim that they should in consequence be bailed out by the government. Hence, it may be desirable to publish these estimates in a form that offers them as guidance for private enterprises without relieving the latter of the responsibility for making decisions regarding their own future investment and production.

In short, planning proposals should be worked out by individuals who use past experience, statistical and mathematical computations, and their own best judgment. The result should be subjected to the democratic process of debate and final political action before it is made official. In addition, the plan should be reviewed each year. Progress or lack of progress should be reported and revisions proposed and adopted on the basis of experience. In this regard, the practice of some United States communities, business firms, and private research organizations may be relevant: they use in their long-term planning a "rolling method" by which every year they review, and if necessary revise, the program for the remaining years of the plan, and then add the estimates for a new, further year at the end.

This method of successive approximation and balancing of goals with programs for public and private activities is less elegant than a strictly mathematical method of decision-making appears to be—at least on paper. But, it seems to us much more realistic, and it has shown results in a number of countries—both industrialized and developing—in which this, or a similarly pragmatic, method has been used.[10]

As already noted, econometric methods can be, and have been, applied within such a pragmatic approach. For example, the relationship between final demand by consumers, business, and government, on the one hand, and the production of specific commodities and services, on the other, can best be tested through the use of input-output coefficients. The internal consistency of the plan with respect to its component parts and to such limiting factors as the labor force, capital, and foreign trade, can also be tested by mathematical methods.[11]

[10] For a survey of planning methods used in various countries see U. N. Economic Commission for Latin America, *Analyses and Projections of Economic Development,* "I. An Introduction to the Technique of Programming" (1955); U. N. Department of Economic and Social Affairs, *Industrialization and Productivity,* Bulletin No. 4 (1961); and U. N. Economic and Social Council, *World Economic Situation, Evaluation of Long-Term Economic Projections* (1960). See also *Planning for Economic and Social Development for Latin America,* Report of a Group of Experts (Pan American Union, August 1961). An international survey of government organization for economic development is being undertaken by the International Institute of Administrative Sciences. Mathematical decision models have been used in the Netherlands, and experiments have been made and are being made with them in the United States and, apparently, also in the Soviet Union. Most planning in the underdeveloped countries has used pragmatic methods, sometimes supplemented by the input-output technique for working out details. However, in some countries, *e.g.,* India, mathematical methods have been effectively used for testing the internal consistency of the plans.

[11] Reference to internal consistency does not exclude the possibility that development in one sector may sometimes be ahead of developments in other sectors. Temporary imbalances may be regarded as part of development strategy, *cf.* Hirschman, *op. cit.,* pp. 62-76.

In these ways, mathematical methods can play an important role in the planning process even in underdeveloped countries without, however, justifying the claim of some of their most ardent proponents that optimum policy choices can best be made by electronic computers. While the incorporation into the planning process of a highly technical complex of equations and calculations may delight econometricians, it may very well alienate the officials responsible for the approval and implementation of the plan. The intelligibility of the plan, especially in the underdeveloped countries, is more important for its political and popular acceptance than is its mathematical sophistication.

Pragmatic planning leaves scope for effective consideration of factors that defy quantification. It also is so flexible that a country can adapt it to the statistical information that is available, and can improve it as more empirical data is developed. It is conceded that the results are not those of "pure science," but involve human judgment with the possibility of error. In addition, recognition that planning contains a large element of judgment, and that mathematics can play only an auxiliary—though nonetheless important—role, prevents the planners from becoming a kind of technocratic elite speaking a mathematical language not understandable either to political leaders or even to well-educated citizens in the countries concerned.

DATA NEEDED FOR PRAGMATIC PLANNING

As already mentioned, all planning rests on empirical data. Comprehensive planning (from the top down, as described above) rests on aggregate estimates of the economy and of its major sectors for the past. The determination of feasible goals for the future rests on data about the country's existing and potential resources—material, human, and financial.

However, there is a view which maintains that estimates of national economic accounts are valid only if they are the final product of a detailed and comprehensive statistical system resting on complete demographic, social, and economic data, which are in effect summarized in the aggregate series. This opinion is in part reflected in the report of the United Nations Statistical Commission responsible in 1958 for preparing a list of the statistical series which "would be of assistance to less developed countries in developing an integrated set of basic statistics for use in programmes of economic and social development."[12]

We are in full accord that every effort should be made to develop the statistical series described in the United Nations list. These include series on population; labor; production; agriculture; forestry; fishing; mining; manufacturing; construction; production of gas and electricity; wholesale, retail, and related service trades; transportation; education, health, and other welfare services; external trade; money and banking, finance, and general prices; government; and personal incomes and conditions of living.

However, the United Nations list does not include national economic accounts or data on capital formation and savings (except for reference in an annex to sample household inquiries on income, consumption, and saving). The omission is justified in the United Nations report on the grounds that, valuable as national economic accounts are in development planning, the information necessary to prepare them will only be forthcoming when there has been a "considerable advancement in the collection of basic data."

This view implies a counsel of perfection in the statistical field that is quite unrealistic not only for underdeveloped countries but for the developed countries as well. It may be conceded that in some countries national economic accounts may have been "constructed" virtually without any reliable statistical basis. Such wholly synthetic (a polite expression for saying that they are taken "out of the air") national economic accounts for the past and the related national economic budgets for the future do little good and much harm. However, our view is that a middle course has to be steered between a frustrating statistical perfectionism, on the one hand, and imaginary statistics produced by wishful thinking, on the other hand.

Fortunately, it has been possible for many underdeveloped countries with inadequate statistics to develop reasonable aggregate estimates of income, production, consumption, investment, savings, and international trade. As soon as reliable employment data are available for a country, it is possible to estimate production by using output-per-man-year ratios from countries with similar economic structures and more advanced statistical information. A comparison of data, such as production per man, average income, and savings ratios, for various

[12] U. N. Statistical Office, *Statistical Series for the Use of Less Developed Countries in Programmes of Economic and Social Development,* Statistical Papers, M 31 (1959), p. 1.

broader programs into which they must fit. Such techniques for relating project analysis to programing would vary quite widely for different countries depending on the relative sizes of their public and private sectors and on many other factors.

More effective methods for making longer-range economic projections also need to be developed. These have to be adapted to varying degrees of availability and reliability of data, and to the differing development needs and possibilities of underdeveloped countries.

Case studies are needed of interindustry and intersectoral relations in different types, and at different stages, of development. Particular attention should be paid to research that would accumulate and analyze data on the more dynamic aspects of such relationships, for example, detailed examples of Hirschman's "backward and forward linkages," and analyses of external economies.

Improved methods for taking into account both the development of the highly monetized sectors of the economy (usually along the seacoast) and the largely subsistence sectors (generally in the hinterland) are required. Such studies should make it possible to reach decisions about the location of future industries in the broad perspective of accessibility to raw materials, distribution of present and potential markets, existing and possible methods of transportation, available and potential sources of energy, and the social and cultural factors determining the labor supply. Considerable work on motivations and attitudes would be involved in research into these economic variables.

In view of the schemes for regional economic integration in various parts of the world, it would be desirable to study the respects in which the national development plans of the member countries need to be harmonized and the methods by which integration might be accomplished.

It would be useful to ascertain the specific sectors, particularly in the private economy, in which planning is useful and desirable and those in which it is not. In which industries is it worthwhile and appropriate for enterprises to prepare individual long-range plans or for the planning authority to formulate industry targets? In which would projections, prepared either by the government or by a private research organization, be sufficient for planning needs? The results should vary from country to country.

A series of case studies could usefully be undertaken of how actual planning decisions have been made in particular countries. Some might focus on the use of specific planning techniques; others on the administrative aspects of the process.

Another problem on which research is needed is the development of better progress reporting and progress evaluation techniques. Requirements in this respect will also vary from country to country.

Administrative Aspects of Development Planning

In most countries, planning is undertaken by government agencies often working in an administrative vacuum. Full integration of the planning process into the normal operations of the government is essential for successful planning. Such integration will differ from country to country, depending on political and administrative institutions. Studies of existing arrangements and of ways to achieve better integration would be valuable.

There is a great need for stimulating much wider public interest in the underdeveloped countries in development planning. Methods need to be improved for involving private enterprises more effectively in the planning process. Also, it would be desirable to explore appropriate arrangements by which educational institutions and private citizen groups could learn about and participate in the planning effort. Some suggestions have been made in this chapter. These need to be explored more thoroughly; the experience of countries that have experimented with such arrangements should be appraised; and recommendations developed for improved methods of private participation in development planning.

While planning and programing must be carried out with the full self-responsibility of the country concerned, considerable help can be given by regional and international organizations, and also by non-governmental research institutions in both the developed and the underdeveloped countries. This is particularly true in the development of planning and programing techniques suitable for different types of countries. In addition, possible regional and international arrangements for a clearing house for factual information, and for preparing projections of future international markets for key commodities should be explored.

3

Research on Rural Problems

ARTHUR T. MOSHER*

W H E N E V E R one thinks about rural development, it is important to keep in mind the multiform variety of physical, economic, and cultural circumstances within which the rural people of the world live. Many, but by no means all, of the low-income rural regions of the world are characterized by dense population, complex social structure, and small, largely subsistence farms, each made up of scattered plots of land. Nevertheless, while it is normal to think of dense population as the rule in such regions, there are vast areas of Africa, parts of the Philippines and Indonesia, and of central South America where population is sparse and considerable quantities of potentially tillable land still go unused. Moreover, there are appreciable settled regions in South America, Africa, and even in Asia where production is largely for subsistence, but where farms are not small and they are not fragmented.

In many, but not all, of these regions there are commercial one-crop plantations of rubber, sugar, tea, coffee, coconuts, and tobacco interspersed among the thousands of small subsistence farms. In other places, as in east central Africa and in the highlands of South America, there are large estates involving varied cropping or combining livestock and crop production. Some of these are operated primarily for profit, but in other places so much social prestige attaches to ownership of large acreages that the profitability of the agricultural operation is of secondary concern, and technology consequently is at a low level. Even in the relatively high-income rural regions of the

* Executive Director, The Council on Economic and Cultural Affairs, Inc.

world, there are numerous pockets where agricultural production at a relatively low level of technology has persisted for centuries.

VARIATIONS IN RATE OF AGRICULTURAL DEVELOPMENT

Of perhaps even greater significance to this study than the variations among types of agriculture, is the variation in the rate at which agricultural development has been taking place within the past two decades in different parts of the world. In Latin America, while Argentina, Uruguay, and Chile, endowed with considerable natural resources for agricultural production, have failed to make substantial progress, Mexico, with much more limited natural advantages, has moved ahead, particularly in the north, at an astounding rate. In Western Europe, there is a dramatic contrast between prewar and postwar agricultural productivity. Japan and Taiwan have enjoyed spectacular agricultural progress in the past fifteen years. India has made gains which are modest when measured against needs but impressive when the dimensions of the problem are considered. Israel is estimated to have increased agricultural production 10 per cent in each of the past six years, and in the United States labor productivity has been rising two and one-half times as rapidly in agriculture as in industry for the past twenty years.

What these differences in rates of agricultural development and these different circumstances in which progress and relative stagnation are now taking place add up to is five facts of great significance to these investigations: First, there is enormous potential for agricultural development in the world. Second, the critical problems are numerous; they vary greatly from region to region; some problems are physical, others are cultural and political; there are no easy answers or panaceas. Third, agriculture is not inherently a primitive industry, since some of the most rapid agricultural development is now taking place in the most industrialized parts of the world, and many forms of agriculture are highly "capital-intensive." Fourth, in research to improve developmental assistance with respect to rural problems, attention should not be focused on low-income regions alone; equally valuable lessons can be learned by examining regions of rapid development and the pockets of persisting low productivity within highly developed and rapidly developing regions. Fifth, agricultural development is not independent of development in other sectors of the economy. Instead, the most rapid agricultural development can only occur where substantial industrial development is taking place, and where social and political developments make their essential contributions.

THE "SPECIAL RURAL PROBLEMS"

In a broad sense, the rural problems in low-income countries are to increase agricultural and other rural production and to maintain or increase the satisfactions of rural life. Stated in more specific categories, these problems embrace production, health, education, rural public works, social organization, and local administration. The "problems" grow largely out of certain characteristics of most low-income regions. No general description is applicable to all such regions, but most low-income regions have not advanced very far from the descriptions that follow and set lower limits from which "developing" countries progress:

A largely *subsistence* agriculture, with the choice of crops chiefly on the basis of utility in family consumption rather than market value, with the meager development of market structure, and with the limited horizon of personal experience and of commercial attitudes that go with these.

A largely *traditional* agriculture, at a low level of technology, that does not stimulate interest in innovation, that does not see practical economic value in knowledge, and in which decision-making is limited to a relatively few choices in production and in consumption.

A general lack of modern medical facilities and of effective measures of environmental sanitation.

A rural population living largely in a pre-literate, tradition-dominated folk culture.

A social structure dominated by the extended family, or caste, or tribe, with traditional social responsibilities that diffuse among many the benefits of above-average performance by any individual, while at the same time providing a kind of social security which individuals are reluctant to abandon.

A feudal or postcolonial pattern of government dominated by the wealthy, the "educated," and the administrators, with a consequent feeling of passive acquiescence and a "waiting for the government" on the part of most rural people even in matters of local concern within the potential power of local people to handle.

Little knowledge by rural people of alternatives within agricultural production and home practices open to them, and very little provision for increasing the range of such alternatives through research.

In the context of the total development of an economy, the importance of rural development rests on two basic facts:

1. The majority of the people in underdeveloped countries now depend on agriculture for their livelihood. Moreover, given the capital costs of industrialization and current rates of population growth, the absolute number of people dependent on agriculture for a living in most of these countries cannot be reduced in the foreseeable future. Most countries will be fortunate if the new employment made possible by industrialization proves adequate to match increases in the size of the labor force.

2. Many of the resources for agricultural production are not transferable to use in other types of production. This being true, and since every country wanting to progress must save and invest, making substantial purchases of capital goods from abroad in the process, no country can afford not to utilize fully every productive resource it now has. The importance of agricultural development, therefore, lies not so much in the fact that it increases the food supply as in the fact that a major part of the productive capacity in these countries is today in agriculture, and many of these productive agricultural resources are not convertible to other uses.

From the standpoint of the criteria of social and political stability, there are some countries with respect to which it could be argued that, for the immediate future, increasing opportunities for the more politically active urban-industrial populations is more important than what does or does not happen in the countryside. However, if the necessary steps are taken to increase agricultural production, more fully utilizing nonconvertible agricultural resources, one result is bound to be greater political awareness and activity among rural folk, and an additional argument for rural development that is not solely economic thus comes into play: namely, to foster a pattern of rural life that can initiate, facilitate, and absorb change within an orderly process of social and political adjustment. Indeed, an enlarging political role for rural people is among the components contributing to agricultural development in any nontotalitarian society.

AGRICULTURAL DEVELOPMENT AND RURAL WELFARE

The various requirements for rural development—subsuming the special rural problems it is our task to consider—may conveniently be summarized under two headings: (1) requirements for agricultural development, and (2) interrelationships between agricultural development and rural welfare.

Agricultural Development

Basically, the requirements for agricultural development are an educated, alert, skillful, venturesome farm population, living within a political, economic, and legal framework offering incentives to effort and conducive to orderly change, and supported by an appropriate set of *services, facilities,* and *public programs.* There is no which-comes-first in this complex, although the activities of developmental assistance lie predominantly in the field of services, facilities, and public programs. This is where it is acceptable to most countries for developmental assistance to take hold. Fortunately, certain of the public programs where assistance is welcome are, when appropriately conducted, among the best opportunities for moving rural people toward greater alertness, new skills and understanding, and greater venturesomeness. And while the political and legal frameworks are widely considered to be too sensitive for outside participation, there are an increasing number of opportunities and invitations for developmental assistance personnel to advise with respect to them.

Beginning where developmental assistance normally begins, agricultural development can be facilitated by an appropriate set of private or public services, facilities, and programs. These include: programs of general education; public investment in roads and communications; private commercial networks or public programs to ensure adequate availability of agricultural requisites: seeds, fertilizers, and implements; adequate market outlets for farm produce; programs of research; agricultural higher education; programs of rural extension education; public investment in irrigation; private or public facilities to provide production credit; programs of rural public health; programs fostering rural organization for voluntary group action.

All of these facilitate agricultural development, but they are of markedly differing importance. At early stages of agricultural development, these varying priorities should be carefully weighed. The most efficient bundle of public programs is probably not the best balanced as between the services, facilities, and programs mentioned in this list, and the most efficient combination varies from country to country with local conditions.

The "rules of the game," the *political, economic,* and *legal framework,* within which the agriculture of any region must operate are important because of their influence on the incentives for farmers to increase production, because they facilitate or inhibit orderly changes in the framework itself (which become necessary as agricultural development proceeds), and because the political process must provide (or fail to provide) the public programs, facilities, and services which agricultural development requires. Laws regarding land tenure and tenancy, taxation, inheritance, civil service, political suffrage, and patterns of national, regional, and local government are among those having the greatest impact on agricultural development. Economic policies with respect to prices and with respect to allocation of public investment are also of great importance.

No matter how many times it may be argued that "what the United States is concerned with is technical assistance, the culture and values of the people must not be disturbed," the fact remains that unless *attitudes and values* do change substantially, development will not come about. From acceptance of nature as beyond influence (except through ritual) those who would contribute to development must shift to viewing nature as manipulable. From dependence on outsiders, people must move to innovation and initiative. From deification of the status quo, they must change to a confident search for the new. Social customs designed to provide insurance against disaster at the margin of subsistence must give way to new customs providing elbow room for risky experimentation and capital formation.

For agricultural development to take place, there must be many such shifts in attitudes and values among farmers and throughout rural communities. But the roles of scientists, merchants, bankers, engineers, and administrators in providing the facilities agricultural development needs, and the roles of legislators and citizens in determining legislation and of editors and broadcasters in molding public opinion mean that agricultural development is not a matter for farmers and agricultural technicians alone, but is a product of the whole way of living, the whole culture, of a nation or of a region. The skills necessary to achieve agricultural development are chiefly those of farmers and agricultural technicians, but the understanding of agricultural development and the attitudes and values which determine its pace are as much those of administrators, politicians, editors, and even the whole politically conscious population through the effect these have on laws and on public programs and policies, as they are those of rural people. Consequently, the solution of some of the most critical rural problems must be achieved in the cities.

Interrelationships of Agricultural Development and Rural Welfare

Agricultural development has to do with production. But farmers are people, members of families and of communities—communities within which they must largely find whatever quality of life and whatever satisfactions of living they are to know. The importance of agricultural development to rural welfare, in the absence of charity, is obvious and universally recognized; it must pay the bill.[1]

The importance of rural welfare to agricultural development is less widely understood. Every pertinent survey has indicated that, throughout most of the range of farm incomes, the higher the achieved average level of living of the farm families of a society, the more responsive farm families in general are to suggested improvements in farm production.[2] The chief aspirations of farm families, verified by every test, are for better education for their children, for better health, or for some other dimension of rural welfare. Greater cash income is a weak incentive when most of it will be drained off to landlords, or dissipated in doles to indigent members of extended families. It is only when elements of a better level of living are available nearby, and purchasable, that greater cash income is an adequate incentive to induce most farmers in low-income countries to increase production.

Consequently, the cause-and-effect relationship runs both ways between levels of rural welfare and agricultural development. Programs dealing with rural welfare, therefore, particularly in forms that are

---

[1] "Rural welfare" is used here in the sense of level of satisfactions, rather than in any sense of the charitable provision of amenities by outsiders.
[2] Within a given society it is frequently the middle income families that are most responsive to innovations.

not charity but are education and encouragement to rural people to bestir themselves to create better facilities for family and community life, are not postponable luxuries but an integral phase of agricultural development as well.

It is against this background of what the special rural problems of low-income countries are, and of the requirements for agricultural development and rural welfare in which these problems can be resolved, that the research necessary to improve developmental assistance is considered.[3]

ROLES OF RESEARCH

There has been a strong tendency in the past to downgrade research projects as part of rural developmental assistance. Sometimes this has been "justified" by the argument that "we already know enough; let's get on with the job." Other times the argument has been that "research is too slow; we must concentrate on projects that get quick results." Those with experience in the field know, however, that the first argument is not sound. We do not know enough. And while some research is time consuming, it should be obvious that many of the research needs outlined in this chapter require neither complicated research techniques nor very much time.

Both of these arguments against research, moreover, ignore the value of the *process* of research as a *teaching tool* in developmental assistance. Rather than being slow, research may be the most rapid operational tool for a number of the specific tasks within developmental assistance.

Hence, there are two roles of research in developmental assistance insofar as the rural problems discussed in this chapter are concerned.[4]

---

[3] For a more extended discussion of these aspects of rural development, see A. T. Mosher, *Technical Cooperation in Latin-American Agriculture* (University of Chicago Press, 1957), Chap. 12. Also Mosher, "Varieties of Extension Education and Community Development," New York State College of Agriculture, Comparative Extension Education Publication No. 2 (1958).

[4] I have not made a rigid distinction between those processes that may be conducted by wholly domestic programs for rural development in each country, and those processes distinctive to developmental assistance involving an "outside" agency. My topic might have made it legitimate to restrict consideration to the latter, but many of the most urgent needs of developmental assistance lie in the field of more accurate understanding of rural development itself, rather than in the distinctive functions of developmental assistance agencies working on rural problems. After the first outline of the chapter was prepared, letters were written to 35 per-

The first is to discover what the United States needs to know in order to carry on developmental assistance more effectively. Here, it is the *results* of research which give it importance. The second is as an operational tool, understandable across cultural differences and neutral with respect to previous beliefs and experience. Here, it is the *method* of research that is important.

AGRICULTURAL TECHNOLOGY

The first group of topics urgently in need of research are those within the field of agricultural technology; and the management of the soils of the humid tropics belongs near the top of this list. The need for this has been well stated by Richard Bradfield in a recent presidential address.[5] Pointing out that the outstanding resources of the humid tropics for plant growth (abundant sunshine and a twelve-month growing period) have tended to deplete the supply of plant nutrients and have "left a surface soil which is acid and has a great capacity for fixing phosphate fertilizer when it is introduced in commerical form," he cites evidence of the rapid regeneration of temperate-zone soils, depleted by prolonged poor management, to support the hypothesis that adequate research on the soils of the humid tropics should bear rich rewards.

A second type of soils research, careful field trials of known soil treatments in the diverse local conditions in which agricultural development is being attempted, is also needed. Here the process may be as rewarding as the results. It is characteristic of primitive agriculture that the soil is generally considered to be the only source of plant nutrients. As agriculture advances, however, the soil becomes primarily the medium to which fertilizers, and frequently water, as well, are applied to support plant growth. The sooner this change in how farm-

---

sons with firsthand experience with the problems involved in Asia, Latin America, and Africa, soliciting their suggestions. Replies were received from 30, listing recent research they had found helpful and suggesting over 150 topics which they feel are urgently in need of study. Some of those topics have been consolidated, and many have been omitted. I am indebted to these correspondents but I have not, in most cases, indicated which correspondent suggested which topics for two reasons: several topics were listed by from two to seven correspondents; and there are confidential reasons for not revealing the source of certain proposals.

[5] "Opportunities for Soil Scientists in Freeing the World from Hunger," International Congress of Soil Science, 1960, published as a reprint by the New York State College of Agriculture.

ers view the soil comes about, the better, and thousands of field plot experiments, conducted largely by local technicians and viewed by as many farmers as possible, are probably the most effective means to this end.

Studies of on-the-farm soil moisture management are badly needed. Experiments conducted by Long[6] and by Indian associates in South India indicate that greater total production might be secured in the vicinity of Bangalore by abandoning one-crop rice culture in favor of two crops annually each of which requires less moisture. There seems little doubt that in many cases, where rainfall is limited and canal irrigation is available, farmers apply too much water at one time. Frequently, this can be traced to patterns of distribution from canals, established without careful research on periodicity and amount of individual waterings for optimum plant growth. In other cases, traditional addiction to a particular food grain has led, in projects of land settlement, to patterns of production not well suited to local rainfall conditions or irrigation possibilities.

Careful economic land classification as a preliminary to land settlement schemes and in preparation for land tenure reorganizations is another high priority need. The history of efforts at agricultural development is strewn with wasted resources and with disappointments based on ill-founded hopes and untested possibilities. Too frequently, a low population density per square mile in humid forests or on semiarid plains has led to the assumption that farmers in high-population agricultural regions would be better off if they moved.

Surveys of variations within small regions of farm production and income should be made. The impression is widespread that all farmers in any region are doing the best that they can with present resources, and that increased production must depend entirely on new techniques and new resources from the outside. Yet whenever studies have been made of variations from farm to farm in low-income regions, it has been discovered that farmers vary greatly in their production and income from essentially the same resources. Popularizing the most productive practices already in use by the best farmers in each small region may frequently be the easiest, as well as the least costly, first step in further development.

Yield trials of strains of crops in use locally should always be, but

[6] Professor Erven J. Long, while a member and Chief of the University of Tennessee ICA Contract team, 1954-1958.

seldom are, the first step in research programs of systematic plant breeding. Quite apart from this, they can open the way for fairly rapid increases in production through popularizing the best locally tested strains, without the elaborate arrangements necessary to multiply and distribute the seeds resulting from experimentation at central research stations.

Surveys of the range of freedom of choice in farm operation should be encouraged. How free are farmers of a particular locality to choose where they will farm, how much land they will till, what crops they will grow, when they will sow, cultivate, and reap, what draft power they will use, what fertilizers they will apply, to whom they will sell their products and when, and how far they will process their products? Any extension service, to be effective, has to begin by stressing improved practices within the power of local farmers to adopt. And a factor in this freedom is the particular bundle of social attitudes, customs, and laws within which each farmer lives. Most farmers tend to list, as their dominant needs, the provision of resources or services which are beyond their present freedom of personal choice. At the same time, technical advisers from another culture tend to ascribe to farmers in the lands to which they go the same range of freedom of choice as is open to farmers in their homelands. Surveys of the present range of freedom of choice in farm operations can give important leads in choosing extension targets, in establishing research priorities, and in deciding what other phases of agricultural development should be tackled and in what order.

Surveys of hand tools, animal-drawn implements, and farm vehicles, and patterns in the use of these, in widely separated but similar agricultural regions, could expedite improved tillage in many parts of the world. Frequently, the tools in traditional use in one region would constitute a substantial technological improvement in another. So far, there are only fragmentary reports of tools and implements in common use in different parts of the monsoon region of South and Southeast Asia. At the same time, there have been many examples of failures in trying to introduce new tools and implements from the outside. The only technical advisers who now have knowledge of these variations, and of successes and failures in adapting tools and implements to local use, are the few who have traveled and worked widely.

Coordinated studies of all types of mechanization in low-income countries could lead to more rapid evolution in the efficient application of power, human and nonhuman, to operations related to agricultural production and marketing. So far, the United States has been much more active in decrying glaring mistakes of massive premature attempts to introduce heavy tractors than it has been in trying to learn the facts about the problem of farm power under various conditions. Meanwhile, there is considerable data bearing on this problem available in the records of ICA operations in Peru, Bolivia, and elsewhere in Latin America. In addition, rapid mechanization is under way on the small farms of Japan, using many types of small tractors and electric motors, and Kyushu University and Japanese agricultural experiment stations are engaged in a series of studies of the economics of this.

In view of the widespread importance of the problem of "slash-and-burn" cultivation in various parts of the world, and of the diverse policies with respect to it now being followed or proposed, comprehensive study of this problem is needed. Slash-and-burn cultivation has been viewed generally as a very primitive type of cultivation, a waste of forest resources, a serious cause of land erosion, and a form of economic activity that should be eliminated. Yet it persists over wide areas in many parts of the world. So far, most studies of this type of human activity have been from the vantage point of a single interest. The greatest attention has been paid to it by anthropologists; the next greatest attention, and the most adverse criticism, has been given it by foresters. I know of only one study, now under way, from the viewpoint of farm management.

THE ROLE OF CAPITAL IN AGRICULTURAL DEVELOPMENT

There are several questions with respect to the role of capital in agricultural development that need study.

What is the nature of the need for capital at early stages of agricultural development? Mellor[7] in a paper not yet published, argues, on the basis of experience largely in India supplemented by brief inquiry in Southeast Asia that, at 1961 stages of agricultural development in those countries, capital is needed chiefly for providing developmental services such as research, extension, and input supply lines rather than for financing farm level purchase of agricultural requisites;

[7] John W. Mellor, Associate Professor of Agricultural Economics, Cornell University.

there are relatively simple changes in farm practices requiring little or no capital that can raise production substantially; and it may very well be possible to finance most or all of the requisites of production needed at later stages of development out of this increased production. This hypothesis should be thoroughly tested, for it goes counter to much current thinking. If it is sustained by further study, it will change many priorities, particularly those with respect to the timing of emphasis on arrangements for production credit.

What is the present effective demand for production credit in agriculture in specific low-income rural regions? Mellor's hypothesis is general, requiring broad study. This question is specific for each of a large number of regions: How much effective demand for production credit is there currently? Answering this question would help to determine priorities in local programs, determining whether attention to credit should receive greater or lesser priority. There would appear to be three possible explanations where the demand for production credit is low, and it is important to determine how far each may be valid: (1) Farmers have enough savings to finance production adequately. (2) Farmers are not convinced that the production expenditures thought by technicians to be profitable are really worth the money. (3) Farmers have deep-seated aversion to borrowing.

What are local social values and motivations with respect to borrowing and with respect to repaying loans? These become important as new credit facilities are proposed and developed. Are there differences in people's feelings of obligation with respect to repaying loans from family members, local merchants, moneylenders, and governmental agencies?

What types of credit institutions have been most successful in meeting needs for agricultural production credit in low-income regions? There are many examples of such institutions for study: various types of "development banks" in Latin American countries; credit for the purchase of seeds and implements to be repaid in kind after harvest; "supervised credit" in Brazil, India, Burma, and elsewhere; the Agricultural Cooperatives and Credit Financing Administration in the Philippines; Farmers' Associations in Japan and Taiwan; and many others. These need to be compared and analyzed, each against its own background and history.

When a given input of proved value is available in insufficient quantity to meet the demand, where should it be applied? A good example of this is fertilizer. If only a limited amount is available, should it be made available in token quantities over a wide geographic area and without respect to the crop? Or should it be made available: only near urban development centers, only in areas emphasizing particular export crops, only for crops having high income elasticity of demand, only for commerical crops already entering substantially into the cash economy, or only in areas with an abundance of complementary resources such as irrigation, fertile soil, well-developed transport? Similar questions arise with respect to the location of irrigation projects, roads, and so forth.

How do rates of return on investments in improved agricultural production compare with rates of return on investments in industry? It is a common assumption that investments in industry yield a higher return, but there is substantial evidence that in labor-rich, capital-poor, low-income agriculture the rate of return on investments in agricultural production is unexpectedly high, frequently much higher than on investments in urban industry. Obviously, these comparative rates of return are of primary importance in all programs of planned investment if capital is to be applied where it will command the greatest return. While this principle cannot, and should not, always be followed, it is important that investments in agriculture not be limited because of false assumptions about comparative returns, particularly when, on the grounds of other considerations, agricultural development is so important to most underdeveloped countries.

EDUCATION AND RURAL DEVELOPMENT

Most people agree that formal schooling is a significant element in rural development. Some go so far as to hold that universal elementary education is so important that it should command all the development resources it can profitably use no matter what other elements may have to be neglected for the time being. This hypothesis merits objective investigation insofar as it may be possible. Some of the questions about the relationship of formal schooling to rural development that need study are the following: What is the valid function of "practical" agricultural high schools in low-income countries?[8] In the past, such schools have been relied on in many countries to provide subor-

[8] Reference here is to dominantly vocational and "practical" high school curricula, terminal in nature and not qualifying students to proceed to the university. Vocational agricultural elective courses in "academic" high schools are another matter.

dinate officials for departments and ministries of agriculture and teachers of agriculture. From now on, however, it is obvious that more thorough training, available only through university study, is necessary for candidates for these posts. Today, "practical" agricultural high schools are being supported in many countries because they "can prepare trained farm operators and skilled agricultural labor for mechanized farms." Is it not probable that on-the-job training and agricultural extension services are more efficient means of agricultural education beyond elementary school for those not going on to the university?

How pertinent is the land-grant college pattern for colleges of agriculture in low-income countries? Here the issue is more the question of integrated administrative responsibility for teaching, research, and extension than it is of content of the teaching itself. There is some question how far it is legitimate to infer from the obvious value of the land-grant college pattern in the United States that this is the best pattern in other, quite different, circumstances, even if it were politically feasible to reproduce it.

What is the best location and affiliation for colleges of agriculture of low-income countries? Most of these colleges of agriculture are small, yet few of them are adjacent to other colleges of major universities. Would it be better for them to be on the same campuses with colleges of arts and sciences where they could share common facilities? Many of them, particularly in former British territories, are parts of ministries of agriculture, members of the teaching staff being civil servants of the ministry rather than having tenure in the colleges. This has disadvantages from the standpoint of building strong faculties. While there is little opportunity for developmental assistance to reorganize or relocate existing colleges, there have been several examples recently of ICA playing a large role in creating new agricultural colleges and rural universities.

What is the best type of education, for the rising generation of a country, at all levels, when rapid economic, social, and political development is the top item on the agenda? One correspondent writes:

Most educational systems in the less-developed countries are patterned after European and American systems. They contain, in many instances, impractical curricula having incomplete applicability to the current and future needs of the students. [Research] studies could aim at discovering educational methods and content most valuable for economic and social development purposes at the elementary, secondary, vocational, adult and special technical levels. They should aim at discovering the types of knowledge, skills, and attitudes related to development needs in different situations and the most effective ways (formal and informal) of delivering them over the long term.

The Basic Education idea espoused by Mahatma Gandhi was designed to build a whole system on the everyday needs of students, but it tended to take the stable, independent village as its objective rather than continuously evolving development to new levels. The Folk High Schools of Denmark similarly broke fresh ground with a type of education specifically designed to meet current needs, giving no hostages to existing educational orthodoxy. Probably any form of education that results in verbal and mathematical literacy and that expands the horizons of students is an asset to rural development. But obviously some types of education and some methods of teaching are better for the purpose than others.

What are the productive and unproductive uses of International Cooperation Administration "participant" programs under which students from abroad come to study in the United States? The participant program is very large. For the most part it places foreign students in courses of study designed to meet the contemporary needs, under American conditions, of American students. In what subjects, and for what purposes, is this participant program an effective technique?

INSTITUTIONAL MEASURES FOR AGRICULTURAL DEVELOPMENT

From the earlier discussion of aspects of rural development, it will be recalled that a considerable number of the elements of agricultural development consist of the legal, commercial, and social institutions within the framework of which agriculture must operate. Developmental assistance becomes involved in practically all of these at one time or another. All of them involve substantial problems, some of which stand out as urgently needing research.

Studies of the economic, social, and political factors and effects of various measures of "land reform" should be made. Many underdeveloped agricultural economies can be described as having, or as having had in the recent past, a feudal or quasi-feudal pattern of land tenure and tenancy. "Land reform" is a battle-cry in every awakened country where such a pattern persists, and it is bound to become an issue in those not yet awakened. It is an issue charged with emotion and widely viewed as a panacea; for these reasons, it needs analysis leading to rational assessment of what it can and cannot accomplish.

It involves intimately interrelated economic, social, and political motives and effects; consequently, it needs simultaneous and coordinated study from all three points of view. A large amount of experience on this problem has accumulated, but no objective evaluation of this widespread experience has been made.

Comparative studies of various types of land settlement projects are also needed. Frequently, for the valid purpose of bringing potentially valuable land resources into more productive use, and too frequently, in the vain hope of relieving population pressures on land already under cultivation, governments embark on various types of programs of land settlement. One research need here is to compare the costs and effects of different types of governmental participation in land settlement: settlements financed and administered by government, including land clearing and preparation for cultivation, and provision of credit for preliminary production needs, and sometimes for family subsistence needs as well; government sponsorship of "cooperative" land clearing and settlement; government provision of access roads only; government provision of access roads, schools, hospitals, and agricultural extension services. It would be helpful to have, for comparison with such governmental efforts, analysis of land settlement schemes financed by private capital, in Latin America and in earlier years in Southeast Asia. Another need is to devise a valid framework for cost-benefit analysis of investment in land settlement schemes to facilitate comparing such programs with others competing for scarce governmental revenues. Techniques being used for this are superficial and inadequate; they leave out many factors involved in the relationships between land settlement and the strength of the national economy.

Institutional arrangements for adaptive agricultural research should be studied. How should regional research stations for varietal and fertilizer trials and other aspects of adaptive research be organized and administered? What type of training is needed for technicians competent to manage routine trials? How much supervision of these technicians is essential? How should experimental field trials and extension demonstration plots be related? Is it feasible for the same personnel to serve both as researchers in branch stations and as extension agents? How, and to what extent, can the administration of such adaptive research best be combined with training new technicians in investigational techniques?

Studies of experience with cooperative societies as agencies for marketing and credit are needed. "Cooperation" has stood very close to "land reform" as a slogan and as a panacea for rural ills. Enthusiasm for cooperatives has persisted in many parts of the world despite repeated failures of cooperative enterprises. The magic of the slogan is so strong that the name cooperative is applied to types of organization making no recognizable application of the classical principles of the Rochdale society of weavers from which the modern cooperative movement sprang. Meanwhile, the problems which cooperative societies are expected to solve are real, and they are of major importance to agricultural development. It is obvious that some type or types of effective organization through which the marketable produce of millions of small farms can move to market, and through which production credit and requisites can be made available to these many small farmers, is essential. And there are examples of successful cooperative societies on a wide scale, notably in Japan and Taiwan, keeping the hope alive that such societies may serve these functions elsewhere.

What is needed is careful multi-country studies of various types of organizations called "cooperatives," of the conditions under which they have arisen, of the problems they have encountered, of the modifications that have been introduced in efforts to solve these problems, of their administrative costs (sometimes hidden in general governmental administrative and auditing budgets as well as in public subsidies), and of the ethical and other cultural elements necessary to their success or responsible for their difficulties.

Institutional changes and problems resulting from the introduction of irrigation should be studied. A prominent phase of many programs of agricultural development is provision of new facilities for irrigation. If the full value of such facilities is to be realized, there must be far-reaching changes in cropping systems, in fertilizing practices, in work patterns, in social relationships, and in legal arrangements for water distribution, payment for irrigation water, and adjudication of disputes. In most cases the planning of irrigation projects is largely in the hands of engineers, and therefore the need for extensive preparation of the people involved and for the provision of new services is usually not recognized until acute problems arise. Despite the seriousness of these problems, there appears never to have been a careful and exhaustive study of them in the special circumstances of low-income countries, to guide preparations for irrigation projects in the future.

PUBLIC INVESTMENT FOR AGRICULTURAL DEVELOPMENT

There are undoubtedly a number of important topics for research with respect to public and private investments of various types undertaken in whole or in part in the interest of agricultural development. These include investments in irrigation facilities, fertilizer and implement factories, mass communications, and market and storage facilities. While agricultural development requires these, they are beyond my competence to evaluate and discuss.

One problem, however, must be mentioned, both because of its great importance and because it bears on an investment in which programs of community development take a major interest. This is the role and economic value of rural roads. A number of knowledgeable and astute observers, the late Professor A. W. Ashby of Oxford among them, have argued that an adequate network of roads and transport deserves first priority in any program of planned development. Two types of studies are needed. One type is small, specific studies of the cost, and economic and social effects, of access roads just after they have been built and three to five years later.[9] The other is more general studies of the role of roads and transport in rural development.

METHODS OF EXTENSION EDUCATION AND COMMUNITY DEVELOPMENT

The great value of programs of extension education and community development lies in the fact that they can be, literally, education for freedom. By confronting rural people with alternatives between which they may choose (where formerly they have lived largely by tradition) and by giving them emotional support while they organize for group action and while they accept responsibility for the results of their own risk-taking decisions, these programs help people learn how to be free men. This transition to freedom is difficult. Nicolas Berdyaev observed, in *Slavery and Freedom*, that "it is easy for a slave

[9] Like the study recently published by the Community Development Research Council of the University of the Philippines, "The Value of Rural Roads."

to become a master; it is easy for a master to become a slave; it is almost impossible for either to become a free man."[10]

Despite their great and unique potential value, programs of extension education and community development in low-income countries have been much less effective than they might be, largely due to false assumptions and inadequate background knowledge. Herein lies the need for considerable research in this field.

The foremost research need here is for more projects involving controlled experimentation with respect to selected variables in extension education or community development methodology. It is amazing, in view of the strong emphasis on extension and community development in developmental assistance, that no more such controlled experimentation has been undertaken. Instead, debates around conference tables result in one decision or another about how to begin, and emphases and methods are continued or dropped as programs proceed on the basis of administrative judgments untested by any experimental comparison of the results of alternatives. I know of only one example of controlled experimentation of this type, carried to completion after three years' trial.[11] It not only led to definite conclusions about the two variables it was set up to test,[12] but its records provided the raw material for several subsequent studies of factors related to performance of extension workers. At a minimum, every country should have several extension or community development projects with built-in provision for keeping the type of records of activities that can be subjected to analysis. But more than this is needed: controlled experimentation, not necessarily with whole projects but with respect to each of a number of specific techniques, is required. Some of the aspects of extension or community development methodology amenable to such experimentation are the following: What background of training is essential for field agents? What are the relative merits of initial concentration on agriculture, felt needs, literacy, village amenities, credit, and provision of requisites? What forms of posters, of leaflets, or of dramatic presentation, are most effective in a particular culture? What concentration of effort, what frequency of contact with individual villages and with individual families is essential for an accepta-

---

[10] Translation (Charles Scribner's Sons, 1944).
[11] The Experimental Extension Project of the Allahabad Agricultural Institute in India.
[12] Correlation between type and amount of previous education of the extension worker and his success as an extension agent; and correlation between nature of initial program emphasis and over-all "practice changes" after a three-year period.

ble rate of change? What frequency and duration of in-service training periods is optimum?

Increases in agricultural production, and in agricultural production per man, are basic. How can extension education and community development be so structured and administered that agriculture receives the primary attention it must have if rural and national development are to be achieved? Three forces impel extension education organizations in low-income countries toward handling several subject matters rather than agriculture alone, and toward taking on one or another of the forms of community development. One is the shortage of public funds and of appropriate personnel. The second is the lack of any distinction between production, consumption, and social amenities in the minds of rural people in low-income countries: life to them is an undivided whole. The third is the proved psychological advantage of responding to "felt needs" over the practice of building a program to pursue objectives predetermined by administrators. In the early stages of rural development, what is needed primarily is *response, change,* and *decision-making*—almost regardless of the subject matter involved.

In practice, the adoption of multi-subject-matter extension and community development programs tends to dilute specific attention to agricultural production. This is partly because the felt needs of rural people are quite diverse. It is partly because the special techniques of most types of community development are more appropriate to securing construction of roads, schools, wells, and drains than they are to achieving changed practices in agricultural production. It is partly because public works and physical facilities are more visible and make a greater impression on visiting officials than do changes in methods of production.

What criteria can be established to help determine when agricultural extension education is more effective if separately organized, and when it is more effective if integrated into a multi-subject-matter community development program? In the past, American technical assistance has helped establish or improve agricultural extension services in some countries, and multi-subject-matter community development programs in others. There are undoubtedly circumstances in which one is more effective than the other. But the decision which should be encouraged has seldom been determined by these differences in circumstances; instead, it has been determined by differences of opinion, even of dogma, and frequently by bitter internal struggle both between and within agencies of the United States government. I am certain that objective study of the performance of the two approaches in the past, in different countries, would yield valuable criteria to help guide future decisions.

What are the separate and joint effects of subsidies to local governments, subsidies to local nongovernmental groups, and technical advice and direction, on local self-help projects? The local self-help group project is the central activity of one form of community development. Normally, these projects are aided both by subsidies in cash or materials and by technical advice and supervision. Are both necessary? What is the relative value of each? Does giving subsidies for initial projects make it unduly difficult to persuade local groups to act without them later on? Can subsidies to local governments be supplanted, at a later date, by the exercise of newly granted local taxing authority? Should subsidies be matched by taxes raised locally?

To what extent, and in what ways, can agricultural extension education and the supply of agricultural requisites be combined? With certain exceptions, extension education in the United States has been able to take it for granted that farmers could purchase, through commercial channels, any new seeds, fertilizers, implements, insecticides, or any other requisites of production they might want to try. This is not the case in much of the world. Consequently, there is a strong tendency to combine the two functions of extension education and the supplying of requisites. There are two basic objections to this combination: first, that it confuses the role of the extension agent for him to try to be both adviser-teacher and merchant; second, that supplying of requisites becomes so time-consuming that it greatly decreases the time available for extension education. Yet the problem persists. Possible new approaches to this problem are suggested in a later section. There is need for more study of the problem to ascertain whether there are ways of combining these two activities without adversely affecting either.[13]

How can interpersonal communication be achieved between extension or community development workers and illiterate or isolated rural people? Carl Taylor writes:

The vast majority of people who work with village people do not really com-

---

[13] One possibility, under Latin American conditions, is to have the office secretary of each extension agent handle the supply of requisites. See Mosher, *Technical Cooperation in Latin-American Agriculture*, pp. 53, 354. But in most of Asia, extension agents have neither secretaries nor offices.

municate with them at all, and I think it is more than a hypothesis to say that the reason they do not is because they do not understand the images and precepts of villagers. . . . I am so convinced that practically no communication takes place that I am sure there is no other topic that is more important to study than this.

What are the communications patterns and channels for the diffusion of news and ideas in various folk cultures? There are numerous recent studies of such channels and patterns among rural Americans. What are the analogous patterns in the largely illiterate societies where much of developmental assistance is carried on? To what extent are the various visual aids, and other specific techniques of extension education used, and what is their effect? It is a common assumption that techniques of extension education effective in the United States are effective everywhere. It is a further general assumption that visual aids are of particular value among illiterate peoples. Considerable emphasis is placed in many programs of developmental assistance on training extension and community development workers in their use. But to what extent do workers use them? And what are the effects when they do? Do these aids really teach? Do they entertain without teaching? Must they be used in conjunction with other teaching techniques? If so, with which ones, for different purposes, in various cultural settings?

How can adequate technical backstopping be given to programs of extension education and community development? In the United States, agricultural extension agents are graduates of agricultural colleges, and they are reinforced by a corps of subject-matter specialists whose specific task it is to keep abreast of new technical developments. They not only relay these to extension agents but also present them directly to meetings of farm operators. In underdeveloped countries, few agricultural extension agents are college graduates. Technically trained personnel are in short supply. Subject-matter extension specialists, apart from the too few research workers, often do not exist. In community development programs, field workers must deal with projects in more than one technical field. And in both extension and community development, in addition to supplying technical information, field agents have the very large and often predominant task of encouraging rural people to begin to overcome the inertia of habitually following traditional patterns. In such circumstances, how can adequate technical backstopping be achieved? Various methods have been and are being tried. Reports of these have yet to be brought together, with each assessed not only with respect to degree of success in its local setting, but also in the light of its probable transferability to other cultural settings.

How can the principles of good extension education be reconciled with crash programs to achieve specific targets of increased production? Agricultural extension as practiced in the United States has seldom, except temporarily in wartime, given any attention to national production needs or goals. Instead, it has concentrated solely on helping individual farmers achieve higher net incomes and a better life. However, in many countries where developmental assistance is active, national governments, faced by inadequate food supplies and limited foreign exchange, are formulating development plans calling for increases, by stated percentages or amounts, in the production of selected crops. A frequent practice is to charge extension and community development services with the responsibility of achieving these production targets. Extension and community development workers claim that such "crash programs" subvert good educational methods and, in the long run, retard the achievement of production increases. Is this true? Need it be true? Are there methods already being used, or new ways of achieving an emphasis on national production targets that are compatible with effective extension teaching? If so, what are they?

I believe there are two methods of achieving this synthesis that should be given greater trial. One method, already tried on a limited scale, is to allocate, arbitrarily, a certain percentage of each field worker's effort to pushing improved practices specific to the increased production of designated crops. In this, reliance is placed wholly on educational methods normal to extension, but response to "felt needs" is restricted to the remaining arbitrary percentage of each field worker's effort. The other method, not yet tried to the best of my knowledge, is analogous to the "Outlook Conferences" common in American extension. In this method, suitable materials would be presented to meetings of farmers in each locality, acquainting them with the nation's production needs. These groups of farmers would then be led in considering these, setting targets for themselves as local contributions to the national effort, and extension agents would then put special efforts into helping to meet these locally determined targets. In the glow of new nationalisms, it might be found that the feeling of having a share in a national effort is as strong an incentive as the prospect of higher personal income—which might, as a consequence, occur in any case.

What amenities of rural living, in each region, do people value most highly? And from which ones do they feel satisfaction over time? A major emphasis of certain types of community development is on improving the amenities of rural life. Which are most important to the people: primarily physical facilities for education, sanitation, and health; organized recreational opportunities; organized dramatic and musical events within the established culture; or others? Which binds people with more loyalty to their locality: the achieved level of social amenities they may enjoy, or the degree of their personal creative involvement in widening the scope of these activities?

What methods have been found effective, or ineffective, for coordinating the technical services of different departments or ministries of the government in tackling specific local problems? Extension education in the United States deals primarily with two broad subjects— agriculture and home economics—and the technical resources to back its efforts are found in a single agency, the land-grant colleges. By contrast, most extension and community development services in underdeveloped countries deal with a variety of subjects. In theory, technical backstopping is to be supplied by departments or ministries of agriculture, education, health, and public works. In practice, the results are not encouraging. Various methods of coordination have been tried in different countries. What has been learned from these efforts, and how far are the lessons applicable in other settings?

THE NATIONAL CULTURE AND RURAL DEVELOPMENT

To revert to an earlier statement, agricultural development does not depend on farmers and agricultural technicians alone; it is a function of the whole culture, the whole way of life of a people. A number of aspects of the impact of national culture on rural development need attention: value systems, local government, taxation, class structure, and foci of decision-making. In addition, the Taylor Hypothesis discussed below needs examination, as well as the relationship between aspects of American culture and the history of rural development here.

Value Systems

The group of topics for research mentioned most frequently by correspondents consulted consists of questions about the value systems, aspirations, and dominant motives of rural people, and of the urban elite of each low-income country. With regard to the rural people, the following questions were included: What are their attitudes toward nature in general and with respect to man's place in the world? What are the dominant aspirations of farmers and of rural people generally? What are their attitudes with respect to social interaction? Are they individualist? Cooperative? Do they feel that cooperative aid should be limited to kinfolk? Extended to close neighbors? To all members of the village? What are their attitudes with respect to family obligation? Do farmers feel free to keep the fruits of increased production for expenditure or for investment, or must they share these with relatives or others in the community? What are their attitudes with respect to land and livestock and to the proper functions and responsibilities of government? How strong is the attachment of rural peoples to particular staple foods in their diet? Does this have ritualistic significance?[14]

One increasingly hears the opinion expressed that the attitudes of the urban elite with respect to rural people and rural development are greater obstacles to agricultural and rural development than the attitudes and values of rural people themselves. Do members of the urban elite believe that rural development is possible? That it is desirable? That it should take second place to industrialization? Do they believe rural people have competence and judgment within themselves, or that they must be given ready-made answers and be told what to do? Are they willing to approve a wide delegation of powers to local government, or do they favor a strongly unitary national form of government? Are they conscious of the strong tendency to spend a disproportionate share of public revenues on public works and services in the capital, and, secondarily, in other urban centers? If conscious of this, what is their attitude with respect to it?

[14] Milton L. Barnett reports that in Venezuela farmers would produce new food crops for sale but would not incorporate them into family diets. Mellor remarks that my statement of the issue is too "black-and-white." He rightly points out that in the study of this and similar value questions the economists' concepts of utility surfaces and of marginal rates of substitution would constitute a more fruitful approach.

Local Government

The topics listed with the second greatest frequency by correspondents as needing research attention are those relating to local self-government. Both in Latin America and throughout much of South and Southeast Asia, agricultural technical advisers are impressed by the feeling of helplessness of rural people with respect to their own governments. Governments seem so far away, so difficult to approach and so enshrouded in red tape. The only participation—and this, for most rural people, only in certain countries—is voting in infrequent national elections. There is next to no opportunity, within the framework of government, for local people to come together and agree to tackle specific local needs, tax themselves to meet the cost, and appoint local officials to carry out the task.[15]

Technical advisers quite generally feel that rural people are ready to move on local issues far more rapidly than current governmental patterns allow. Many of them place local government above land reform in order of priority. Obviously, this is a sensitive area for developmental assistance, yet it is vital to rural development in any free society, and there are, in fact, several instances of technical advisers being asked to advise on, draft legislation for, and help to establish local self-government. Some of the questions needing study are the following: What have been the successes and failures in attempts to establish or strengthen local self-government? Can evolution toward local government proceed by stages, with power to tax being the last authority granted, or should taxing authority be part of the first stage? Where there has been a measure of local government, largely judicial, in a relatively static culture in the past, what are the problems in converting this to largely executive local government, competent to plan and carry out new projects as part of orderly and dynamic development? Is the educational phase of establishing local government an appropriate activity for a community development program, or should it be separately administered?[16]

[15] Two exceptions to this are Indonesia and Taiwan, where local government is real, active, and effective.

[16] In the Philippines and in certain states in India, increasing local government is a major objective and activity of community development programs.

Impact of Taxation

There are at least five aspects of the impact of taxation on rural development that merit study: (1) the deterrent effect of low land taxes on agricultural development in cases where land is held in large estates primarily for purposes of social prestige or, in any size of holdings, for speculation; (2) the possible use of tax exemption incentives for certain types of improved land use; (3) the possibilities, limits, and effects of using the taxing power to accumulate savings for investment; (4) the possibilities of the labor tax as a phase of building and maintaining local public services; and (5) the economic, social, and political effects of granting taxing power to rural local governmental entities.

Impact of Class Structure

One of the knotty problems of development arises from the fact that practically all of the personnel of development agencies are drawn from the urban elite, and educated in schools and colleges patterned on foreign models, with the result that they have difficulty in achieving effective rapport with village people. Trained in a rationalistic approach, they do not communicate easily with rural people whose ways of thought are more holistic and whose logic is tempered by local experience. Analysis of the performance of extension workers at the Allahabad Agricultural Institute in India revealed decided differential impact depending on the caste of individual farmers and the caste or other religious affiliation of extension workers. In the Andean countries of South America, rapport and response are quite different between extension workers, on the one hand, and "Indian" and "non-Indian" farmers, on the other. Each of these problems hints at the substantial impact of class structure on measures for rural development, indicating that better understanding of this problem would be helpful.

Factors Influencing Decisions

To what extent are decisions about agricultural production—what to grow, what requisites to purchase, when to cultivate, whether or not to borrow for productive investment—made by the male "farm operator"? To what extent are these family decisions? To what extent are they determined by the social pressure of neighbors, by tradition, or by a communal organization of production? If land reform is to be achieved, who must make the critical decisions? Who are involved in decision-making with respect to village sanitation, new feeder roads, new schools? Who must make the decisions if commercial fertilizers are to be used in quantity? These questions are important partly because of the relation they may have to the rate of development in any culture. They are important also, where developmental assistance is involved, because a technical adviser tends to assume that the pattern is similar to that of his homeland, or that of another foreign country in which he has worked.

What, in each region, are the effective incentives to increase agricultural production? Some rural programs are postulated on the assumption that nothing is needed except proof that certain practices will increase production; others on the assumption that improved amenities of village life—better sanitation, roads, and water supply—will call forth increased production. The new "Package Plan" in India introduces assured forward prices as an incentive. Some observers believe a ready supply of desirable consumer goods in local shops will do the trick. Some argue that raising the aspirations of village women through home demonstration agents can be a major factor. Some programs appeal to farmers to increase production "because the nation needs it." These incentives are not equally potent in any one place, and their relative strength varies from place to place and from time to time. This is a topic on which economists, social psychologists, and anthropologists might well join forces.

What have been the factors which, in different regions and countries, have been primarily instrumental in getting the agricultural economy moving again after a period of stagnation? This question is frequently raised, illustrated by one or two examples, and with the implication that a broader study would yield important clues toward establishing priorities in agricultural development. The significance of studying this question lies in the contribution such study can make to identifying the variety of requirements for agricultural development rather than in indicating priorities. One consultant emphasizes the role of the migration of groups of persons with more highly developed skills. Another underscores the transforming influence of new roads and improved communications. Another points to the influence of general elementary education. I know of instances where the trigger influence seems to have been eradication of malaria (in Minas Gerais, Brazil and in the Terai region of India), the introduction of irrigation, or the evaporation of a fatalistic attitude in the heat of political demand for independence. It is a question worthy of study, provided it is not understood to reveal a panacea or a universally valid "trigger role" for a particular influence.

The Taylor Hypothesis

Along with other research on the relationship between the national culture and rural development, there is need for careful testing of the hypothesis advanced by Dr. Carl C. Taylor: "that so-called tradition-ridden peasants will not be inhibited by their sanctions and taboos [value systems] if they are approached with alternative ways of doing things which they are already doing, and the doing of which yields them immediate, obvious results." It is easy to become immobilized by considering all possible difficulties. It is easy to confuse research interests that are imperative to operational effectiveness with those that are largely of academic interest only. Taylor suggests, and I agree, that the United States can get on with the job without waiting for exhaustive studies of certain cultural differences. This does not mean that more exhaustive studies may not allow the United States at a later stage to increase operational efficiency substantially. It does warn against losing operational momentum and against being frightened by apparent complexities.

Rural Development and American Culture

The Taylor Hypothesis, in addition to being intrinsically important, provides an easy transition to what may be the most important topic for research considered in this section, if not in all of rural developmental assistance, namely: *What is the relevance to rural development of specific attitudes and values prominent in American culture?* It may be that, in becoming aware of cultural differences among peoples, and of the multiform influences of aspects of these cultures on rural development, specialists are in danger of concluding that to get along in other cultures they must master their ways almost to the point of adopting them.

If attitudes and values are such important determinants of rates of development, why did rapid rural development begin so much earlier and accelerate so much more rapidly in the United States than in many other places? Americans now going abroad in developmental assistance are the inheritors of those attitudes and values which accelerated this development, and, to greater or lesser degree, they embody them. What is it that they have to contribute that is of greatest value? Is it their tractors, their centrifuges, their scientific concepts, the dollars in their pockets? Or is it their attitude toward nature? Their willingness to risk ridicule in order to try a new method? Their ways of dealing with peers, "superiors," and "subordinates" within an organization? Their sense of time as a valuable asset? Their propensity to want to measure with precision? Their literal use of language? Their readiness to classify and generalize? The value they place on formal schooling? Their preference for local over national government? Their willingness to delegate responsibility coupled with distrust of concentrations of power? Their preference for pragmatism instead of for dogma? Their acceptance of some right to equal consideration of all persons? Their concern for the underdog? Their preference of the new to the old?[17]

In any such studies, due consideration must be given to other factors. Certainly America was blessed with abundant natural resources. It could create a new civilization in a new, largely empty, land. It did not have to transform an established feudal culture in a crowded land into something different. It was effectively separated from foreign tyrannies. Nevertheless, why was it that thousands left an uncrowded (by any other than American standards) East to settle Oklahoma, without roads, schools, hospitals, seeds, or credit supplied by "the government," whereas elaborate subsidies seem necessary to get settlers into Mindanao, South Sumatra, eastern Bolivia, southern Venezuela? What was it about the "climate of investment" that brought European capital in large amounts into nineteenth century America without the guarantees implicit in colonialism? What is it about American culture that impels voluntary private philanthropy into "distressed areas" long before governmental action is even considered?

There may be two sides to this question of "attitudes and values" in developmental assistance. The United States has been forced by its

---

[17] This listing is illustrative only; it is in no sense a list of considered hypotheses. These are items that come easily to mind to try to make a point: the point that Americans need to search their own cultural background to try to determine what is pertinent to the rate of "development" and what is not.

experience in low-income countries to recognize that noneconomic aspects of culture are powerful forces affecting the rate of development there. Is it not time the United States really studied the extent to which the noneconomic aspects of its own culture have affected its own development? The American government is in a position now as it has never been before to make such studies, by bringing to them an increasing knowledge of contrasting cultural components in many different settings of resource endowment, population density, and institutional history, around the world. Only when such studies have been made will the United States be able to answer with assurance the question: What really does America have to contribute via developmental assistance?

NEW APPROACHES WORTHY OF PILOT
PROJECT EXPERIMENTATION

There are several specific types of rural development projects that merit thorough testing in the form of pilot projects.

Adaptive Research as a Major Operational Activity

The widespread needs for many field trials of crop varieties and of fertilizer response together with studies of the economics of these; for studies of variations within small regions in farm production and income; for studies of the range of freedom of choice in farm operation; for adequate technical backstopping of agricultural extension; and for effective techniques of training in research procedures have all been noted. It would seem worthwhile to experiment with a new type of field project, combining an experiment station with its program confined to adaptive and farm economic research, and an agricultural extension service throughout the surrounding countryside within a radius of ten to fifteen miles.

The adaptive research would be valuable both for its results and for the training involved in carrying it out. The cooperation between technical advisers and local technicians, being centered in learning together, would help bridge problems of understanding due to cultural differences, and help minimize mistakes of technical advisers due to lack of experience in the region. Having such a program of adaptive research at the center of an extension project might, in addition to being highly effective locally, prove to be a more efficient and a faster way of multiplying extension projects throughout a large region or country than methods now in use. By double-staffing the first few such projects, the most competent local technicians could be transferred year by year, to start similar new projects, and the combination of adaptive research and extension, probably not by the same staff but in close collaboration, might provide far more effective in-service training for extension workers than the prolonged training in special centers, which is the normal practice now. Such a plan would also avoid the widespread tendency to postpone regional adaptive research until after a strong central experiment station is well-established.

Education Programs for Merchants, Bankers, and Moneylenders

The close dependence of response to effective extension education for farmers on ready availability of the requisites of agricultural production has been noted. The problem introduced when the extension agent is asked to handle sales and distribution of these requisites has also been mentioned. Has anyone experimented with a program of extension education to village merchants to see whether this could induce them to stock new articles, thus meeting the needs of farmers for requisites through normal commercial channels? A merchant accustomed to dealing only in staple consumption items faces real problems in shifting to dealing in these production requisites: there is not a preexisting predictable demand; the need for most such articles is highly seasonal (in many cases a week's difference in time of availability is crucial); periodicity in size of inventory is much greater. What would happen if a program were set up to work with rural bankers and moneylenders? One experience in the Philippines has demonstrated that a local bank can meet the credit needs for a rapidly expanding poultry and swine industry and do it profitably.[18] This example resulted from the unaided imagination and creativity of a local banker, but is it not possible that an appropriate extension education program could multiply such instances?

In many cultures, the merchant and the moneylender are cast in the role of exploitative villains to be eliminated. But their functions are essential, and there is considerable evidence that their profits, in

---

[18] The Tanauan Branch of the Philippine Banking Corporation.

most cases, are not exorbitant since their costs, particularly in credit, are high. Perhaps it would be better to help them adapt their present skills to the new needs of a dynamic agriculture than to try to replace them. Research on the costs and returns of these small agriculture-related businesses and on factors affecting their efficiency would be needed in connection with such programs.

A Publicly Supported Advertising Program

In North America and Western Europe a considerable amount of the propaganda for changed practices in agriculture is provided not by public programs of extension education but by private advertising. In low-income countries, however, both cultural history and the small and highly local nature of merchandizing firms makes integrated advertising campaigns not feasible if left to private support. Also, much advertising that does appear is of doubtful reliability. But what would happen if, in addition to extension education programs for merchants, publicly supported advertising campaigns for selected and tested production requisites were provided? Such a program would be much simpler to administer than a wholly governmental agency to merchandize such requisites direct. It would utilize the present skills of village merchants and add what might be a very effective stimulus to increased use of these requisites, reinforcing the impact of extension education for farmers. It would be possible, of course, to phrase this proposal in a way to make it just "another extension approach," but the nature of this approach is probably best indicated by calling it advertising, and it would be more effective if it named the merchants from whom the requisites could be obtained and published the prices of each article.[19] This could easily be combined with another public service of substantial benefit to agricultural development—regular dissemination of market information for farm products.

Use of Radio in Agricultural Development Programs

The potential value of radio for mass programs of agricultural development is great enough to warrant further experimentation and

---

[19] Such public-supported advertising would have to be accompanied by enforced regulations to maintain product quality and to suppress adulteration.

the elimination of the obstacles to its most effective use. The economic and technical difficulties of such programs have been drastically reduced in recent years by the availability of inexpensive and dependable transistor radios operating on flashlight batteries. There have been a number of experiments, mostly small, involving use of radio in extension education, and one immediate need is to consolidate the knowledge gained through them. So far, most such experiments have lacked one or another of the elements for success on a large scale.

1. To be most effective in extension education, radio broadcasts must be in the local dialect of rural people. The validity of this has been indicated by experiments at Silliman University in the Philippines. In many cases, however, the insistence of governmental broadcasting monopolies on using the "pure" form of a new "national language" has prevented adherence to this principle.

2. Much of the broadcasting should be done by persons who are known to the listeners as local extension workers. One of the characteristics of cultures in low-income regions is that, to be trusted and believed, the speaker must be a personal friend. Radio broadcasting lacks this feature if done largely by persons with whom listeners are not personally acquainted.

3. Radio broadcasting is more effective when listeners are familiar with the mechanics of broadcasting and when broadcasts include transmission of programs originating in villages. Silliman University has made effective use of programs recorded in villages, with the village people both participating and observing. It has broadcast discussions recorded in the villages on topics of agricultural development and village improvement, and village performances of music and drama.

Exploratory Projects of "Enclosure"

There is considerable evidence that fragmentation of holdings (in the form of one "farm" composed of a number of noncontiguous fields) is not, in itself, as inefficient as it is widely believed to be. But uncontrolled livestock, or herded livestock in unregulated numbers, grazing on common lands, is another matter. One would think that the importance attached to enclosure in the economic history of Great Britain, and to the barbed-wire war in the history of the American western plains, would have led to attempts at some exploratory projects of enclosure in countries like India. So far, however, they have not.

The "Outlook Conference"

This proposal, mentioned earlier, would substitute targets set locally by farmers themselves for local targets set nationally and laid on extension workers as an obligation. The extension or community development staff would acquaint farmers with national needs and work with them in setting local production targets for themselves. What are needed, in the way of some pilot projects, are arrangements for comparing both the production response and the psychological effects of the two methods.

Mass Media and Other Concentrated
Education of Urban Elites

Would it not be worthwhile to experiment with a few projects aimed at apprising a whole urban elite of the reasons for the importance of, and the steps needed to achieve, agricultural and rural development? For the most part, the efforts of developmental assistance to accelerate agricultural and rural development are aimed at rural people and at agricultural technicians and administrators. Yet many of the programs, investments, and legal and political changes necessary to agricultural development depend more on the attitudes and decisions of the urban elite of low-income countries than on those of rural people. Feature articles in newspapers and magazines, radio broadcasts (primarily news of local rural events but with interpretive comments regarding their significance), movie shorts, public meetings, speakers' services for private organizations, special seminars, and weekend informal conferences for invited guests, are among the possibilities. Some of these are now being used to a limited extent. What is here proposed is exploratory experimentation with integrated and more extensive use of these methods aimed specifically at achieving rapid education of urban public opinion on specific topics crucially related to agricultural and rural development. For the future, revision of the curricula of schools and colleges to place greater emphasis on those elements of understanding and knowledge essential to both rural and national development should be encouraged, but that will not do the present urgent job of changing urban attitudes with respect to rural development.

Experimentation with the
"Village-Cluster" Proposal

Nothing has been said so far in this discussion about the important topic of rural industries, nor about the urgent need for increasing nonagricultural employment opportunities. Mention has been made of the problem of identifying and developing those amenities of rural life that will make it more satisfying. The need has been stressed to strengthen commercial availability of agricultural requisites and to improve marketing channels for farm products.

Albert Mayer, initiator of and consultant to the pioneer Etawah Project in India, has given focus to a proposal for a concerted attack on these problems. His proposal is, in essence, that certain plans should be developed and executed for "clusters" of villages: plans including the development of small industries within easy distance of people's present homes, commercial services, secondary schools, and other activities and amenities of rural living. In the context of developmental assistance on special rural problems, and particularly with the extension of developmental assistance in recent years to include town and regional planning, this is a proposal that merits several exploratory projects.

SPECIAL REGIONAL PROBLEMS

Two special problems of a regional nature have been brought out by consultants: the need for at least one really first-class agricultural experiment station in each major region of the world; and the group of urgent special problems of rural development in Africa.

Without contradicting what has been said above about the advantage of concentrating first on adaptive and farm economic research in each country, there is urgent need for at least one first-class central research station, for basic as well as applied agricultural research, in each major region of the world. So far, American aid to such projects has been left to private technical assistance agencies, primarily the Rockefeller Foundation. Other governments have aided such projects in at least two instances. This may be an appropriate activity for cooperative action together with the governments of other nations now providing developmental assistance.

Two consultants, particularly, have urged the need for special research on the problems of rural development in Africa. The topics
they suggest as needing study are the following: a summary of what is
known, technologically and sociologically, about the transformation
of African agriculture; the social, economic, and political factors affecting the determination of a recommended pattern for peasant agriculture in the rain forest zone, the savannah zone, and the arid zone
of Africa; and devising an inexpensive agricultural extension service
for the countryside of Africa, armed with effective techniques of im-
parting scientific knowledge and technical information to African
farmers.

ADMINISTRATION OF DEVELOPMENTAL ASSISTANCE

Most of the research mentioned in the foregoing sections is related
to improving programs of rural development whether developmental
assistance is involved or not. In this section, research needs in connection with developmental assistance itself will be discussed, as these
needs show themselves in agricultural and related programs overseas.

What are the comparative merits of the *servicio,* of joint commis-
sions, and of advisory missions, as agencies of agricultural technical
cooperation? Informal comparisons of two of these administrative devices, with respect to conditions in Latin America only, were made
five years ago, incidental to a broader study.[20] A similar study is needed
covering experience in other parts of the world.

Where should technical advisers be "headquartered"? In capital
cities? In ministries of agriculture? In office buildings of the United
States Operations Mission? All sorts of answers have been given to this
question. It has never, to my knowledge, been objectively studied.

What is the suitability of the college contract as a device for developing agricultural colleges? An analysis is past due of the college contract as a device of developmental assistance, comparing it with the
potentialities of similar aid provided directly by ICA. The college
contract has substantial advantages, both to the United States college
and to operations in the field. At the same time, it has been used, in

---

[20] Philip M. Glick, *The Administration of Technical Assistance: Growth in the
Americas* (University of Chicago Press, 1957), Chap. 2; Mosher, *Technical Cooperation
in Latin American Agriculture,* pp. 323-38.

many cases, in inappropriate ways. It has been covertly and not-so-covertly opposed by some field administrators of ICA. It should be re-examined.

What is the optimum degree of discretionary latitude for field administrators of developmental assistance? This question will never be finally settled, but it merits a sound independent study at this time. Conditions from country to country vary so much that considerable discretionary latitude seems advisable. How much exists? Is there a consensus among field administrators on how much latitude they have? Is the staff as distinct from the line organization of ICA such that field administrators have appropriate staff support in considering alternative program possibilities within their present authority?

What is the validity of the "counterpart" concept in developmental assistance? In theory, a technical adviser works closely with one counterpart so that the counterpart may carry on after the technical adviser departs. In practice, there are serious problems. The counterpart may have had so much less training and experience than the adviser that he cannot be brought to competence within the two-year term. He may have had as much or more training and experience, in which case there is a serious psychological obstacle to considering himself a "learner." Differences in individual temperament between the adviser and a single counterpart may inhibit rapport, whereas if an adviser works with several persons not formally designated as counterparts, there is more probability that productive rapport will be established with at least some of them. The counterpart may be transferred to quite different responsibilities while the adviser is still present or soon after he leaves, thus defeating the specific purpose of the relationship.

What is the counterpart's perception of his role? What are the "bands of misunderstanding"[21] between advisers and counterparts, unsuspected in some cases and exaggerated in others, that cause friction and prevent full cooperation? What is the adviser's perception of his own role and his perception of his counterpart's role? If study of these questions could result in a brief handbook on the adviser-counterpart relationship, its purposes and possible problems, this might help. But there still remains the question whether the adviser and single counterpart arrangement is sufficiently promising to continue its use as a general practice.

[21] Howard Beers' phrase.

What is the influence of political considerations on selection and location of developmental projects? Frequently, it is discovered that a project is undertaken, or is located in a certain place, because congressman so-and-so or "the minister" or "the president" wants it thus. Part of the problem may arise from lack of objective criteria, understandably phrased, that might be applied to decisions on project selection and location. Frequently, also, developmental assistance personnel are unaware of the positive role political influence can play in furthering developmental plans.

What background of professional training and experience is most effective for the diagnostic role with respect to what is needed for developmental assistance in a particular country at a particular time? As must be obvious from the number and dissimilarity of the many elements of, and influences on, rural development, the diagnostic task of determining what to help with, how, and when, is a very difficult one. The predominant economic criteria in fashion a few years ago have been widely challenged by new knowledge and experience in the recent past. The ICA Career Development Institute at Johns Hopkins University is getting at this problem pragmatically. Meanwhile, additional study of it seems warranted. Some observers feel that American deans of colleges of agriculture and directors of experiment stations are more likely than others, in the absence of additional training, to have the qualifications for such a role.

What criteria can be set up for evaluating programs of rural development? It is inevitable as well as imperative that judgments be made continuously about what to continue and what to drop and about how to modify on-going programs. Within this process, some quantitative measures are valid and useful, and field personnel in developmental assistance need to know what they are. At the same time, if developmental assistance is to be of optimum productivity, its activities must not be limited to those whose effects can be quantitatively measured.

THE TECHNICAL ADVISER

A major study is needed analyzing the roles performed by technical advisers in agricultural extension, research, community development, and health. An adequate theoretical framework and appropriate methodology for such a study is at hand.[22] This analysis should be made of all relevant roles within several United States Operations Missions, in the Food and Agriculture Organization of the United Nations, and in private agencies, with similar analyses of the roles of those in the relevant counter positions in the host government. Such a study would be helpful at two points: (1) it would facilitate modifications in administrative procedures and in the nature of assignments so as to increase the positive contributions of individual advisers and reduce conflicts and working at cross-purposes between different advisers and different technical divisions of the same agency; (2) it would be helpful in reformulating policies relative to the recruitment and training of advisers.

In studying the problems of recruiting technical advisers, the need is not for a single research project but rather for careful investigation of a cluster of related questions. What are the personality characteristics and technical training and experience related to successful field performance in each of the roles played by developmental assistance field personnel? What incentives are effective in recruiting the particular types of personnel needed in developmental assistance? What recruiting methods are needed in order to find and secure such personnel? What are the most frequent and the most serious obstacles to recruiting the most appropriate personnel? What is needed to provide means of gaining professional recognition by personnel in developmental assistance? To what degree is a common program of orientation appropriate for the wide variety of roles for which personnel must be recruited, and what should the content of this orientation be?

There are many criticisms of the policy of frequently transferring technical advisers. What can be learned from the policy of the past few years of keeping an adviser in a particular country not longer than four years, and often transferring him after such period to a different part of the world? Has this proved beneficial? Both aspects of the policy have been criticized. What seem to be the facts?

TOWARD BETTER UTILIZATION OF PRESENT KNOWLEDGE

If the knowledge gained through research and experience is to be effective in improving developmental assistance, it is important that

[22] See Neal C. Gross and Others, *Explorations in Role Analysis: Studies of the School Superintendency Role* (John Wiley & Sons, 1958).

it be consolidated into useful form and be readily available in every low-income country, as well as in every training center in the United States. To this end, the following concluding suggestions are made:

A circulating library of agricultural development and developmental assistance should be established in each country, with a reference librarian on each United States Operations Mission staff. Arrangements should be made to have what is now known, in its present forms, available to every technical adviser in the field and to all of those with whom he is working. The librarian should make this information readily available to busy field workers and keep the library well organized and up-to-date.

A set of handbooks should be prepared, summarizing present knowledge on topics of general importance to rural developmental assistance. Technical advisers need library facilities, but present knowledge is recorded in many types of documents and in various scientific jargons. There is widespread and valid demand for a series of handbooks that summarize those selected portions of present knowledge most frequently useful to technical advisers, presented in a form for ready comprehension and easy use. Such handbooks should draw for their materials both on pertinent general knowledge from past research and on the experience of recent programs of developmental assistance. Handbooks are needed on the following subjects: tropical crops and soils, and pest and disease control in the tropics; methods and special problems of conducting adaptive research, simple farm economic surveys, and village social studies; hand tools and animal-drawn implements; village and farm methods of water supply and environmental sanitation; extension and community development methods specifically for low-income countries; choice of projects and operational devices for agricultural and rural development; the role of the technical adviser and of counterparts in developmental assistance; principles and methods of local government in rural areas.

Materials particularly pertinent to each country should be collated. In addition to the general handbooks, each technician needs to have at his finger tips the results of research conducted locally and related to his task. Two forms of collations would be particularly useful. One is a summary of the results of local research with respect to agriculture and rural life. The other is a cumulative history of developmental assistance in each country: What has been tried? What were the results? What special problems have arisen?

A consolidated review of theories and speculations regarding agricultural development should be made. There is no agreed theory of agricultural development. Several are implicit in this essay. The research projects listed earlier would provide considerable additional data. Meanwhile, there is no one book in which one can find a summary of the various theories propounded or implicit in policies adopted and procedures employed. A comprehensive review of the literature in this field, with references to sources, noting areas of agreement and conflict, and stating which theories appear to be supported by what empirical data, would be most helpful.

A history of programs and projects of planned or guided change should be written.[23] Perhaps the lessons of these programs could be summarized in a single book. Perhaps it would be better to have a "guide" to existing records, together with a well-annotated bibliography; or a combination of the two. The difficulty with the "guide and annotated bibliography" for this purpose is that many important records are out-of-print, many have never been published, and those that are still available are in several languages. Despite the problems, an enormous amount of experience has accumulated in many sorts of programs of planned or guided change, and the lessons of this experience should be widely available.

Regional subject-matter specialists within ICA should regularly visit technical advisers to consult on program rather than on administration. Technical advisers need the counsel and comradeship of regional subject-matter specialists who have no administrative responsibility, and who can perform a liaison role within a group of countries in one part of the world. Such specialists could, at the same time, take an active part in research projects related to agricultural development, and they would be useful policy advisers to headquarters administrators.

SUMMARY AND PRIORITIES

Research is much more than a staff activity preparatory to agricultural development or preliminary to developmental assistance. Since

[23] The differences between what is proposed here and the "Handbook on Extension and Community Development Methods" proposed above are two: the experiences of whole programs would be considered in this history, and a wider range of types of programs would be covered.

an important phase of agricultural development is to move from a fatalistic acceptance of the ways of nature to a systematic manipulation of natural law to achieve agreed results, the experience of engaging directly in research may be one of the most fruitful ways of achieving this revolution of outlook. Inasmuch as technical advisers and local counterparts come from different cultures, speaking languages in which it is frequently difficult even to find acceptable verbal translations to represent key concepts, the field experience of engaging together in systematic examination of local conditions and in joint searches for locally valid improved practices may be one of the easiest ways of establishing meaningful communication. Since, in many cases, local attitudes, customs, and taboos seem to stand in the way of development, perhaps joint, objective examination of the impact of these on specific steps toward agricultural development would be a more effective way to modify them than verbal discussion of the respective merits of the attitudinal fruits of different "cultures" and of different historical developments.[24]

Consequently, in reviewing the needs for research to improve developmental assistance, more is being done than listing needs for "prior homework." In fact, the subject-matter opportunities are listed for what could well become a most important operational component of developmental assistance in the field.

Research needs have been discussed in the foregoing pages under subject-matter headings. It may be useful to summarize them here more by types of research and by geographic scope, since, when it comes to implementation, each research need must be tackled by an appropriate agency or unit. These research needs fall into two broad types: (1) those requiring comprehensive multi-country studies, comparing similar and contrasting experience and drawing reasonable conclusions; (2) those involving careful examination of local conditions, local cultural traits, local practices and locally available "improvements" for each particular region.[25]

Two refinements of this reclassification would be useful. One would be a rating of these needs from the standpoint of "researchability." Many of the topics listed here are ones on which more wisdom is needed but they are not easily amenable to "research." No attempt is

[24] Arthur E. Morgan, among others, advanced this view in 1948 in the "Report of the Universities' Commission" in India.
[25] A number of multi-country studies would be more fruitful if they could utilize the results of many local studies of this second type.

made here to indicate degree of "researchability," since this can best be judged by experts in the many fields and disciplines in which these topics lie.

The other refinement would be to give some indication of the relative importance of the different topics, thus indicating priorities in research. I have already done this to some extent, primarily by omitting discussion of two thirds of the topics suggested for consideration by correspondents. Thus I deem important all of the topics discussed. Among topics discussed, however, an indication of priorities is given in Tables 3.1, 3.2, and 3.3 at the end of the essay, in the notation opposite each topic in the right-hand margin. In this notation, 1 indicates high priority, 2 indicates the second order of priority, and 3 indicates the third order of priority, but still important. Two ratings are given. The one to the left is my rating. That to the right is the average rating of those correspondents whose ratings had been received by the date of this final draft. Thus, the notation 2-1.5 would indicate that, to me, the topic is of the second order of priority while to the correspondents it stands half way between the first and second orders of priority.

Research Needs Requiring Multi-Country Studies

Thirty-one of the topics discussed in this essay and listed in Table 3.1 call for research drawing its data from a number of different countries. This does not mean that research on any one of a number of these topics in a single country would not be valuable. It does mean, however, that these are topics on which results from a study in a single country should not be considered to be generally applicable in others. It also means that comparisons between countries, while not absolutely necessary in all cases, are likely to be particularly helpful in uncovering pertinent factors which a single-country study is likely to overlook.

Consequently, these are topics best explored by independent or centralized agencies in a position to administer multi-country studies. In cases where one of these topics is studied in a single country, it would be helpful if the methodology of the study could be reviewed by a central agency before the study is carried out, in an attempt to promote comparability among individual studies in different countries. It is partly because of the importance and the special requirements of multi-country studies such as these that I have, in another context, proposed the establishing of an independent Institute of Agricultural Development, primarily to promote, finance, and conduct research in this general field.

Research on Local Problems, Country by Country

Twenty-two of the topics needing research, and listed in Table 3.2, call for investigation of local conditions, local practices, and local possibilities in each of the regions where developmental assistance operates.

The priorities assigned to these topics in Table 3.2 should be treated gingerly, for in practice quite a different criterion of selection should come into play. These are the research topics particularly amenable to study as an operational part of developmental assistance. Consequently, an important criterion in selection is this: What topics are such that the process of tackling them can make an appreciable contribution, at a given time, to the growth in competence and understanding of local technicians and farmers?

I would lay it down as a general proposition that every field research project in developmental assistance should include a substantial training component. That is, every field research project should be so conducted that it trains men in research methods. If this is to take place, projects must be of the degree of simplicity or of complexity that potential trainees are ready for.

The *results* of all of the research suggested herein are needed. In choosing from among these many topics, those should be selected in which the *process* is as fruitful as possible at each given point in time.

New Approaches Worthy of Pilot Project Experimentation

The previous section of this chapter advances certain proposals for new approaches in rural developmental assistance that I believe are worthy of pilot project experimentation. Two of the proposals are rated fairly high by the correspondents: adaptive agronomic and farm economic research, coupled with extension, as a major operational activity; and an extension education program to village merchants, bankers, and moneylenders, backed by appropriate research.

The others were given medium to low ratings by the correspondents. These priorities are summarized in Table 3.3.

CONCURRENT RESEARCH AND ACTION

There is no other way to proceed with a task where the almost infinite complexities and potentialities of human behavior are involved, except "prematurely" and in partial knowledge. This is true not only in the beginning, but throughout the process.

The situation leading to developmental assistance was, and is, urgent and desperate. The United States was right to plunge in, and it must not now let any impulse to research slow its action programs. But, fortunately, no such conflict arises.

Needs for research at this point are as much opportunities for more effective modes of continuing action in the field as they are preparation for the future. In its defensible haste in getting into developmental assistance, the United States assumed it had more answers than was, in fact, the case. However, in view of the problems of human pride, on both sides, inevitably involved in every form of cross-cultural cooperation, the United States may be in a stronger position now for not knowing the answers. In tackling some of the problems outlined in this essay as learners together with friends in other countries, the United States may have opportunities for more effective forms of developmental assistance in the years ahead.

TABLE 3.1

Research Needs Requiring Multi-Country Studies

TOPIC	PRIORITY	
	MOSHER	CORRESPONDENTS
Suitability of college contracts	1	1.2
Communication with illiterate and isolated peoples	1	1.3
Distinctive curricular needs for rapid economic and social development	1	1.3
Role and function of the technical adviser	1	1.3
Consequences of different patterns of land settlement	1	1.3
Factors affecting recruitment of technical advisers	1	1.4
Effective uses of ICA Participant Program	1	1.4
Validity of the "counterpart" concept	1	1.5
Economic, social, and political factors in land reform	1	1.6
Technical back-stopping for extension and community development	1	1.6
Cultural traits conducive to rapid development	1	1.7
Types of production credit institutions	1	1.7
Communications patterns and channels in folk cultures	1	1.7
Preparation for the diagnostic role in developmental assistance	1	1.7
Where should technical advisers be headquartered	1	1.7
Changes and problems introduced by irrigation	1	1.9
Relative rates of return to capital in agriculture and industry	1	1.9
How secure adequate emphasis by community development programs on agricultural production	1	2
Experience with cooperative societies	1	2
Agricultural Extension or Community Development?	1.5	a
Surveys of hand tools, implements, farm vehicles	1.5	1.5
Optimum discretionary latitude for field administrators	1.5	1.7
Relative merits of *servicios,* joint commissions, and advisory missions	2	1.4
Evaluating programs of rural development	2	1.8
Arrangements for adaptive agricultural research	2	1.9
Role of subsidies and technical aid in self-help projects	2	2
Can agricultural extension and supply of requisites be combined?	2	2.1
Pertinence of land-grant college pattern	2	2.2
Coordinating technical services of different ministries	2	2.4
Studies of "slash-and-burn" cultivation	2	a
Effect of transfers of technical advisers	2	a
Influence of political considerations on project selection and location	2	2.4
Effective location and affiliation of colleges of agriculture	3	1.7
Contribution of practical agricultural high schools	3	1.7
Factors which have ended periods of stagnation	3	a

a This topic was added or differently stated in the final draft, so consultants had no opportunity to give it a priority rating.

TABLE 3.2

Research on Local Problems, Country-by-Country

TOPIC	PRIORITY	
	MOSHER	CORRESPONDENTS
Place to apply limited capital inputs	1	a
Relative strength of different incentives to increase production	1	a
Range of freedom of choice in farm operation	1	a
The role and economic value of rural roads	1	1.1
Studies related to local government	1	1.3
Farm-to-farm variations in production and income	1	1.3
Yield trials of strains of crops in use locally	1	1.4
Controlled experimentation on selected techniques of extension education and community development	1	1.4
Management of soils of the humid tropics	1	1.4
Studies of local value systems	1	1.4
Studies of the foci of decision-making	1	1.4
Field trials of soil treatments	1	1.5
The Taylor Hypothesis	1	1.6
Relative value assigned to different amenities of rural life	1	1.9
Values and motivations regarding borrowing and repaying loans	1	a
Nature of the need for capital in agricultural production	1.5	1.4
Studies of on-the-farm moisture management	1.5	1.5
Economic land classification	1.5	1.6
Present effective demand for production credit	1.5	1.7
Effectiveness and extent of use of visual aids	1.5	1.7
Studies of the impact of taxation on rural development	1.5	2
Impact of class structure on rural development	2	1.8
Studies of the economics of farm mechanization	2	1.9
Effect on extension education of "crash" production programs	2	2
	3	2.4

a This topic was added or differently stated in the final draft, so consultants had no opportunity to give it a priority rating.

TABLE 3.3

New Approaches Worthy of Pilot Project Experimentation

TOPIC	PRIORITY	
	MOSHER	CORRESPONDENTS
Adaptive research coupled with extension as a major operational activity		
An extension education program to village merchants, bankers, and moneylenders	1	1.1
Extended and more effective use of radio	1	1.6
Education of the urban elite in the requirements for agricultural development	1	1.8
The "outlook conference" approach to extension emphasis on national production targets	1	2
Experimentation with the Village Cluster proposal	1	2.7
Exploratory projects of "enclosure"	1.5	1.8
Publicly supported advertising of agricultural production requisites	1.5	2.1
	2	2.3

4

Technological Change in the Less Developed Areas

R. S. ECKAUS*

THE URGENCY OF ECONOMIC DEVELOPMENT in the less developed areas of the world is now generally agreed on, even though not so long ago such development was widely regarded as of only marginal concern for United States policy. In any case, the premise having achieved wide acceptance, there need be less distraction from the issues of understanding and implementing economic growth in the less developed areas. There is also general agreement that technological change has a central role in the improvement of the economic conditions of the peoples of the less developed areas. There is less appreciation of the problems of adopting technologies that will use the resources available as effectively as possible to achieve the growth desired. The less developed areas vary in their natural resource endowments, the structure of their economies, their current capabilities, and their future objectives. Unskilled labor is nearly always relatively abundant, while skills and capital equipment are relatively scarce. The degree to which technologies are suited to these different resource availabilities and to the achievement of growth targets determines their aptness for use.

Technological change is important for the less developed areas but is opposed by strong forces of tradition that attempt to forestall the consequent social changes. Thorough study is required in order to de-

* Associate Professor of Economics, Brandeis University and Research Associate, Massachusetts Institute of Technology, Center for International Studies.

cide which technologies will contribute most to economic growth and to find methods of implementation that will facilitate rather than counteract the change.

The discussion that follows will concentrate on technological change in an industrial context; neither related sociological changes nor technological change in agriculture will be considered except in so far as some of the broader generalizations may be applicable.

THE ROLE OF TECHNOLOGICAL CHANGE
IN UNDERDEVELOPED AREAS

Although there is agreement that technological change is important in underdeveloped areas, there is no unanimity on why it is important or on its most important features. It may not be necessary to decide on its most significant role, but it is necessary to appreciate the various influences it exerts.

The role most commonly assigned to technological change is the achievement of a more rapid rate of economic growth and improvement of the standard of living than would otherwise be possible. The belief is quite widely held that in modern technology there is the means by which the less developed areas can avoid or reduce the sacrifices and the time span required to achieve a satisfactory level and rate of economic development. Certainly there is a substantially larger inventory of technology that can be drawn on now than there was when economic modernization began in the nineteenth century. If this body of knowledge can be made available to the less developed areas, they will undoubtedly progress more rapidly than would otherwise be possible. Although technological transfer will make the tasks easier, it is almost never costless and seldom, if ever, will yield something in the way of output for nothing but a new idea. So the essential economic problems remain of finding the techniques that impose the least sacrifices for achieving specified targets of future output.

Recent economic research on the growth of the United States has reinforced the general impression that, quantitatively, technological change has been a major causal influence. Studies such as those of M. Abramowitz, J. W. Kendrick, and R. M. Solow indicate that ordinary capital accumulation and growth in the labor force can alone account for only 10 to 20 per cent of the economic growth in the

United States in the past half century or so.[1] It is by no means clear that all of the remainder is due to technological change,[2] but there is a general consensus that it is a substantial factor. These studies, therefore, reinforce the impression of the importance of technological change in the development of the less developed areas.

Technological characteristics have a major role in many of the most widely discussed problems of economic development. The possibilities and the significance of "balanced growth" in economic development depend to a considerable extent on the character of technology. Economic programing, the relative roles of agricultural and industrial development, and significance of "external economies" are likewise related to the technology of the various sectors. For such reasons the problem of optimal choice of technology which will be discussed below has been a central theme in development literature.

A less common conception of the role of technological change in the underdeveloped areas is that it should provide *new* technologies especially adapted to their resources and conditions. This approach recognizes the differences that prevail in the relative availabilities of productive factors in the less developed as compared to the more advanced areas. Most of modern technology has been developed in and for the latter areas and is, therefore, less obviously suited to the conditions of underdeveloped areas. Facilitating technological change in this conception means research to find new production methods suited to the less developed areas and implementing them there.[3]

In a number of analyses the touchstone of a country's prospects for development is its ability to initiate continuing technological change. Professor Everett Hagen makes this the heart of his theory.[4] One has the impression from Professor Hagen that it is both a necessary and

[1] Moses Abramowitz, "Resource and Output Trends in the United States since 1870," *American Economic Review, Papers and Proceedings*, Vol. 56 (May 1956), pp. 5-23, reprinted as National Bureau of Economic Research, *Occasional Paper 52* (1956); John W. Kendrick, "Productivity Trends, Capital and Labor," *Review of Economics and Statistics*, Vol. 37 (August 1956), pp. 248-57, reprinted as National Bureau of Economic Research, *Occasional Paper 53* (1956); R. M. Solow, "Technical Change and the Aggregate Production Function," *Review of Economics and Statistics*, Vol. 39 (August 1957), pp. 312-20.

[2] E. Domar refers to it as the "residual." See his as yet unpublished paper, "On the Measurement of Technological Change," which surveys and analyzes the methodology of such measurements.

[3] This is an avenue that is being explored at the Massachusetts Institute of Technology by the Center for International Studies and is discussed in the recent staff paper of the Stanford Research Institute, *Scientific Research and Progress in Newly-Developing Countries*.

[4] See E. E. Hagen, "How Economic Growth Begins: A General Theory Applied to Japan," *Public Opinion Quarterly*, Vol. 22 (Fall 1958), pp. 373-90.

sufficient condition for economic development to occur. The rate at which technological change can be implemented is not independent of other economic conditions, to be sure, and there is great scope for all the tools of economic policy. Initiation of technological change is the key, however, and this requires initiators: enterprisers, who play the central role in Professor Hagen's cosmogony. The most important issues in development are, therefore, the emergence of such individuals and the psychological and cultural factors that account for them. These define the crucial areas of research for understanding of the basic problems of development.

Professor Hagen's emphasis is reminiscent of that found in a number of other analysts of economic growth, though none have carried research into the factors which create the entrepreneurial personality so far as he has. Yet the view that the role of the entrepreneur in initiating technological change must certainly be an important factor in development is reinforced by the fact that it has been stressed by Joseph Schumpeter[5] and even earlier historians and analysts of capitalist development.[6]

In addition technological change is regarded by many persons concerned with the advancement of underdeveloped areas as one of the major instruments for necessary changes in the general social structure. There is no doubt that this structure to a considerable extent always reflects former economic and technical patterns. Though these may once have represented an optimal adaptation to the existing conditions, the social patterns that facilitate economic growth are likely to be different. As a result, old adaptations become modern barriers. Technological change is undoubtedly powerful in destroying the rationale of old social roles and demanding new ones. A special aspect of this is the effect of technological change on the distribution of income and, therefore, on the division of income between spending and saving. Since capital scarcity is one of the common features of the less developed areas, the effect of a new technology on saving is sometimes regarded as its most significant feature.[7]

The conclusion that technological change has a number of impor-

---

[5] J. Schumpeter, *Business Cycles* (McGraw-Hill, 1939).

[6] The classical references are Max Weber, *The Protestant Ethic and the Spirit of Capitalism* (Scribner, 1930) and R. H. Tawney, *Religion and the Rise of Capitalism* (Harcourt, 1926).

[7] Walter Galenson and Harvey Leibenstein, "Investment Criteria, Productivity and Economic Development," *Quarterly Journal of Economics*, Vol. 69 (August 1955), pp. 343-70.

tant effects in economic development is hardly challengeable. That does not, however, mean that all types of technological change are equally feasible and desirable in the process of growth or that the underdeveloped areas are intended to become technological facsimiles of the advanced areas. Nor are the means of introducing and disseminating technological change at all obvious. The criteria for technological change and the means of facilitating it must be developed in terms of the influences it is intended to have. All the influences described here are related to growth via increases in the amount of and the productivity of the available resources. Generally, the relation is direct, though in some cases, to be mentioned, it may be inverse.

The first job in discussing technological transfer is to establish a terminology and methodology of measuring technology. These can then be used to address the issues involved in making the optimal choice of technology.

MEASURING TECHNOLOGY AND MAKING AN OPTIMAL CHOICE

It is easy but misleading to assume that everyone knows what is meant by a particular technology. A little experience in discussing technology with engineers and businessmen is enough to show that lack of a common terminology is a major source of confusion. Clearing it up will take us far along the path toward deciding what research is necessary.

The ordinary engineering names or descriptions of technology are usually qualitative and may refer to a set of physical or chemical processes. A technology may be described in terms of some basic physical equations in which the variables are physical quantities such as material weights and volumes or electrical energy or heat inputs. Often a technology will be described and summarized in terms of the name of a particular piece of physical equipment. Thus, an engineer or a businessman or a foreign aid official may discuss the introduction of high-speed automatic lathes in India as a particular technological change. Or they may refer to the Frasch process for sulfur extraction or some particular chemical process for which the equations are well-known.

These are deceptively easy ways of discussing technology. They are easy because they are connotative; they convey a general meaning, at least to people versed in the terminology. But they are deceptive because by themselves they do not convey a precise, quantitative indication of all the inputs and outputs required. It is necessary to *measure* a technology in order to arrive at an appreciation of its significance. The economist has developed the conceptual tools but has not gone very far in giving them empirical content. The engineer has his own set of concepts, which do have empirical content but are not the most suitable for economic analysis. Therefore, for the means of measurement the skills of the engineer and the economist must be combined.

A technology is defined by an economist by identifying and measuring the various inputs of productive resources that are used to create a certain output.[8] The economist has usually had recourse to such global terms as capital, land (natural resources), and labor, which are not unfamiliar to the businessman as he often discusses his firm in somewhat similar words. These terms do not discriminate sufficiently between alternative types of resources, however, and thus do not match the types of inputs the engineer will ordinarily specify as required for a particular output. Basically, however, the approaches are the same. Though an engineer may sometimes start from the most basic materials, energy, and chemical change concepts, in working through his design procedure he will end up with the values of machinery and material of each type, electrical power, and labor of various skills required for a specified output. What is mainly needed between the engineer and the economist is some reconciliation of vocabularies.

The differences which exist in terminology do not vitiate the main point that ultimately technology is defined both by economists and engineers in terms of the amounts of inputs necessary to achieve a particular output. This permits the comparisons and evaluations that are the necessary basis for the formulation of a policy which must itself be in quantitative terms.

This concept of a technology as something that can be measured and precisely defined will be useful in future discussions. It is not an overstatement to say that it is absolutely necessary if any headway is to be made in attacking the various problems mentioned above of finding, choosing, and transferring appropriate technologies. For example, the quantitative notion of a technology permits the distinction

[8] In linear programing terms this is called an "activity."

confined to increasing the productivity of the amount used of only one productive factor, such as labor or machines of particular types, is quite misleading.

The criteria for optimal choice of technique in developing economies start from the static criterion and consist of modifications of it that arise from the many problems involving time in an essential way, the statement of different goals, and the imposition of additional constraints. In a dynamic context, for example, differences in the gestation period of production processes and in their durability must also be taken into account in choosing the technology which in turn determines the relative intensity with which productive factors are used. As between processes with equal input requirements and equal outputs, the one with the quicker payoff is to be preferred. When a faster return requires having more inputs or getting less output, again an economic question arises.[9]

If the goal is to increase the rate of growth, another set of influences related to but not purely technological must be taken into account. Different technologies which use different combinations of labor, capital plant and equipment and materials will give rise to different distributions of incomes. Each income distribution will have its own savings characteristics and, therefore, will differ in the amounts of resources that will be made available for further investment and economic growth. In this way, there may be a specific savings and investment potential associated with each type of technology. The choice of technology in the context of a developing country must take this feature as well as the immediate contribution to output into account.[10]

The choice of technology in developing economies involves other features not generally considered in a static context. Economies of scale, which do not fit easily into static economic analysis may be an essential feature in a developing country. One type of technology may have external effects, as in labor training, which tip the scales in its direction.

These issues may be illustrated and made more concrete by a few examples. The recent Chinese experiment with small iron ore smelting furnaces provides a frequently cited example of a technological

[9] In this case the best procedure, put briefly, is that which gives the highest present discounted value.

[10] A substantial literature exists on this problem. The recent article by Prof. Hollis B. Chenery, "Comparative Advantage and Development Policy," *American Economic Review*, Vol. 51 (March 1961), pp. 18-51; and the book by A. K. Sen, *Choice of Techniques* (Oxford, 1960), are good guides into this area.

revival supposedly more suited to their conditions than the methods now generally in use as it requires a great deal of the abundant labor which they have. However, the experiment appears to have been virtually dropped; it is likely that the process was simply physically inefficient. The small furnaces undoubtedly required more fuel per unit of output and possibly more capital also, as well as more labor.

On the other hand, it is not unusual to find plants embodying the most modern technologies in the less developed areas, using a good deal of equipment per worker and relatively little labor with a very high average productivity. This may be justified on several grounds. Sometimes it is argued that such methods are the only physically efficient ones, or, that, even at the low wages prevailing, they are economically more efficient than methods that use more of the abundant labor which is available. Both of these answers, if they were true, would be adequate reasons, but, as stated above, it would be wrong to justify a technology solely on the grounds that it increased the productivity of the workers in the plant.[11] It is, after all, the productivity of the entire labor force and the output of the entire economy which is important for development.

To illustrate the impact of changes in technology on savings patterns, the possible implications of a land reform program can be cited. In some of the less developed areas of the world, land reform programs increase the labor intensity of cultivation by breaking up large landholdings and distributing them in parcels to individual families. This means that a change in technology as well as a change in property relationships is involved. The effect may very well be in such cases to increase output per acre or per hectare and total output, though output per man would fall. A further effect might be that an increased proportion of the total output is consumed as the result of its wider distribution in the hands of the workers of the land, and that total saving is reduced. This in turn would tend to impede further over-all progress by reducing the total investment possible.

The problems of measurement are handled best in the context of investigation of the characteristics of particular technologies and so will be discussed in the next section. On the other hand, the principles of optimal choice of technology can be investigated and estab-

[11] As an example of this kind of reasoning see Richard L. Meier, "Automation and Economic Development," *Bulletin of the Atomic Scientists*, Vol. 10 (April 1954), pp. 129-33.

lished before they need to be invested with facts and numbers. The logic of making optimal choices has by no means been completely explored in spite of the extensive literature cited above. More work is needed in order to integrate the rules for optimal choice into an overall programing framework. In the present state of knowledge the choice issue is usually analyzed for projects as if they are and could be considered separately from each other and independently of the overall growth pattern of a country.

There are analytical tools which, when given empirical content, can be used to establish the *consistency* of various projects in an overall plan. These are best represented by the input-output approach first developed by Professor Wassily W. Leontief at Harvard University[12] and, perhaps most skillfully used in application to underdeveloped areas by Professor Chenery.[13] Where input-output methods cannot be applied, something equivalent has to be developed for the purpose of establishing over-all consistency in economic programing. The development of input-output type information must, therefore, be seriously considered in research plans for any underdeveloped area. However, it would be premature to put such research on the current agenda for every country. In many areas the economic programing currently required is not sufficiently complex or elaborate to require the full input-output apparatus to establish consistency. In these and other cases, the quality of the statistical data available may not warrant the empirical effort involved. Where the data make the project feasible, various methods of constructing input-output tables should be considered. These are by no means completely settled in themselves so that in this, as in other fields, alternative approaches should not be foreclosed by a premature commitment to a particular method.

The problem of optimality is logically and practically distinct from that of consistency. Though input-output tables will help establish the latter, more is required for the former problem. The theoretical framework necessary for forming policy has not yet been completed, though theoretical programing models exist which give useful insights and are of value as partial guides. Relevant work is going on,[14] but

[12] *Studies in the Structure of the American Economy, Theoretical and Empirical Explorations in Input-Output Analysis,* Harvard Economic Research Project (Oxford University Press, 1953).

[13] For example, "The Role of Industrialization in Investment Programs," *American Economic Review, Papers and Proceedings,* Vol. 45 (May 1955), pp. 40-57.

[14] For example, S. Chakravarty, *The Logic of Investment Planning* (North-Holland Publishing Co., Amsterdam, 1960), and "The Use of Shadow Prices in Programme

much more needs to be done. Again, for some countries, the priorities are so obvious and the opportunities so limited that no highly sophisticated tests of optimality and consistency are necessary. For other areas, with greater scope for choice and action and better data availabilities, the problems of formulating a consistent and optimal development program are pressing ones.

The recent attempts to place United States economic aid on a long-term basis highlight the need. This country may soon be asking recipients of our economic aid to prepare long-term development programs. Yet the means to do this are not fully available. Therefore, more research is necessary just to get a good start.

The problem of optimal choice of technology can be treated with the full generality with which it needs to be treated only in the context of complete, consistent, and optimal programs. Though it will always be necessary to make pragmatic compromises with inadequate methods and data, the nature of the inadequacies should be recognized.

This conclusion can be illustrated by another type of reference. One of the sectors in which the choice of technology is most important for underdeveloped areas is transportation. Transportation systems can be based on railroads and locomotives and rolling stock of various types, or highways and buses, trucks, and cars, or some combination of the two systems. The choice of methods is a choice of technology. Yet it is obviously not one that can be made in abstraction from the rest of the economy for the choice itself will determine how the rest of the economy develops. That is, it is not legitimate to ask "What is the optimal technology to move so many ton-miles of freight?" and then choose a technology of railroads or highways and buses, and leave it at that, because the answer to the question will change the way the question is formulated; specifically it will change the number of ton-miles which have to be transported to achieve the economic development specified.[15]

Lacking a fully general way of treating the problem, partial solutions may have to be accepted, but that does not justify being per-

---

Evaluation" (unpublished); Hollis B. Chenery, "The Interdependence of Investment Decisions," in Moses Abramowitz *et al.*, *The Allocation of Economic Resources* (Stanford University Press, 1959); R. S. Eckaus and L. Lefeber, "Capital Formation and Economic Growth: A Theoretical and Empirical Analysis" (unpublished).

[15] See Louis Lefeber, *Allocation in Space: Production, Transport, and Industrial Location* (Amsterdam, Holland, 1958).

manently satisfied with second best. There should be a major effort to improve the ability of countries to take into account the full ramifications of technological choice: to have that choice fully sensitive to the targets specified, on the one hand, and to have the choice feed back and affect the targets to be chosen on the other hand. The analytical problems are among the most complex faced by economists. Research work in this area may seem far removed from the pressing issues of economic development because of its abstraction. Yet it is only by pursuing the abstractions that models can be formulated which, when given empirical content, will provide concrete guidance in particular circumstances.

There are relatively few individuals working in this area, and nearly all of them are in academic institutions. The nature of the research, which must include tentative theorizing also suggests that academic institutions or private research organizations are the proper location for such work. It is likely to be done best if the injunction to make a contribution to development programing is clear, though full scope is given for theoretical development.

FINDING TECHNOLOGIES ADAPTED TO THE CONDITIONS OF UNDERDEVELOPED AREAS

There are two aspects to finding technologies adapted to the conditions of underdeveloped areas. The first constitutes searching among already known technologies; the second involves research to find new technical methods especially suited to the unique conditions of underdeveloped areas. Both aspects will be discussed below, but it will help to clarify the issues if another question is discussed first—why the choice of technology is less difficult in advanced than in underdeveloped areas.

In principle the problems of technological change in advanced countries are not different from those in underdeveloped areas, but practically they are of a different magnitude. The technological changes occurring, or in prospect, are first of all pervasive and profound departures from previously used techniques. These have become imbued with cultural traditions so that a change in production methods requires fundamental adjustments in all aspects of the society. By comparison technological innovations in advanced countries are, for the most part, marginal changes occurring in societies more readily adaptable to change.

Secondly, technological changes in underdeveloped areas are nearly always imported from advanced countries. The characteristic differences in the relative availabilities of the various productive resources in advanced and underdeveloped areas have already been pointed out. As a result, while some of the technological imports may economize on all factors and be physically more efficient than existing techniques, other imported techniques may very well economize on the wrong factors. For example, while it may make good sense to substitute capital equipment for United States labor at three dollars an hour, it may not be sensible in other countries where equivalent labor is, say, three dollars a day, or three dollars for two days, or even less.

Technological change is a more obvious problem in the less developed areas and attracts more attention and greater pressures. It is done more consciously, more publicly, and more often under government control if not under its direction. In advanced countries it occurs regularly with less public attention and seldom with government interference.

Not only do the less developed countries face more difficulties in adopting changes in technology than do the economically more advanced countries, they have much more difficulty in generating new technologies especially suited to their conditions. The overwhelming part of the research and development which is currently going on to develop new technologies is in advanced countries and directed toward their conditions. The amount of technological research directed especially at the problems of underdeveloped countries is virtually negligible.[16]

The research facilities in the less developed countries are themselves quite limited while research in the advanced areas is directed to their own technical problems. The relative poverty and slow growth rates of the less developed countries means that they have not constituted a substantial market which has warranted the attention of those private companies that sponsor technical research. Lack of knowledge of the needs and potential requirements in such areas has also contributed to their neglect. Academic research in the advanced countries is preoccupied mainly with problems in the forefront of scientific and engineering sophistication. Rightly or wrongly the applications

---

[16] The national scientific research institutes such as those of India and Pakistan do concern themselves with these problems to some extent.

are directed primarily at the conditions found in the already developed countries.

It should, therefore, not be surprising that finding and implementing appropriate technological changes include some of the most difficult problems in economic development. However, these problems once identified are, themselves, amenable to research.

The Present State of Knowledge about Technology

In spite of the central role technology plays in economic theory in general, and in development theory in particular, economists know relatively little about it, though it is customary to assume a lot. For example, the degree of variability of inputs of productive resources is an important aspect of a number of significant issues of economic development such as the feasibility and desirability of balanced growth. Yet there are few available facts on the extent of input variability. Likewise, economies of scale in production are widely admitted to be an important consideration in development. Yet there is relatively little information of the specific and quantitative character necessary to be useful in understanding and assisting development. External economies and differences in the technological characteristics of the various producing sectors are also frequently cited, but factually elusive phenomena. The importance of training labor with the skills required to modernize production is well recognized, and education programs are prepared with that objective in mind. In fact, however, there is almost no data generally available that specifies the precise amounts of the various skills required to operate different kinds of technologies. In the absence of such information much of educational policy amounts to calling for more of all types of educated labor. While it is true that more of all types of education is necessary for development, there are differences in the degree of urgency of the requirements for some skills as compared to others.

Though economics has been relatively successful in preparing a framework for the analysis of the relative suitability of alternative techniques of production and in generating the right questions which need to be asked about technology in order to make choices among alternatives, economists have not gone far in answering the questions. This has not prevented the formation of quite strong views on the factual issues. As a matter of faith some economists insist that there must be a wide range of variability of inputs into any productive process. Less frequently, the reverse is held to be true: that there is no effective choice whatsoever. Similarly, strong and opposite views exist on the importance of economies of scale and "external effects," with relatively little specific information on these issues.

The existing engineering literature in turn provides relatively little information of the type desired. The relevant part of this literature is that dealing with the design of production processes and most of this is concerned with the principles of some particular aspect of a production system. Complete working specifications with all the inputs and outputs described in detail are almost never available.

Though there are many examples of the effective transfer of technology from advanced to underdeveloped countries by engineers and businessmen, there are many other examples of application of inappropriate technologies. There is a tendency among some engineers to believe that the "best practice" in the United Kingdom, Switzerland, or the United States is the best practice everywhere. It is understandable that engineers whose experience has been mainly or exclusively in the context of advanced countries should not fully appreciate the economic significance of the application of different technologies in less developed areas. Moreover, it is easier to reproduce existing designs than to start from scratch with a complete rethinking and reworking of the technology of some process.

There are tendencies also in business organizations which would lead to the implementation of inappropriate technologies in the less developed areas. Among the indigenous business leaders there is often an inclination toward a kind of conspicuous emulation of technology which brings them to adopt the latest and most "up-to-date" equipment rather than that best suited to local conditions. Among foreign investors one frequently finds attitudes similar to that found in some engineers that "best practice" does not depend on the locality. Moreover, where there have been successful adaptations of technology to local conditions, it is only rarely that these are written up in the detail necessary to permit consideration of their transfer to other relatively underdeveloped regions. Thus there is relatively little business literature to which one can refer for guidance.

The particular difficulties of this research area may be illustrated by comparing it with the extensive empirical research that has been done on consumer saving and spending patterns. A wealth of detailed information about consumer budgets at various levels of income and in urban and rural areas exists not only in advanced but in many of the less developed regions as the result of the collection of national statistics and sample surveys of budget patterns. Certainly the information is not completely adequate any place, but enough has been generated to permit this to become a major field of economic research. Unfortunately, national statistics are nowhere available with the detail necessary to yield information about technology on which choices could be based. It is even doubtful that macroeconomic data are useful for this purpose though undoubtedly significant for inferences about the aggregative influences of technology and changes in it.[17] On the microeconomic level, no survey technique similar to the household budget studies can be applied to the study of technology. Though consumer budget studies are expensive, the responsiveness of consumers as well as other features of the problem, such as the convenience of general categories of consumption, make mass surveys feasible. Business firms, on the other hand, are notoriously close about their affairs and for understandable reasons. Moreover, the heterogeneity of inputs and outputs makes the collection of data more difficult. Comparison is also more difficult due to the different impact of local production conditions, firm organization, past technological adaptations, and so on.

Yet the type of information essential to understand and assist in the transfer of the most useful kinds of technology to the less developed areas is information at the microeconomic level. Both the aggregative and input-output research mentioned above would also be more useful if this type of additional information were available.

The increasingly obvious need for information about technology is spurring research by economists though the work is still at the beginning.[18] Some of the studies at the macroeconomic level have already been mentioned. More of these are necessary, yet by themselves they cannot penetrate to the causes of the changes which they observe, at least with the type of aggregative data available.

Input-output tables and their associated empirical studies on "technological coefficients" are useful tools of research and programing as pointed out earlier. Yet such technological coefficients are not revealing about production processes at the firm level as they are again too aggregative, combining as they do many different types of firms and

[17] R. M. Solow, *op. cit.* and R. S. Eckaus and L. Lefeber, *op. cit.*
[18] See U.N. Department of Economic and Social Affairs, "Report on the Meeting of the Expert Working Group on Industrial Development Programming Data," May 17-19, 1961.

products. It is even somewhat misleading to call the numbers in the input-output tables "technological" coefficients. They reflect many other than technological influences as, for example, the degree of vertical integration in plants and the amount of subcontracting which occurs in a particular industry.

Agriculture is classically the sector in which there has been the most work on the detailed characteristics of particular types of production and the alternative inputs required. Investigators in this area have also occasionally extended their interest to related food processing operations.[19] The work is by no means finished, and there are particular deficiencies in the research on the types of agriculture found in underdeveloped areas. Moreover, since local conditions are to such a great extent controlling in this sector, there is a greater need for matching the research to the particular situation. The investigation of disguised unemployment in agriculture in the South of Italy, which was sponsored by the Italy Project of the M.I.T. Center for International Studies, is an example of the application of survey methods to a problem closely related to the resources and technologies available there.

In the area of industrial technologies, the Netherlands Economic Institute at the instigation of Professor Tinbergen has adopted a fundamental approach and has turned out studies on woodworking, weaving, and lathing. This Institute, as well as the Division of Industrialization of the Department of Economic Affairs of the United Nations, has studied in detail particular construction and earth-moving processes. The Economic Commission for Latin America in cooperation with the Division of Industrialization is currently studying alternative methods of investigating the technology of industrial sectors to provide information in the forms most useful for implementation of industry in the less developed areas. One approach currently being followed is an extension of the process analysis first developed at the Rand Corporation by Hoffenberg, Manne, H. Markowitz, and A. J. Rowe. This is a research procedure which begins by measuring inputs at the most basic level of industrial processes. It will be discussed below.

The Center for International Studies at M.I.T. has had a continuing interest in this type of research. Work done there and sponsored

---

[19] See, for example, W. H. Nicholls, *Labor Productivity Functions in Meat Packing* (University of Chicago Press, 1948).

between processes that are physically efficient and those that are not and thus makes it possible to focus on only those processes which might be economically efficient. In comparing any two technologies, one is physically inefficient if it uses more of all productive inputs or even more of any one input, if all its other requirements are the same. There is never any point in using physically inefficient technologies; it amounts to an absolute waste of resources.

When alternative technologies require, for the same level of output, more of some productive factors but less of others, the economic issue arises: Which is the best technological process to use in a given situation? This is the problem of making the optimal choice of technology which was referred to previously. Though the problem need not be resolved here, it is important to pose it. As alternative processes are considered in discussing the transfer of technology to underdeveloped areas, the criteria for choice must be kept clearly in mind.

The optimal allocation or combination of resources in production, which is equivalent to the choice of technology, is an old problem in economics and fully discussed in the context of a static economy. In such circumstances the rule for choice is, roughly, to use that combination of techniques in the various sectors which, over-all will employ productive factors in proportions as close as possible to the proportions in which the resources are available. This is entirely consistent with using factors in different intensities in different sectors, for optimal allocation requires that resources make the same *relative* contributions to output in the various types of production. Thus, capital-intensive methods in producing electric power in central stations and labor-intensive agricultural methods, for example, may both be optimal for particular countries. The criterion for optimal choice does not involve maximizing either the productivity of the employed labor force, the equipment used, or of any other particular resource input. Its objective is to maximize the total output that can be obtained from *all* the resources *available* to the country. Even with such an optimal allocation, the productivity of any one factor such as the labor employed in some particular line of production can be increased by choosing a different technology which is, say, more capital-intensive. That, however, will always involve a greater loss of output in other sectors. Of course, any costless method of increasing the productivity of labor or any other resource ought always to be seized, but such methods seldom exist. A criterion for choice of technology which is also by Brandeis University and financed by the Rockefeller Foundation, though based on United States data, is intended to provide information that will be useful in the less developed regions. A study of labor skill requirements, which is quite far along, when adapted to such areas, can provide the basis for detailed recommendations for educational and vocational training. This is also the purpose of the study of foundry processes which has been started. In addition, economists have been exploring with members of the engineering faculty the possibility of establishing a group to develop new technologies or new adaptations of old technologies especially suited to the conditions of underdeveloped areas.

Another type of work which deserves mention is that done by the Stanford Research Institute on small industry. Their published studies are not confined to consideration of the most appropriate technology and, in fact, do not generally treat this subject at great length.

In addition, the work of the International Cooperation Administration itself in providing engineering assistance and helping to improve technical standards should not be slighted.

Research Needs and Methods for Finding Suitable Technologies

It is useful in tackling a problem which one knows in advance to be complex and hedged about with conceptual, empirical, and policy restrictions to state clearly both objectives and the optimal empirical information. Though these may not be fully achievable, if they are kept in mind, they point the directions in which to try to move and help in assessing the significance of the inevitable compromises.

The economist has long known what data should be available in order to make the best possible decisions regarding the use of technology. One ought to know the full range of alternative technologies. Referring to the terminology developed at the beginning of this section, the optimal set of information would be that which gave in quantitative terms all the productive resources required to achieve each output level. This would necessarily include specification of the time pattern of inputs and outputs.

The optimal set of information may be unobtainable, but stating what it is helps to indicate the type of research that should be done. It should involve quantitative investigation of alternative technologies. Even if the complete range cannot be known, the investigation ought to be pushed toward the more intensive use of the more abundant factors in underdeveloped areas and away from the scarce factors. Since the relative availabilities of productive resources will vary from area to area and from time to time, the study of technology must be a continuing program of research but a major initial effort can cover much of the ground necessary.

Fundamentally there are two approaches to such studies. One is the investigation of actual production systems which have been or are now in operation. The other is the design of alternative production systems, which amounts to simulation of production processes. These approaches are complementary and reinforcing though each has its own set of advantages and disadvantages. The former has the special virtue of realism. It impels the investigator to consider issues which might otherwise have been passed over. It may also reveal the reflexive or feedback effects of economic and other social forces on the organization of the production process itself. It requires an accounting of both inputs and outputs, and this in turn implies a previous study of the production process to determine the set of categories and measurements which will best reflect the output mix, the input components, and so on.

Real systems always involve adaptations to local conditions and may reflect a quite special set of practices. It may also be difficult first to find and then to measure the inputs and outputs for the variety of technologies in operation. This suggests the advantage in combining such studies with simulation or design of production processes using different combinations of inputs. Once a simulation model is set up, it can yield information over a wide range of alternative methods and of alternative employment requirements of various types of skills and various material, equipment, and power inputs. On the other hand, however assiduous the attempts to reproduce the conditions likely to be found in the less developed areas, simulation necessarily involves some abstraction. While that also widens the scope and generality of the conclusions in one sense, it decreases their immediate applicability.

This is not the occasion to enter into the details of measurement, but it is useful to describe briefly just a few of the conceptual and practical problems involved in order to indicate more precisely the nature of the studies contemplated.[20] In some industries the outputs

---

[20] For details see R. S. Eckaus, "The Choice of Technology in Economic Develop-

are reasonably homogeneous or have some common feature so that they can be converted into comparable units. In these cases it is feasible to make comparisons of inputs on a plant basis, and the problems revolve around finding the input categories that will reveal the significant variations in technology. Though concerned with a different problem and therefore not providing the detail desired for the present purposes, the estimates of capital coefficients by the Office of the Chief Economist of the Bureau of Mines provide an excellent example of this approach. These studies were based on records of existing plants and were centered on mineral extraction and processing. For each "product," the amounts of each type of input necessary to expand capacity by one unit were computed. The capital coefficients computed from these studies are, of course, only one of the items of information desired as a basis for considering a transfer of technology. The studies provide good examples of methods of resolving product and input comparisons. However, they also indicate the inadequacy for our purposes of studies based on existing designs alone, as there is no basis for supposing that these designs are generally optimal for underdeveloped countries.

There are industries in which the product is quite heterogeneous so that it is difficult to find a high common denominator in the comparison of inputs and technologies. The answer then is to turn to an examination of the particular subprocesses involved and to compare inputs on this basis. The output of metal machining shops is quite varied, for example, though they use many of the common cutting, grinding, and forming processes. In this sector a comparison of technologies at the process level is likely to be the most rewarding approach. One of the best examples is "An Analysis of Machine Tool Substitution Possibilities," by A. J. Rowe and H. Markowitz.[21]

The objective of the studies proposed here is to create, in a readily usable form, a body of knowledge of alternative technologies which, though not exactly fitting any particular case, would indicate concretely the range of technological substitutions possible. Though it is commonly said that scientific and technical knowledge is universally available, this is an understatement of the real difficulties of obtaining such information in the less developed areas. The fundamental

ment," Center for International Studies, M.I.T.; and "On the Methods of Investigation of Factor Proportions," Center for International Studies, M.I.T.

[21] Rand Corporation (June 1953).

principles may be known, but knowledge of their most effective application and organization is not easy to come by. The purpose of organizing the studies described and obtaining the technological knowledge is precisely to speed the transfer of this applied information.

Though theoretical issues will undoubtedly be involved in the studies of technology suggested here, these need not be expressed when the results are made available to overseas aid missions. The material must be presented in a way in which local engineers and businessmen can understand the suggestions made. Guidance should also be supplied for testing whether the suggestions are appropriate in the local conditions and for exploring the possibility of other, still better adaptations. The studies call for considerable ingenuity whatever the method used. Dogmatism about techniques should be avoided so that there is as much chance as possible for optimum adjustment to local factor endowments along the lines discussed earlier. However, the argument for such adjustment is not meant to prejudge the issue whether the most advanced technology available is or is not appropriate for use in the less developed regions. In some lines of production and in some areas it may very well turn out to be so because of the tremendous production rates that can be achieved. In other sectors it may not be so. The argument here is primarily of the necessity for having information on which to make a judgment.

The engineer must eventually be the source of the technical information necessary, but in developing this information, cooperation between the engineer and the economist is essential. The economist lacks the basic technical information necessary to establish the most effective set of categories and to measure inputs and outputs in ways which will facilitate comparisons. On the other hand, the engineer can profit from the help of the economist in deciding in which directions, in terms of saving scarce resources, the design of production systems should be pushed.

The studies may be organized and distributed in a variety of ways. Bound handbooks suggest a rather more definitive treatment of a technical area than may in fact be feasible in the face of the many new situations that will undoubtedly arise. Loose leaf files to which new case studies and designs may be added as they are developed provide a means of collection and dissemination of technological information that is more in accordance with the probable pattern of its accumulation.

One source of information which should be tapped and made more widely available is the experience of technical assistance personnel in the overseas missions. Working as they do with actual problems and adaptations of technology, they may provide valuable ideas if their experience is properly collated into a general file. To be most valuable the information should, as with the other studies, be quantitative in nature. One should hesitate to suggest additional paperwork for overseas officers; intensive interviews provide a research method less demanding on them and probably capable of better results.[22]

The types of studies recommended as important for one area will be less so for another. Agricultural development is important everywhere. This sector probably already has more information in the requisite form than any other sector, though additional effort in collecting and organizing the material is undoubtedly necessary. Civil engineering projects of various types are also of general importance and much more work on alternative construction techniques is desirable.[23] Housing and other types of construction are also of great significance and deserve more ingenious study. Again a great deal of information already exists which needs to be collated but original studies on the potentialities of local building methods and materials would also be desirable. Transportation is another sector in which the implications of alternative emphases on road and rail technologies are by no means fully understood though of great importance. A listing of research topics and the assignment of priorities is a preliminary step deserving special thought.

An aspect of production methods that requires special attention is the labor skill requirements. Labor skills themselves are one dimension for substitution of productive resources and are relatively scarce even in the less developed areas in which labor, in general, is quite abundant. Skills are in many ways like capital resources, yet, because of the methods of creating this type of capital and its other unique features, they require special consideration. For example, because of the in-

[22] Examples of the use of such techniques for other purposes are in J. Montgomery, "Field Organization, Administrative Relationships and Foreign Aid Policies," *Public Policy*, Vol. 10 (1960), Carl J. Friedrich and Seymour E. Harris, eds.; "Political Dimensions of Foreign Aid," *Tradition, Values, and Socio-Economic Development*, Ralph J. D. Braibanti and Joseph J. Spengler, eds. (Duke University Press, 1961); and John D. Montgomery, *Politics of Foreign Aid: An Analysis Based on American Experience in Southeast Asia*, forthcoming; also a recent project by the Center for Development Research and Training of the African Studies Program of Boston University.

[23] See U. N. Department of Economic and Social Affairs, *Industrialization and Productivity*, Bulletin No. 4 (1961). This journal has had several articles relevant to this subject.

alienability of labor, it is likely that there would be underinvestment in education and training if all of it were left as a "business" decision. That is why it is necessary to have an over-all judgment on the education and skill requirements associated with different types of technology. This is not a suggestion for research on the methodology of education but for research on what kinds of education and training are necessary for the labor force in the less developed areas, using the technologies best adapted to their conditions. Relatively little work on this latter subject has been done in spite of its significance, but there is an increasing amount of interest in this area.[24]

In some sectors or aspects of the economy so many different industries, types of production, and aspects of economic life are bound together that what is required is an over-all or "systems" approach, or what the economist calls a model of "general interdependence." Without such an approach essential features are lost. Transportation and location of industries provide a good example. Separate studies of the technology of transportation are necessary as described above, but they are less useful piecemeal than in a general approach that encompasses not only the technology of particular processes but their economic relations with the location of industrial and population centers.

This suggests another related area that calls for a comprehensive approach: urban studies. Here again many specific studies of alternative technologies are required. The need is particularly pressing because of the rapid rate of urbanization that is occurring and the high costs of the various urban services required. Technologies and designs for the various aspects of urban life have been transferred from advanced to less developed areas almost without change. It is possible that such transfer is warranted, that no other organizations and technologies can be found which would be more economical in terms of the resources available. On the other hand, studies of urbanization problems from the point of view of the economist are relatively scarce, and much more needs to be done in the way proposed here by measurement of inputs and outputs.[25]

Of the studies proposed here, some are necessarily quite large, and others can be subdivided into many parts. Studies of many technological processes can be done on a small scale whereas other processes and

[24] See R. S. Eckaus, "On the Comparison of Physical and Human Capital," Center for International Studies, M.I.T.

[25] As an exception, see the studies jointly supported by SVIMEZ and the Italy Project of the Center for International Studies, M.I.T. on municipal costs in cities of various sizes.

issues such as those of transport or urban problems, involving many facets of economics and technology as they do, must necessarily be on a larger scale. For some of the studies, academic or research organizations can be used quite efficiently and may be particularly suited to the more theoretical investigations. At least partial knowledge of the topics discussed here and the competence to do more research are widely distributed. Therefore, for the most effective use of the available research potential, it is suggested that research on particular types of technology should also be dispersed, though special responsibilities may be assigned to particular organizations, especially where a broader range of problems is involved.

Such dispersal of research imposes more stringent requirements on the central organization for coordination, planning, and collating all the studies. As pointed out above, the foreign aid organization is itself a potential source of useful information on technology. Therefore, it seems necessary that a research organization should be developed within the foreign aid administration. Its functions in this area would include planning and supervision of research projects subcontracted to private individuals and institutions as well as collection and collation of data from internal sources. There is no intention in these proposals that such a research unit be foreclosed from having a wide scope. The suggestion is only that the potential of the research personnel committed to academic and other institutions should be mobilized as fully as possible.

The development of new technologies or adaptation of old technologies for the less developed areas poses different problems than the survey and measurement of existing methods of production. The finding of new techniques requires scientific and engineering projects, though they will be done most effectively with the cooperation of economists. Reasons for the relative neglect of this type of scientific and engineering research were set out above. Certain common difficulties arise in the contemplation of this research area by engineers and scientists. Due to lack of familiarity they do not identify the crucial problems to their own satisfaction and do not always fully appreciate the inapplicability of existing technologies. To engineers and scientists in industry and in academic faculties who are accustomed to work for specific "customers," the lack of a technical statement of the problems creates an aura of vagueness in objectives to which they are not accustomed. Finally, and quite importantly, there have been no sources of funds for sponsoring research on the technical problems of underdeveloped areas, and therefore no effective way for these problems to compete for research time and laboratory space. This type of research has been virtually neglected, in large part because the availability of funds for research on national defense and sophisticated production systems has monopolized the available resources. However, there is an increasing amount of interest in the technical problems of underdeveloped areas by both the research organizations of private companies and academic engineers and scientists.

The terms of reference of research to find new technical methods may be defined in broad or narrow terms depending on the skills and interests and facilities available. At M.I.T. members of the Center for International Studies and the engineering faculty have conferred on a program of research on the development of small-scale energy sources for underdeveloped areas which would cover a range of engineering fields. On the other hand, such a specific project as the preparation of a fish powder as a dietary supplement has also been discussed tentatively. Implementation of this research depends primarily on the availability of funds for the purpose.

Most of the research of this type might best be done outside of government in existing academic and private facilities, again because of the commitment of personnel to these institutions. That would not foreclose a certain amount of direct effort by a government agency. In any case, to stimulate, organize, and supervise this engineering research, a high level of technical and scientific as well as economic competence must be created in the foreign aid organization.

An undertaking by the United States government to sponsor research for the improvement of the conditions of the less developed regions would make a direct contribution to our foreign aid effort. It would also stand as a symbol of the commitment of some of our best minds and research facilities directly to foreign assistance. By example and direct cooperation it might influence the scientific and engineering talent in the underdeveloped areas to attack their own problems more vigorously. Certainly no miracles should be expected or promised. There are no cheap and easy ways to prosperity, but it may be possible to increase substantially the potential rate of development by creating technologies particularly suited to the less developed areas rather than by simply transferring technologies designed for the most advanced countries and different economic conditions.

Such a mobilization of the engineering and scientific resources in this country should be related to the previous research projects pro-

posed on the investigation of existing technologies. The latter will undoubtedly throw up research topics and stimulate development along
new lines.

RESEARCH ON PROBLEMS OF IMPLEMENTING
TECHNOLOGICAL CHANGE

Implementation is often not a problem which is, for practical purposes, separate from those of finding and choosing among alternative
technologies. The latter activities are usually undertaken by a public
or private entrepreneur only when there is a clear prior commitment
to act on the choice made. On the other hand, lack of entrepreneur-
ship is a commonly observed phenomenon even when the potentialities of alternative technologies seem to have been well established. In
these latter cases, the problem of the implementation phase emerges
as a distinct issue.

In turning to this issue the present discussion will be confined to
the organizational and social and psychological aspects of it. The barriers to implementation of new technology that are created directly by
such economic constraints as, for example, the shortage of savings and
foreign exchange and high interest rates, will not be dealt with here.
In view of the central place these problems have had in economists'
discussions of foreign assistance programs, there should be no danger
that inadequate appreciation of them will be assumed if they are omitted from consideration at this point. Likewise implementation depends on the availability of particular skills in the labor force, and
this in turn suggests the usefulness of research on labor training programs and skill requirements, as was mentioned earlier. Another chapter is directed to these problems, so they also will not be discussed
here.

The Social Barriers to Technological Change[26]

Widespread reluctance to adopt new technologies, even those whose
superiority seems overwhelmingly obvious, is a commonly observed

[26] In this section I rely in part on the research of Prof. Everett Hagen of the
Center for International Studies, M.I.T. See, for example, "How Economic Growth
Begins: A General Theory Applied to Japan," *Public Opinion Quarterly*, Vol. 32
(Fall 1958), pp. 373-90. Prof. Hagen is, of course, not responsible for my interpreta-
tions.

phenomenon. It is often attributed to "backward" or "irrational" ways of thought which can be changed only in the slow process of education and modernization of societies. On this, two types of observations must be made. First of all, there ought to be a healthy respect for local skepticism of new methods. "Peasant wisdom" is, to be sure, sometimes only ignorance and superstition. Sometimes, however, it turns out to contain an important kernel of truth. The examples of the former can be multiplied; beliefs that certain foods are poisonous, that only a particular crop can be grown on particular lands and so on. But examples can also be cited of projects which have foundered on the very difficulties predicted by local producers.

Objections to new and thoroughly tested procedures are often encountered that apparently can be nothing else but irrational once appropriate investigations have been made of the technical objections of local producers. To this a second response is required. There must be a full appreciation of the disruption of life that is caused by new technologies. These are important even in those advanced countries that might be expected to have adjusted to change as a way of life. One has only to mention the dislocation and uneasiness in many cities of the United States due to the current wave of automation of production processes. In the less developed areas, where technological changes disrupt a traditional society which is often without flexibility and the means to adjust to change, the threat is very great. In the face of this threat, it is natural that there should be a reluctance to embrace the enemy.[27]

It is convenient to talk of the disruptive effects of technological change on society as a whole, but this is only a useful generalization of what it does to groups and individuals within the society. If they are in fact desirable changes, the new technologies will permit cheaper production than would otherwise have been possible. However, they will seldom, if ever, be confined to products entirely new and complementary to those already produced. Thus, these changes are bound to displace workers, destroy existing market positions and disturb established social relations. There is little point in claiming that the over-all economic growth which is engendered will make everyone better off on balance or permit adjustment into new lines of investment and labor. Though that hopefully would be true, the danger to

[27] The volume *Human Problems in Technological Change: A Case Book,* Edward H. Spicer, ed. (Russell Sage Foundation, 1952), is full of such cases.

the displaced individual is immediate and pressing. The reward is tentative and distant, and there are at best only slim reserves that can act as a cushion for the adjustments required.

Self-interest is not defined narrowly in terms of economic improvement in any society, but in terms of the total adjustment to the community. Where status depends on or can be achieved by material advancement, technological change that achieves it will be attractive to some people at least. But where status is associated primarily with other features of social adjustment, technological change may even be abhorrent. For example, there are places in which the landowner or owner of an industrial firm is expected to act as the benevolent patron of his working force, to be a kind of super father figure. In such circumstances to introduce a technological change that would displace part of his labor force, would expose the owner to profound social criticism, so much so that he may not even be able to conceive of such an innovation.

This suggests another aspect of technological change that needs to be stressed. Not only does it often require new skills but it requires that new roles be filled. There may have been no exact counterpart in a society for the function of a supervisor or a foreman in a plant or even for a solitary worker at a machine. So the technological change may demand economic functions from the labor force that have not previously been performed. The inability of a society to adjust easily to these new requirements is another barrier to the implementation of technological change. Social prestige is often, but not always, associated with economic functions. The criteria by which the new economic roles are filled and, therefore, the criteria by which social prestige is distributed as a result of a new technology are likely to be completely alien to a traditional community and another source of hostility to technological change. A good example of such a pattern of behavior, is the impact of the accelerating economic development of the South on race relations there.

This suggests the significance of Professor Hagen's argument that the innovators of technological change in the less developed areas are most likely to come mainly from groups in the society which, for one reason or another, are disaffected. They must, of course, at the same time have effective opportunities to become innovators rather than being so completely suppressed as to have become more or less passive. It is not necessary to go into the detail of Professor Hagen's theory of personality adjustments to appreciate these conclusions. However, if technological change becomes associated primarily with such disaffected groups, that in itself may create another barrier to such change.

Self-interest has a powerful logic that can lead to a correct intuition of the indirect as well as direct effects of a particular technological change. Thus, many forces of a community are likely to be mobilized against it as its pervasive effects are perceived. These cannot be concealed or denied; they are, in fact, part of the object of technological change. It is disruptive and destructive of the status quo in spheres beyond the purely economic. It is unsettling; that is the social essence of it.

There is no point, therefore, in denying the existence of psychological and social barriers to technological change or in underestimating their importance by reducing them to "irrational" or "anthropological" quirks. They are real and rational in the total social context. Since they cannot be hidden or denied, the only recourse is to try to understand them in order to predict their effects and to smooth the adjustments required.

Research on Social Barriers to Technological Change

It has long been a complaint of some anthropologists and sociologists that their advice has not been asked about problems of development. This is partly because the questions that should be addressed to such specialists have not been obvious and partly because such specialists have not been concrete about what questions they think are important and can be answered by them. These are, however, the specialists who should be asked about the significance of cultural barriers to particular technological changes and the means of facilitating such changes. Their responses must be based on accurate knowledge of exactly what the changes entail in terms of changes in the quantity and quality of the labor force required, organization of work and so on. Information from the detailed studies of technology suggested in the preceding section would therefore be essential in this connection.[28]

In retrospect it has been possible for sociologists and anthropolo-

---

[28] An interesting start along these lines has been made by S. H. Udy, Jr., *Organization of Work: A Comparative Analysis of Production Among Nonindustrial Peoples* (Human Relations, 1959).

gists to say, for example, that a wage system would not work in a particular area because the workers were only interested in earning the price of a wife, after which they quit. Presumably, it would be possible to make predictions about the labor force as well. Research is undoubtedly required to develop methods as well as a body of reference knowledge. Here again it would pay to arrange close coordination with the engineers and economists measuring and developing technology.

Another useful type of research would be on the sources of the innovators who emerge to introduce new technologies. This may reveal some patterns of social mobility that are more acceptable than others. For example, in many of the less developed regions, participation in industrial or mercantile activity carries less social status than entering a professional career. This means that a law or an engineering education may become the route of ambitious individuals who wish to satisfy the social status requirements of a career but also want the material success obtainable from technological innovation. Relatively little is known about such patterns of movement. More knowledge would lead to a better appreciation of the social function of various types of education and the relative significance of their encouragement.

Experiments with Institutional Arrangements that Facilitate Technological Change

There are a variety of difficulties in improving technology which may be lumped under the heading of institutional or organizational problems. Wide dissemination of knowledge is one such problem. Handbooks and files may contain much useful information that may be applied only slowly in the absence of effective demonstration. Therefore, some effort in experimentation with alternative methods of spreading knowledge is desirable. The method of establishing model farms in agriculture for demonstration of techniques is well-known. These have sometimes been criticized as unrealistic in their use of equipment or methods not feasible in typical local farm conditions. There should be a continuing experiment to find organizational approaches that, on the one hand, will be most faithful to the local context and, on the other hand, make the best use of resources generally available to the typical farmer.

It would also be worthwhile to experiment with this demonstration method in industry. There are ample historical precedents or analogies: for example, in the development of Japan, governmental firms played a pioneering role in industry before giving way to private firms. Though industrial institutes and classroom training programs can be useful, they would be even more useful in combination with practical experience with particular technologies. In this sector also, there should be special care to reproduce for such model firms the conditions generally found in the industry in terms of the typical resource availabilities.

A related problem is the development of pilot plant facilities to test operationally new techniques developed in laboratories or considered for transplanting from different conditions. Lack of such facilities can be a major bottleneck in the implementation of new technologies. In considering this particular difficulty, it would be most useful to have information based on the various ways in which it is resolved not only in the United States and other advanced countries but in less advanced areas as well.

In applying new technologies, adaptations to local conditions are nearly always necessary. There are "bugs" even in the most carefully planned production systems. These obstacles in achieving full-scale operation and effective use of resources are likely to be particularly important in underdeveloped countries since so many of the production organizations and types of outputs are relatively new, and engineering skills by comparison rare. This suggests the usefulness of having on tap a corps of consultants to whom the local technical problems could be posed as they arise. In this the foreign aid administration might best act as a clearing house, matching inquiries against *expertise* rather than hiring a permanent staff of such consultants. However, to be a reliable clearing house, it must develop efficient means of reporting such problems and of finding the expert advisers. A variety of organizational methods are possible here and again research to determine which are most effective would be a desirable preliminary step.

There are many training or development programs for personnel at all levels, from management to semiskilled labor, which are being sponsored by the United States foreign aid administration. These are undoubtedly filling a pressing need, and there probably should be more of them. There is, however, also a need for better understanding of general and vocational education methods. A review of the literature in this country indicates that there is in fact relatively little understanding of vocational education methodology in this country in spite of the considerable amount of vocational education being undertaken. To be specific, there can be no doubt that effective vocational education methods exist, but there is little appreciation of their relative efficiency.[29] This is certainly an area that warrants a substantially expanded research program.

The Role of Foreign Investments and Consulting Firms in Implementing Technological Change

Foreign investment has been one of the most significant carriers of technological change from the advanced to the less developed areas. Without judging the question whether the choice of techniques has always been optimal or the methods of implementation most effective, there can be little doubt that a considerable amount of experience has been accumulated. This must surely contain useful lessons if studied systematically and within a framework which would permit comparisons with other types of data. For certain industries and aspects of technological transfer, such studies should have a high priority. A number of fruitful research areas spring to mind: case studies on problems of opening new plants, evaluation of choice of technology, and evolution of special adaptations are examples.

There are other types of study that require comparison of plants in different countries. For example, it has been claimed that there are differences in the qualities of the labor force in different countries even when it has had similar training, or become urbanized. One difference may be in the intensity or consistency of application of workers. Such variations, if they exist, should surely be taken into account in the choice of technology to be implemented. Yet this accounting can be done adequately only when quantitative information is available. One way of obtaining such estimates under more or less properly controlled conditions is by observation and measurement in foreign plants of enterprises using approximately similar production methods.

Since foreign investments often have a somewhat unique identification in the less developed areas, it might also be possible to study the

[29] See Matthew Radom, "Measuring the Results of Training," *Conference Report, Sixth Annual Institute for Training Specialists*, May 28-June 1, 1956, pp. 93-99.

diffusion of technology by movement of workers from these enterprises. This type of movement of workers is recognized as an important factor in spreading technological change, but the factors controlling it are inadequately understood at this point.

Modern technological knowledge is undoubtedly concentrated in the business enterprises of advanced countries. It is probably also true, though perhaps to a lesser degree, that the ability to adapt technology to the special conditions of the less developed areas is centered in such enterprises. This knowledge is much less than fully utilized abroad, however, due to the suspicion of direct foreign investment and the uncertainty engendered which discourages such foreign investment. One of the results has been that, while the role of the production enterprises of advanced countries in transferring technology has been inhibited, the role of the consulting firm has been considerably expanded. There are fewer constraints on the use of foreign consulting firms because their role is considered to be confined to technical advice rather than involving ownership and control of production facilities. This may have effects both on the type of technology used and on the effectiveness with which it is implemented. In any case it means that one of the most significant concentrations of skill in developing technology is not being used most effectively.

It would be useful to survey the possible interest in United States firms in undertaking consulting activities or other types of mutually useful relations with plants in underdeveloped areas other than direct investment. Consideration should be given in advance to the forms this might take and the organizational problems involved.

The proposals here will not be entirely new to the United States economic assistance programs. Indeed in many ways they have already been anticipated by existing projects of the International Cooperation Administration, and the suggestions are not intended to derogate those efforts. Increased understanding is required, however, to improve the efficiency of existing operations and support the larger range and scale of foreign assistance envisaged. American foreign aid programs are working in many areas without the substantial reservoir of knowledge on which they should be based. The research programs described above are intended to help provide such knowledge in the form of concrete guidelines for improving the effectiveness of the transfer of technology to the less developed areas.

5

The Role of Education
in Development

MARY JEAN BOWMAN AND C. ARNOLD ANDERSON*

THAT EDUCATION IS ONE OF THE FEW SURE ROADS to economic progress is a contemporary creed. But there are too few facts with which to support this faith, and stated in the usual way it is far too vague. We need to know *how* education enters into political or economic transformation, in what ways it interacts with other social processes, and in what sorts of time patterns. For which parts of the labor force is literacy essential? What, under various conditions, is the most fruitful allocation of resources between secondary and primary schooling, and with what distribution of responsibilities and costs? In what form and in which circumstances should technological training be given priority over academic? How do patterns of incentive and aspiration affect the outcome of this or that kind of schooling? How can incentives be modified to improve the contribution of education to diverse sorts of change? How different are the methods for transferring "know-how" from those that spread knowledge? When, where, and to what extent should resources be devoted to the formation of human capital rather than physical capital? Are there situations in which education may even obstruct economic advance? Though these questions are asked and even boldly answered by planners and economic advisers, the answers commonly are sophistic and wishful. Estimates of man-power needs and their educational implications facilitate planning, but they contribute little to identifying the ways in which this or that sort of education might impinge on the economy.

* Comparative Education Center, University of Chicago.

The role of education in political development is as important, diverse, and ambiguous as its role in economic development—though naive faith in its efficacy may be less prevalent. With the expansion of national planning and the shift of decision-making from local community or tribe to the national scene, widespread education is increasingly a necessary condition of political participation, but it is not a sufficient condition. It may also undergird coercive regimes. What distribution of education of what kinds by what agencies conduces to one or another political development in what circumstances? What are the probable, and the unlikely, sequences of educational-economic-political phases?

Questions such as these exemplify the basic orientation of this chapter. They stem from the two major goals that underlie American policies of technical assistance and related programs: (1) facilitation of popular participation in government and (2) rising levels of material well-being among the less developed nations. Research as such is not policy-making, but it has a significant policy role. Research can identify critical situations and the directions and occasionally the quantitative impacts of alternative strategies. All policy involves a gamble, even a no-action policy; research may improve the odds.

None of the important politico-economic questions can be answered by viewing education as a separate system, apart from the surrounding society. In this chapter, therefore, intra-educational projects are considered only as they are important to understanding the place of education in an evolving social order. "Education" is defined to include schooling, training on the job, extension services, and mass communication. This is something less than the educational aspects of all human experience, but it is considerably more than formal schooling. The interconnections among the various sorts of education are of major importance. Also, one cannot ignore the fact that research may itself be a powerful agency of education. Given this relatively broad definition of education, there has been selective emphasis in this chapter, conditioned in part by topics covered by other contributors to this volume. For example, only passing attention is given to political issues since political development is the theme of another chapter.

It would be a mistake to assume that one takes up these problems innocent of knowledge. Much of the overwhelming mass of empirical and theoretical background work in the social sciences is relevant. Studies of educational developments in the early stages of Western industrialization and in Soviet and Japanese experience have been made. Pertinent field studies in less developed countries have begun to appear.[1]

A THEORETICAL FRAMEWORK

Five basic propositions underlie the approach to growth taken in this chapter and condition the kinds of hypotheses deemed important in identifying promising research.

1. Economic growth is a process of structural transformation. Because it involves basic changes in the structure of a society, it cannot be understood by empirical or theoretical approaches that assume too simple a continuity or that look primarily at aggregates and averages.

2. There are many alternative combinations of factors that can foster growth or prevent it. But there are limits to the substitutions consistent with given levels of development. This holds both within the educational sphere and as between education and other programs.

3. Attitudes and preferences within a population strongly condition the interplay between education and other aspects of development; they are also variables subject to change and influenced by the nature of perceived opportunities.

4. The "multiplier" and "external economies" concepts of the economists and the rates-of-diffusion analyses of geographers and sociologists constitute a promising framework for dealing with development. Sustained, relatively rapid growth depends on the strength of the multipliers.

5. The concept of "balanced growth" is either a contradiction in terms or highly ambiguous. Decidedly unbalanced growth may be the only potentially rapid growth for many underdeveloped countries. A

[1] Among these are: Arthur T. Mosher, *Technical Cooperation in Latin-American Agriculture* (University of Chicago Press, 1956); Bryce Ryan, "The Dilemmas of Education in Ceylon," *Comparative Education Review*, Vol. 4 (October 1960), pp. 84-92; Susan Elkan, "Primary School Leavers in Uganda," *ibid.*, pp. 102-09; Walter Elkan, *Migrants and Proletarians* (London: Oxford University Press, 1960) ; D. N. Majumdar *et al.*, *Social Contours of an Industrial City: Social Survey of Kanpur 1954-56* (Bombay: Asia Publishing Co., 1960), pp. 128-29; India Planning Commission, *Educated Persons in India*, Manpower Studies No. 9. Field studies completed or in progress by students at the Comparative Education Center, University of Chicago, include work on universities and the role of their students in Indonesian political life and studies of secondary schooling in the economic life of Ghana and of the Guianas. See Comparative Education Center, University of Chicago, *1959-60 Report.*

breakthrough may call for planned imbalance. This does not, however, mean there is no need for coordination between educational and other developments nor does it reject the principle of complementarity in regard to the components of a concentrated push—perhaps best described as selectively focused "integrated sets."

Probably Johan Åkerman has put more stress than any other economist on the significance of structural transformation in his theory of structural limits and transitions, which relates to political events as well as to endogenous economic change.[2] Though he has concentrated on the histories of today's industrialized nations, his work suggests questions about earlier stages of development and by implication about the role of education in different settings. Following his line of thinking, formal schooling and other types of education probably play different roles in some settings than in others. (This amounts to incorporating point 2 in point 1.)

Starting from a more orthodox orientation, Eric Lundberg reaches a similar position but within a single major structural frame. He cites Solow and Aukrust[3] who with other writers, especially at the National Bureau of Economic Research, demonstrate that increases in physical capital together with increases in the labor force explain only a part of the rise in national incomes since 1929. He then poses the question: Does this mean that allocation among investments is unimportant to economic growth? That is, if the total is relatively unimportant, can its parts be important? He concludes that they can be, and are. The averages are misleading, including declining as well as expanding industries; marginal rates of return on investments in the latter may be very high and play a major part in growth even though returns in the more stagnant sectors may be small or negative. This general proposition relates to early as well as later stages of development; applied to education, it requires consideration of marginal returns to different components in the education mix under varying conditions.

Though Åkerman's and Lundberg's views differ in many ways, both challenge implicitly the meaning of "balanced" growth. Indeed that

---

[2] Johan Akerman, *Theory of Industrialism* (Lund: Gleerup, 1960).
[3] Lundberg's thesis was stated in a recent lecture at Chicago; his analysis is based in part on an interview study in Sweden. See R. M. Solow, "Technical Change and the Aggregate Production Function," *Review of Economics and Statistics* (August 1957); O. Aukrust and J. Bjerke, "Real Capital in Norway," *Income and Wealth Series VIII* (London: Bowes, 1959).

notion is questioned by conceiving of growth as structural change, especially when growth and structural change are rapid. Taken together with the more sociological studies of the influence of attitudes on societal processes and with the many studies of diffusion processes, such considerations lead to proposition (5).

Though most Western writers of late have argued for balanced development, there are important exceptions. Moreover, there is a respectable history behind some elements in the unbalanced growth approach. It is clearly involved in Joseph Schumpeter's cycle theory and in Edwin Gay's stress on "disruptive innovating energy." More recently related but different arguments have been presented by Hirschman and Streeten, among others,[4] and even Nurkse admits a possible positive role for successive limited imbalances as a growth mechanism (distinguishing the mechanism from the social end of "balanced development").[5] Soviet economists recently have been pursuing the idea of planned imbalance for growth, which is hardly surprising in the light of Soviet economic history. Amidst complex and mathematical models, one basic idea is essentially simple: rapid growth occurs, and must occur, unevenly, by concentrating effort now in one sphere and then (after a period of only partial digestion) in another. The arguments do not center on planning versus a "free" economy; in the Soviet as in the Schumpeter and Gay conceptions imbalances are important, though they differ with respect to how much imbalance occurs, in what forms, with what timing, and at what costs.

The position taken in this chapter shares the conception of successive imbalances as part of the growth mechanism, and it rests in part on some of the same economic arguments. However, it is in much greater degree a social-science as distinct from a strictly economic approach. It pays more attention to variations in socio-economic starting points, and there is a broader sort of multiplier and diffusion theory at its core.

This brings us back to propositions (3) and (4) concerning attitudes and diffusion. A few remarks here will anticipate later discussion. Because growth, especially in take-off and early stages, changes attitudes (by plan or incidentally), it necessarily entails conflict. Criticisms of aid programs commonly give too little recognition to this fact. Edu-

---

[4] Albert O. Hirschman, *The Strategy of Economic Development* (Yale University Press, 1958). Paul Streeten, "Unbalanced Growth," *Oxford Economic Papers,* New Series, Vol. 11 (1959), pp. 167-91.
[5] Ragnar Nurkse, "Notes on Unbalanced Growth," *ibid.,* pp. 295-97.

cation that feeds into growth in such circumstances becomes entangled with complex processes of transforming attitudes; it is therefore inevitably a threat as well as a promise. Moreover, the less favorable the prevailing attitudes with respect to change, the more likely it is that a breakthrough will require concentrated efforts at particular points in the economy and in the educational system, with periods of highly visible and relatively extreme imbalance. Yet imbalance does not assure growth and may throttle it. Growth depends on unleashing multiplier and diffusion processes. These are not merely the multipliers of the economist's money-flow models or his external economies and interindustry employment and investment multipliers; they are also attitude and education multipliers.[6] They do not occur evenly through time and space. A more generalized multiplier and diffusion theory is needed, one that joins the approaches of the economist with those of other social sciences, and one that takes the time element more explicitly into account along with possible discontinuities and minimal reaction thresholds.[7] Education falls into place in this sort of framework.

Finally, a sixth basic proposition should perhaps be added, though it is a derivative of what has been said. The fact that single factors in development cannot be isolated means that to understand the part education plays in any given situation (or the failure of educational advance to be followed by other sorts of development) requires viewing education in a broad context. Alternative sets of critical factors, each necessary for growth but alone insufficient, must be found. Both dissection of "education" into components and consideration of noneducational factors are involved. If this view is correct, attempts to assess the influence of education by studying aggregate inputs and outputs, while essential in plotting the scale of possible contribution from the human factor, must be inconclusive. Yet approaches from one or another special angle, a bit at a time, are the unavoidable steps in making a rounded picture. The crude data summarized below are such partial abstractions, used here mainly as bases for rapid incursions into vaguely known territory.

---

[6] Some other aspects of the problem are discussed by C. Arnold Anderson in "The Impact of the Educational System on Technological Change and Modernization," in UNESCO, North American Conference on the Social Implications of Industrialization, 1960 (forthcoming).
[7] Ragnar Frisch's well-known contributions to a more positive conception of the role of time in economic analysis are relevant here.

AN EMPIRICAL OVERVIEW OF ASSOCIATIONS
BETWEEN EDUCATION AND INCOME

Briefly, comparisons made by the authors between educational indexes and per capita incomes around the world revealed the following:[8]

1. Correlations of literacy rates with income were very loose, and nonlinear. Only countries with 90 per cent literacy or better had 1955 per capita incomes of over $500, and, where literacy rates were under 30 per cent, incomes were under $200. However, countries with incomes under $100 had literacy rates ranging up to 60 per cent and those with incomes between $100 and $200 included countries with literacy as high as 70 to 80 per cent. Moreover, in the 30 to 70 per cent literacy range there was virtually no correlation between literacy and income.

2. Correlations between 1955 income and elementary school attendance in the 1930's were moderate ($r^2 = .59$) but lower than the reverse sequence relating 1938 income to 1950-1954 elementary school attendance ($r^2 = .71$). When countries with literacy rates of over 90 per cent in 1950-1954 were excluded, both correlations were lowered, but the difference between the two variances was sharpened, with r^2 values of .21 and .57 respectively.

3. Excluding countries with 90 per cent or more literate in 1950-1954, post-primary enrollment rates added virtually nothing to the correlation between 1950-1954 literacy and 1955 per capita incomes. The zero order correlation gave an r^2 of .43 and adding post-primary enrollment rates raised this only to .44.

4. Far Eastern countries had low incomes relative to their education indexes. However, for the world as a whole the amount of cultivated land per capita provided no explanation of the income variance unexplained by the various education indexes. Neither did measures of energy potentials.

5. South American countries manifested diverse patterns, but predominantly they were characterized by stagnation in both educational

---

[8] This analysis is to be published under the title "Concerning the Role of Education in Development" in a forthcoming symposium sponsored by the University of Chicago Committee for the Comparative Study of New Nations, Clifford Geertz, ed.

and income development after reaching an intermediate educational position.

These findings point up the importance of examining the processes by which education may enter into and interact with other factors in economic development. Clearly, there are problems not only of take-off but also of sustaining educational diffusion as well as economic growth. Clearly, also, a relatively large elite is no guarantee of progress in the less developed areas. There can be wasteful investments in education as in any other sphere. And potentially fruitful investments in education can be wasted by failure of the society to make effective use of its educated people. It is against this background that research needs and priorities are outlined.

THE NATURE OF RESEARCH AND ITS ROLES

A few of the important questions concerning the place of education in economic and political development have been suggested by the foregoing brief summary. Some of these and other questions will be discussed further from the particular standpoint of research potentials and priorities.

Feasibility of Research

An inventory of what one would like to know does not establish a list of research priorities until the question of "researchability" has been faced. This question has overlapping political, time, and data dimensions.

Political blockages within the United States are presumably within its control as a nation. Other limitations lie in the politics of the less developed nations and in their attitudes toward the United States. In some countries no local research is possible, in others the opportunities are subject to varying degrees of political restriction, and these interferences change over time.

The time element places two quite different kinds of limitations on research. One of these is imposed by political instabilities and anti-Western developments in host countries. Under such conditions research projects requiring a long period for completion may be a poor gamble as research, but some of them might nevertheless be the best gamble as action programs. The second major limitation arising from short-time horizons, which may also be primarily political, relates to impatience for results, either at home or abroad. Many intrinsically suitable research projects are impractical only because of strict time limitations. It is perhaps in this time dimension that the real, as distinct from the superficial, differences between the interests and priorities of government and university are to be found. Results promised ten years hence are of little help to the man who must make a decision today or in a couple of years. On the other hand, if research had been started ten years ago, its findings could be used today in formulating policy. Such research should be given a high priority now on behalf of the policy makers of 1970.

The need in research is often a need for time to cumulate a series of coordinated research efforts, each of which can make a contribution in its own right along the way. Long-time horizons in designing, financing, and executing research are essential for coordinating this cumulation of data and for theory construction. Comparability in sequential short-term studies are the steps to broader research goals. There are also research projects of great potential value that require a long follow-up period; assessment of the effects of education and experience on intelligence and competence is an example. Others, more important for the developing countries, are pilot experiments in the transfer of know-how.

Data limitations are most serious in problems requiring information about the past. These and other gaps in data may be remediable but only at high cost. An underdeveloped country is one where policy-making is often seemingly deliberate but where the necessary information is almost totally lacking. Hence newer methods of collecting data must be utilized—such as sample censuses or polling—but these necessities highlight the fact that there is a cost as well as a benefit side to the determination of research priorities.

Too often a problem is deemed intractable either because it cannot be attacked by some particular set of methods or because it has been too vaguely defined. Effective research on the role of education in social change calls for versatility in methods and broad competence. Skill in the more sophisticated mathematical techniques comes at the bottom of the list. Well-oriented "grubbing" is more essential.

Research as an Action Program

Research is learning, and it can be teaching. Research as such, whatever the findings, is a form of education for the participants—whether the problem concerns fertilizers for tropical soils or the spread of secondary schooling. Participation in research induces skill in methods and points of view that are intimately bound up with the broader processes of "modernization" of a society. This kind of learning can make a major contribution to economic and political development, provided the research is well designed and nationals of host countries are active participants at high as well as subordinate levels.

It would be difficult to overestimate the value of research as an action program in aid strategy. Mosher argues this ably with respect to agriculture, but the point is equally relevant in virtually every sector of development. We suggest two sets of considerations that should be weighed in balancing such projects on the role of education in society against other topics and in deciding among research projects in education.

First, "hard" research in the natural sciences is often politically neutral and conveys much prestige—obvious advantages when political tensions limit opportunities for social science investigations. There is a strong argument for fostering cooperative hard research at an early stage as a first step, provided subsequent fanning out into social science studies at an early date can be assured. But, second, some kinds of cooperative social science research, and in particular that on the relations between education and the economy, can play a more powerful role in development precisely because they require objective examination of politico-economic processes. Host country participation is particularly important here. It is strategic to tie research into action programs as small-scale experiments. Opportunities for such linkages in technical assistance for agriculture are innumerable; equally promising but largely unexplored are assistance programs and research with respect to enterprise-linked training in nonagricultural sectors.

To specify that research has strategic value as part of an action program is thus to introduce inevitably the question of the aid programs themselves. In particular it becomes important to assess what kinds of assistance programs are most promising as social experiments and how they can be planned to maximize the feedback between economic programs, fresh research endeavors, and action programs.

SUGGESTED RESEARCH PROJECTS

To make a list of projects is to select from an indefinite number of possibilities. Hence a list is in itself a first step in specifying priorities. In the following discussion suggestions are grouped under four main headings: (1) educational methods and the products of the schools; (2) the diffusion of education; (3) costs of education, mobilization of resources, and distribution of the burden; and (4) the role of education in economic development.

We start with the most explicitly intra-educational topics, though none of them is totally so. Category (4) is the broadest, but includes only a part of the "economics of education" viewed in relation to development. Putting this another way, returns to investment in education depend on the quality of the "product," on how readily schooling is diffused through self-generating processes, on the costs entailed, and on the ways in which graduates of the schools are integrated into economic life. Heading (4) concentrates on the last of these. However, the four categories overlap at many points, and a particular research project may contain elements that would fall under more than one of them.

No project directly relating education to politics has been listed though this does not imply any underestimation of the place of education in civic life. In part it is sheer evasion; specifications for such research are particularly difficult. Fortunately, the most critical problems in this sphere are important, and in similar ways, for economic development. Viewed in the latter context, they center around the cultivation of a broad spectrum of educated persons and the integration of an independent, critical, and practical-minded middle class into the economy.[9] The other side of this picture is the stultification of development and the political malaise associated with the growth of unemployed pseudo-intellectuals and their obsession with bureaucratic sinecures.

Educational Methods and the Products of the Schools

Crosscultural studies in the learning process and elementary teaching. Direct transfer of Western school practices has proved surprisingly

---

[9] In using the expression "practical minded" we do not imply that men who realistically assess opportunities and express their preferences by seeking white-collar or government jobs are foolish from the point of view of their personal advantages.

easy in some underdeveloped countries, though more commonly it has been a formalized parody of the Western elementary school that has initially taken root. But as the scale of school operations expands, the shortcomings of the transplanted variants of Western-type schools have been revealed. So far discussion of this topic has dealt mainly with what not to do, offering few suggestions for adapting the universal tasks of transmitting literacy and necessary familiarity with numbers. It is not sufficient to talk about making schools "practical" or "adapting" the school to the culture; the imperatives of modernization give priority to Western content for large parts of the curriculum over local cultural peculiarities. But, how far can Western teaching methods help? There can be no doubt that aid programs in this sphere have sometimes tried to transplant the shell instead of going back to the fundamentals that may have accounted for success in the West. Fresh research on adaptations in elementary education in different cultural settings is needed. Studies of this kind can help also on problems of teacher supply and in resolving some of the dilemmas of quality versus quantity in the spread of education.

Comparative testing to establish achievement profiles. Comparisons of achievement in school subjects can be made between countries or between types of schools within countries. Establishment of profiles of attainments for different dimensions and kinds of school performance not only serves to evaluate the work of the schools but supplies important information about the quality of human capital entering the economy. As in other efforts to evaluate the impact of the schools and the character of their products, one must relate the findings to a matrix of variables that identify the supporting and the inhibiting factors in the environment within which the schools operate. This must be done with special prudence in the least developed countries, or it may aggravate propensities toward an excessively academic school system, a caution that does not apply to the study of examination systems.

Study of examination systems. This kind of project makes a good entry into many educational problems and illuminates many functions of schools. Modification of examinations in favorable circumstances can open the door toward needed educational and even broader socioeconomic reforms, though in isolation it is unlikely to be successful.[10]

[10] See Benjamin S. Bloom, *The Improvement of University Examinations* (Delhi: University Grants Commission, 1961) and *Evaluation in Secondary Schools* (New Delhi: All-India Council for Secondary Education, 1958).

As yet only scattered bits of information are available about the inter-play between examinations and the supply of needed skills, emergence of maltrained people, or undue centralization of economic decisions; that these relations can be critical is known.[11]

Factors determining literacy thresholds and literacy retention. Though this is a comparatively simple problem, it is vital for the pro-grams of mass education in many nations. Until the average duration of schooling reaches a certain point, loss of literacy predominates and much of the investment in schooling is wasted. But literacy retention depends also on inducements to its use. Of special interest are experi-ments in the use of communication media outside the schools and the operation of extra-school programs encouraging continuous use of literacy among people with little education.

Comparative field studies of educational attitudes and expectations. Continuation in school and selection of various types of middle or sec-ondary schooling are strongly influenced by parental and community attitudes, which are closely influenced in turn by opportunities and by complex sentiments about modernization. Such studies should be combined with follow-up of subsequent occupations and attitude changes, using readily available control groups in other sectors of the population. It is possible also to launch experiments on the attitude effects of teaching methods, academic-vocational mix of curricula, on-the-job training programs, and so forth.

A widespread problem reported by many observers in the less devel-oped countries is the limited conception of what an "educated" man should do—or has coming to him. The problem lies partly in the be-lated appreciation of opportunities in business and the low prestige of manual work, combined with exaggerated prestige attached to white-collar jobs.[12] There is commonly a pronounced passivity and se-curity mindedness that exaggerates the failure to visualize any oppor-

[11] "If care is not taken, the excessive importance attached to diplomas and especially the fact that they give direct access to every kind of public office will lead to atrophy in the private economy sector, a plethora of "white collar" workers and a pretense of development which is the very negation of reality." E. Valin, *The Value of Examina-tions: A Technical Study Carried Out in Lebanon,* UNESCO Educational Studies and Documents No. 40 (1961), p. 8.

[12] Once again the anthropologist may object that these images are realistic, but the issue is not the "realism" with which individuals assess prestige. The prestige of certain jobs is "exaggerated" in terms of a societal goal assumed here: advance toward higher levels of material well-being. It should be noted that the comparatively high civil service incomes are often pegged; the elite tax people to pay themselves independently of their productivity. Economically, these incomes may be quite unrealistic, though to the striver for a post they are very real indeed.

tunity for individual initiative, even where capital or credit facilities are available. Attitudes are not independent of opportunities, nor would mere change of attitudes, even if it could be brought about directly, alone bring an economic breakthrough. But search for ways to influence attitudes through the educational system is essential in evaluating an educational strategy for development.

The general-vocational curriculum balance and job adaptability. Though this topic overlaps the foregoing items, it deserves special attention. Collation of the mass of data available in many countries and accumulation of both contemporary and historical case studies is needed.[13]

Responses of educators to pilot-school projects. Where pilot-school projects have been inaugurated, their students would presumably be included in other studies already described. But here emphasis is on the processes of transfer of educational methods and content from teachers in one cultural setting to those in another, and in the special influence of pilot schools on diffusion of educational innovations. Have the demonstrations been absorbed into local practice or do they constitute merely another route for escape from the demands of the local situation, to be abandoned when the Westerners depart? What circumstances maximize the influence of such projects? Which of these conditions lie in the local milieu and which in the assistance program itself? Pilot schools are only one example of many kinds of experiments in crosscultural transfer of educational orientations and methods. Another that is particularly amenable to analysis in terms of "teacher-orientation" transfer is agricultural extension work.

The Diffusion of Education

International comparison of factors influencing the diffusion of elementary schooling in the less developed nations today. There are wide divergences among the populations of developing countries in their readiness to make active use of chances for elementary schooling. This variation in readiness is concealed by the unanimity among national leaders in paying lip service to educational goals; to be "for" education is respectable everywhere. Judged by their policies, however, some

---

[13] Soviet educational history is particularly illuminating on this topic.

leaders display a qualified enthusiasm; more important, large parts of the population in most countries remain uninterested. Yet, given favorable circumstances, there can be quick growth in popular zeal for education.

Studies in this area would aim at establishing types of time sequences in the over-all diffusion of elementary schooling and the factors associated with these types. Intensive analysis of the educational transformations in a number of the developing countries are needed, with proper attention to relating such investigations to other studies of growth. In large part, readiness reflects past educational history; the spread of education as of other cultural traits tends to follow the usual growth curve. Countries now having, say, only 10 per cent literacy are in a quite different position from those with 40 per cent. But there may be plateaus of stagnation; for example, national figures may show that 30 per cent are literate or that 30 per cent complete six primary grades, but in each case the persons making up this 30 per cent may be concentrated in one part of the country or one ethnic group. For the other 70 per cent, the problem may be similar to that faced by the country with 10 per cent literacy. The factors conducive to educational diffusion must be known before an effective educational strategy can be formulated.

Five broad sets of factors and associated hypotheses may be suggested as key points for such investigations; their study will throw light on many other problems as well: (1) degree of polarization of the society or, on the other hand, the presence of a continuum of communication among various socioeconomic groups in the population (Mosher's property-ownership patterns constitute a corollary of this point); (2) the presence or absence of supportive mass communication media and auxiliary adult education and extension programs; (3) spatial patterns of population distribution, settlement patterns, and communication or transport networks; (4) the nature of and grounds for patterns of noneconomic motivation to acquire literacy—as religious motivation in Burma and Colonial North America; (5) perhaps most important, existence of visible occupational opportunities for graduates of the schools. Most of the same factors are equally important in diffusion of secondary education.

Educational effort as such may be a key strategy for encouraging growth, but even to list the above factors is to point to the potential importance for education of changes on other fronts. Innumerable projects offer opportunities for identifying factors that impede educational advance in particular countries.

Studies of the social status aspects of education in developing countries. Under what conditions does academic secondary education spread through the population, along what channels, and at what rates? Where does it become dammed up? Does diversification of a school system foster diffusion, and if so how? What categories of the population are recruited into one or another kind of training, and why? Apart from their direct bearing on education, these topics have implications for the development of an independent middle class capable of maintaining economic and political advance.[14]

Costs of Education, Resource Mobilization, and Distribution of Burden

Analysis of the opportunity costs of education in less developed countries. The real costs of education are what is given up in diverting resources into this activity—the opportunity costs. The term is used here in a narrower sense, however; that is, contributions the students would otherwise be making by their work. Opportunity cost studies in this sense form an important part of over-all assessment of cost, and are needed also to clear up some common misunderstandings.

It is frequently contended that peasants cannot spare their children from work in the fields, but in many societies children of school age do little such work.[15] In other contexts, paradoxically, it is said that the marginal product of the labor of these children is zero. Also, there is much confusion surrounding the effects on opportunity cost of unemployment, underemployment, and the institutional factors conditioning the roles played by age in the occupational structure—problems that are important in formulating educational investment policies. It is time that research on the economics of education dig into these questions.

[14] The influence of parental status on educational diffusion has received an unusual amount of research attention in advanced societies; but most of it refers to recent decades and the pattern of successive diffusion waves has received little attention. Similar work in developing societies has barely begun, as is true of archival study of the situation in early Western history and in Japan.

[15] See the study of Egya, Ghana by Philip Foster and also his forthcoming study of secondary schools in Ghana; see also Susan Elkan, *op. cit.*

The private opportunity costs of shifting children from production into schools need to be differentiated from the social costs. The possible effects of compulsory school attendance on agricultural practices and on extension programs are often ignored. This is one of the few instances in which, at least for the elementary school ages, it may be possible to have the cake and eat it.

Analysis of opportunity costs for higher and secondary education involves the same confusions, but something is added; namely, what the graduates of the next lower level of schools do.

The supply of teachers. Shortage of teachers is frequently a genuine bottleneck in extending educational opportunities. The most severe bottlenecks occur at different points for different societies and at different stages of development. However, at three points "shortage" is virtually universal.

One of these is shared by the already industrialized countries; there always will be a "shortage" of superlative teachers. The other principal shortages are of teachers in rural schools and of individuals qualified to teach scientific and technological subjects by demonstration rather than by memorization. This latter deficiency is aggravated by customs and considerations in regard to occupational prestige. One may sometimes find two men teaching a class, the professor who talks and a trained assistant who does the manual manipulation. The wastage of trained men is obvious. Moreover, the demonstration of professional status may well be more appreciated than the importance of the subject—and the image of the working assistant is a very negative way of conditioning students to *do* things.

In recommending research on problems of teacher supply, it is not our intention to suggest additional inventories of man power and projections of "needs" associated with some hoped-for extension of schools. Such surveys are merely a basis for research. To go behind the supply estimates to their underlying factors, entails "search" for unused or underused resources, for the incentives that could bring them into use, and for possible modifications in educational policies that can make more effective use of the resources that are available.

On this last point, it is essential to examine the effects of accepted "standards" of teacher qualifications on teacher supply. It is also essential to know whether these standards are distorted in the context of alternatives for employment and in the light of the potential as against the actual roles of schools in economic and political life.[16] The self-conceptions of teachers play a central role in this situation. Teachers remain unused sometimes because they will not take certain types of positions or will not leave urban centers or their native province. In other cases teaching is viewed as a temporary halt on the road to political office. Special attention needs to be given also to assessing the untapped local resources of potential teachers.

Research on teacher supply ties in with many other aspects of education. It is related to research on educational methods and on the kind of people turned out by the schools. It is linked to study of the processes by which education becomes diffused and with the ways a society uses its trained man power. For many reasons, this offers a particularly apt point of attack on a series of related problems.

All international exchange of persons, broadly, is an exchange of "teachers." In some of the developing countries foreign personnel constitute the core of the teaching staff in secondary schools and universities. Other than in the very short run, however, these foreign teachers can form only a small fraction of the staff.[17]

Distribution of the financial burden. Countries vary widely in how they distribute costs between central and local governments and between government and private sources, but education is a large item in the public budget nearly everywhere. Though studies of public finance must be undertaken for many reasons having little to do with education, there are special problems and opportunities with regard to school finance that demand attention.

A salient contrast between less and more developed countries lies in the greater importance in the former of the subsistence sector of the economy. Where this sector is relatively large, the effective ways of drawing private resources into the public domain may be quite different. For example, there may be a legitimate place for using a *corvée* to build schools (and roads) in lieu of money taxes.[18] Most of the other

[16] This question of realistic standards in relation to resource limitations and development goals and requirements is a pervasive one. For example, to apply American or Swedish or British standards in training physicians in most of the developing countries is more likely to retard than to hasten provision of better health care among the population as a whole.

[17] Studies relevant to decisions in the United States as to what kinds of teachers can serve most effectively in certain countries are unlikely to bear much relation to the teacher supply projects suggested here.

[18] Readers may be reminded of the American tradition of housing and boarding the rural teacher in rotation at the pupil's homes.

problems have their analogues to at least some degree in the more advanced countries.

Distribution of responsibility between local communities and central government is an issue that takes on a special cast where tribal or similar units are involved. Financial decisions and strategies for manipulating educational incentives are interrelated; thus diffusion and finance studies contribute jointly to decisions concerning the geographic locus of the burden of school support.

There is a parallel set of questions concerning distribution of the costs between public and private sectors. These include the sensitive questions of stipends and loans: to whom they will be granted, for what kinds or levels of schooling, with what conditions about later job commitment—and whether they are warranted at all. This brings us back again to the problem of teacher supply and to the complex problems relating to public subsidy of various kinds of educational endeavors.

Research cannot answer these questions outright, but it can identify possible courses of action and the probable outcomes from alternative policies. Studies of public finance in the developing countries may seldom be fundamental social science research, but objective analysis of its socioeconomic facets is vital for improving the allocation of scarce resources for development, and it can contribute to pointing up some new (and old) types of assistance projects that may be especially promising.

The Role of Education in Economic Development

Interpreted sufficiently broadly, "the role of education in development" would include many of the items already listed. However, the emphasis here is on the way education enters into economic activity, rather than on what it costs or how resources are mobilized for it, the nature or quality of those services, or their diffusion.

A question often asked but not as yet answered is: What is the part played by literacy and primary education in economic advance? As usually posed, this tacitly assumes too simple a conception of the factors in development. To spell out a design for study of the contribution of primary education to development would lead into innumerable other topics, many of them already mentioned. However, two broad hypotheses suggested by the evidence already at hand are worth noting here as indicative of kinds of questions to which the projects listed might be directed.

First, as the data summarized in an earlier section suggest, gains from a literate minority may level off rather quickly and remain level until education has been built up to a point at which widespread trans-formation of the economy is possible. There is perhaps an educational threshold for primary schooling that must be reached before further extension of such schooling can be brought into economic play. But some countries seem to offer exceptions. Longitudinal as well as cross-section data for particular countries are clearly needed. The variant situations particularly need investigation. These comments suggest a further hypothesis that is important in its own right even if the fore-going one does not stand up.

This second hypothesis relates to the socioeconomic milieu of education, and it pertains perhaps more to secondary and higher than to primary education. A polarization of society and an absence of communication among the peoples of that society may inhibit effective economic use of any given level of schooling even when it has not checked the spread of such schooling. The loose but positive correlations between "competitive" political systems and economic development (referred to by Hagen in Chapter 1) may well relate mainly to the existence of a middle class. Some of the exceptions in Hagen's chapter would cease to be exceptions if this redefinition were adopted. However, to say this is also to point to the fallacy of considering status structures as unidimensional. Our second hypothesis then has two variants (and could of course have more). One of these, in line with the way it was initially stated, focuses on the "communication" factor; the other emphasizes the emergence and growth of a mundanely active "middle class," whether or not it is "deviant" in origin.

This raises a question that is often asked and answered, after a fashion, because policy demands an answer. What is the appropriate educational mix in various situations or stages in development? Presumably, the impact of primary education depends partly on a certain spread of advanced education. But the availability of complementary skills created in the higher schools is only one of the reasons for such a relationship. Another may well be the effects of the people with intermediate schooling, along with others having primary and higher training, on the social status communication networks, and hence on what opportunities are perceived and acted on. Again, noneducational conditions influence education's role in economic change as in political "democratization." What educational and noneducational strategies weaken social polarization and foster growth of a middle stratum, given various starting points? Studies of factors in educational diffusion and of the use of education in economic life are here joined.

Research on the economic effects of education does not divide neatly into subtopics. The list of suggestions that follows distinguishes by types of research methods, especially historical versus field studies, as much as by the main questions posed.

Historical research on the relations between spread of literacy and elementary education and the occupational structure. While an adequate theoretical base for analysis of the role of education in development of the "new" nations cannot be constructed merely by identifying historical sequences and correlates in the earlier history of the West, that history can nevertheless serve to check some hypotheses and suggest others. One of the main questions calling for investigation is that of the interplay between the spread of literacy and elementary education in the early stages of the agricultural and industrial revolutions in Western countries and Japan. Such studies would examine the diffusion of schooling among status categories and geographic areas and development sequences in the spread of education, growth of markets, and changing occupational structures.

Historical research on the training of key groups in the industrial labor force and in entrepreneurial ranks. Despite the many educational histories, economic histories, and histories of particular industries, research concerned explicitly with the sources and training of key groups in economic life is only beginning. To study engineers and machinists in various countries is one example.[19] Another would be to build on work already done concerning the early Iron Masters of Britain and of Tsarist Russia, and so on. Some studies might of course be wider in scope and embrace merchants in general, entrepreneurs, or skilled workers within a particular country. There is reason to think that development can proceed with relatively small numbers of trained men provided these are linked in the proper manner geographically and in terms of status relations. Probably also "imports" of skill have always been major factors.

19 W. H. G. Armytage, *A Social History of Engineering* (London: Faber, 1961).

Case studies of the twentieth century history of Latin America. These countries are of particular interest because of their European populations and their stagnation under seemingly favorable circumstances. The extent of development also varies considerably among them. Broad studies incorporating in varying degree most of the topics listed in this chapter are called for.

Special studies of the effects of education of rural populations on agricultural progress. Cases might be selected to approximate controlled experiments, though special cases like Denmark and Japan are also of great interest. One would examine changes in agricultural practices and productivity in areas (within or among countries) that are similar in some critical respects but differ in the spread of general elementary education, and in the presence or absence of agricultural extension and other forms of adult education. There is an especially strong case for cooperative research of this kind linked to experimental programs within a host country, projects in which there is explicit provision for study of control areas matching those in which assistance programs are undertaken.

Factors influencing relations between education and labor force "commitment." Lack of a committed labor force is often cited as a major obstacle to economic advance. Identification with the job, responsibility for tasks, and adaptation to nonfamilistic organizations call for varying modification of prior patterns in the host country, but they require also modifications of Western institutions imported into new areas. Intra-educational factors affecting commitment includes types of schools and methods of teaching as well as levels of schooling. But the degree to which these educational influences carry over into vocational performance reflects also many extra-school features of the society. These topics are well suited to experimental research linked to assistance programs.

Investigations of the efficacy of enterprise-linked training in developing economies. The term "enterprise-linked" has been used here deliberately to encompass a considerable range of activities, from on-the-job training in the lesser skills and strictly vocational apprenticeship to academic schooling provided by private concerns. There would be several facets of such studies, even excluding variations in the legal and financial setting. Who is trained, how recruited, from what sectors of the population? What are the perceptions and attitudes concerning education and jobs of the new entrants? How are these attitudes and perceptions changed? How do those receiving one or another sort of training compare in subsequent work efficiency and adaptability? And how do the new entrants and the "graduates" compare in these respects with comparable groups that have not had this experience, including those receiving technological training versus those in academic schools? Do the higher-level trainees see this program as another facet of bureaucratic life and posts in the organization as the security equivalents (whether or not at equal "prestige" ratings) of jobs in the government, or do they perceive and act on perceptions of less traditional economic opportunities elsewhere? To what extent, if at all, are attitudes of disdain for practical engineering, for example, modified or even overcome? What skills are developed, and how much adaptability?

To be able to interpret differences in the answers to some of these questions, one must simultaneously look into the factors that might explain them. In particular, for example, are they associated with prior training, with the kinds of education in the enterprise-linked program, with teaching methods and examples set by teachers, with family backgrounds of the students, with expectation (whether legally bolstered or not) of more or less permanent jobs in the firm?

The importance of this kind of research goes far beyond what would be justified by the present modest scale of enterprise-linked training. Opportunity perceptions and prestige images impede effective use of educated men in economic development. These images are by no means divorced from reality, and they reflect the traditional exaltation of bureaucratic employment and its links with higher and even secondary schooling. Also, transfer of "know-how" is far more difficult than teaching school subjects or narrow craft skills, depending as it does more closely on participant experience.

Innovation in enterprise-linked training is one of the potentially most promising strategies for orientation toward progress in a kind of society congenial to the freedoms treasured in the West. It brings jobs and education more closely together in a meaningful setting consistent with economic advance. It offers exceptional opportunities for transfer of know-how[20] and for development of a cadre of trained, practical men. There are many possible variants. In addition to those already

---

[20] In this connection see Eckaus' discussion in Chapter 4 of experiments with institutional arrangements that facilitate technological change and of the role of foreign investments and consulting firms in implementing such change.

tried, it should be possible, for example, to combine intern periods on the job with courses in higher and secondary technical schools and with credit arrangements and business advisory services for those trained.[21] But these types of programs will call for innovations in educational finance also.

The costs and financing of enterprise-linked training. Even in the already industrialized countries, it takes a long time to train a whole cohort of workers in a new plant as compared to the time needed to fit a few new men into a going operation. These special problems in the developing countries have received scant attention. To be sure, there is general appreciation of the inadequate managerial skills and lack of a committed labor force. But there is a tougher problem that is not solely one of unfavorable attitudes. In the developing countries, virtually all new enterprises are in some degree "infant industries," whatever the capabilities of their managers, especially if the technology calls for a skilled labor force. The foregoing are contributory factors encouraging the introduction of modern plants and capital-intensive processes despite the large "labor surplus."

Assessment of the training costs for launching a particular new enterprise is mainly the task of business consultants and managers. But research into the magnitude and implications of these costs is needed as a basis for public policy.

The preceding discussion refers only to those costs that are typically borne by the enterprise where there are neither subsidies to training nor legal requirements for training of local employees. Such requirements are feasible without subsidy only when there are special reasons for a firm to locate in a particular country and its prospective profits will cover what amounts to a "training tax." Oil and mineral exploitation furnish the best examples, but these are not the best settings for the kinds of enterprise-linked training that will most facilitate development. Cases of governments subsidizing training in private enterprises without trying to take over the enterprises have not come to our attention. Material for research on training costs is available, for example, in records of some British enterprises in colonial territories. Various host-country mixed enterprises (notably in India) and public

---

[21] There are other possible combinations. The Mexican government did not require that the Sears Roebuck Co. institute a training program, but its stipulation that a large part of the inventory be purchased in Mexico led Sears to inaugurate a kind of business-management advisory service. The learning aspects of this program warrant study.

enterprises are also available for study and may prove more important. Moreover, Soviet experience is particularly relevant.

Given data for realistic appraisal of this problem, research into new methods for financing enterprise-linked training may well throw fresh light on a whole series of policy problems and strategy potentials for development.

Studies of the civilian impact of training in military service. Military schools would of course be included in any case in the strictly educational studies. Here attention is directed to military-linked training as preparation for civilian roles, asking questions similar to those raised in connection with enterprise-linked training.

TOP PRIORITIES

Priorities presuppose specification of purposes. In the present context there are two highly relevant policy goals: (1) raising levels of living in the developing countries and spreading these gains among the population; (2) facilitating democratic participation in political decision-making and freedom to dissent from policies of the party in power—development and acceptance of a "loyal opposition." Faint-hearted local acceptance of these goals throttles assistance programs and may limit research opportunities, but it does not impugn the use of these goals as guides for a priority ranking of research topics and methods.

Basic Criteria

Priorities in research should be accorded those projects that give greatest promise of identifying reaction thresholds and the most potent multipliers. But this proposition is equally valid for those interested in "basic" research, since identification of strategic factors requires fundamental insight into societal processes. Two kinds of multipliers are involved, both of which require a large enough initial impact to surmount thresholds. First, there are the self-generating processes within education, calling for studies of the factors in educational diffusion and studies of complementarities and substitutions among these factors. Second, there are intersector multipliers, the supportive interplay between educational and economic (and political) development. Critical here is the integration of education into economic life. Cutting across the research proposals given priority below, and imbedded in some of them, there should be special stress on investigation of educational and cultural transfer as part of or in coordination with development assistance projects (or with experimental projects of host countries). High priority should be accorded also to research in which colleagues from host countries are active participants. Not only can such projects become valuable training programs; in many situations they are shrewd strategy for accomplishment of other ends.

High on any priority list also must be more diligent exploration of what is in the files of the aid agencies and the heads of its staffs. Buried there are unusually valuable materials for research that would be of special pertinence for policy-making. What has been the experience of the International Cooperation Administration with educational assistance programs and with education by means of noneducational projects? What factors in the environments and programs have been associated with success and failure—viewing these criteria more deeply than publicity? Much that has been learned is being lost and will have to be learned over again. The Congress, concerned with United States investment in development assistance, has in our view been negligent in not establishing large funds for research parallel to American assistance programs.

Six Top-Priority Research Topics

Under headings that cut across the categories used in previous pages, the urgency of research on the following topics is emphasized.

Teacher supply problems, preferably conducted on the ground in several developing countries. Teacher supplies are critical in educational development, they have quantity and quality and locational dimensions. They are tied up with a whole complex of interconnected problems concerning resource use for development. Moreover, a focus on teacher supply problems can be an exceptionally useful route into related studies; it is a handy starting point since the subjects are readily available for inquiry. The problem gains importance from the prevalence of what we believe to be fallacious tactics in teacher recruitment and from the relative ease with which policy can be modified.

The diffusion of education and its influence on diffusion of other traits. Such studies can make important contributions to social science theory and method. They are highly pertinent for policy-making in the developing countries and for American assistance policies. Jointly with the next item, they offer an especially promising approach for cutting into problems of stagnation after take-off.

The role of education in social mobility in developing countries. Such work combines analysis of the social status dimensions of educational diffusion with analysis of job destinations. What influence has education of this or that type had (as compared, for example, with the pulls of hunger and money) in moving people from one kind of work and orientation to another? Such studies can identify strategies contributing to the emergence and strengthening of the middle strata.

Exploration of the possibilities in various media of rural education. Media can be used separately and in combination as agencies for injecting skill in decision-making into farm populations. Plans for educational research should be part of every agricultural assistance program.

Education of elites. The usual questions about how much resources to put into secondary and higher as against elementary education are of the second order. The first order questions relate to the nature of the elites, their training, what they can do, and in what ways they can become more effective agents of change. Unfortunately, powerful local elite groups can veto both program and research proposals; hence there is need for a strategy of introducing this kind of research. This information can usually be obtained in projects dealing with status mobility or with enterprise-linked training. Also, it could be a by-product of man-power surveys or of a study of examination systems; if this focus were built into such studies, they would have higher priority than otherwise.

Experimentation in the use and subsidization of enterprise-linked training. Educational research (broadly defined) must be built into programs of enterprise-linked training. On the action front, experimentation in enterprise-linked training is justified on several scores. First, it is economically justified because of the "infant industry," or, in more respectable technical economics, the "external economies of scale" problem in its human resource form. It is justified, that is, as providing a boost over the big hump between now and the point at which the "economies of scale" that depend on existence of an experienced intermediate-level labor force can be reached. It provides one channel for integrating education more effectively into economic life and getting intersector multipliers moving. Also, it may be that experiments of this kind will provide the most effective methods of transferring higher level know-how from foreigners to the inhabitants of the host country—including in the process the adaptations that are needed for successful transplantation. (The latter specification suggests some of the experimentation and research problems that may be peculiar to a transfer situation.) And action programs of these kinds are justified as one of the few ways in which aid programs may help foster development of a genuine middle class.

But like other assistance programs, these would be gambles; some almost certainly might fail to come up to what had been hoped of them. Others might be surprisingly successful. Parallel research that could identify the reasons for these successes and failures should obviously have extremely high priority. Over time, the research contributions should multiply, both in their basic scientific value and in the assistance they would provide to men responsible for policy changes and for sponsoring trials of new approaches or in new locations.

Insufficient Knowledge

Neither policy makers nor scholars have produced a doctrine of political development, a relatively sophisticated and flexible set of propositions which would supply a yardstick for evaluating the consequences of particular events or guidance on how to act in a given situation. Until a workable doctrine is elaborated and confirmed, each government operator must use his own judgment on an *ad hoc* basis, guessing rather than judging the consequences of events or of actions.

Western political studies have usually focused on the governmental structure, the way in which individuals gain and hold governmental power and use it for the ends they set. Yet comprehending changes in governmental forms, political practices, and the public purposes for which government power is used, particularly in emerging countries, requires broadening the intellectual field to include insights drawn from sociology, social psychology, economics, and history. This is particularly true in transitional societies which are experiencing social and technological changes even more rapidly than they are absorbing political changes. Thus, to examine political development embraces a spectrum of the social sciences as they apply to exotic environments that Western social science has not yet studied in detail, except for the work of the anthropologists who have rarely been concerned with the problems of organizing political power.

Although the organization and distribution of political power is a central concern of this chapter, the succeeding section will suggest the interdisciplinary breadth of perspectives that must be brought to bear on the problem of political growth.

PRELIMINARY RESEARCH AGENDA ON FOREIGN ASSISTANCE
AS AN INSTRUMENT TO PROMOTE POLITICAL GROWTH

In considering the problems of political growth, the nine functions of government identified above will be discussed. For each of these a different set of questions and hypotheses concerning the relation of foreign assistance to political development will be raised. As is obvious, these functions are not presented in their order of priority. Each political system will have its own primary weaknesses to be corrected and therefore its own set of priorities. These nine functions of government are interwoven; their separation for purposes of analysis is artificial.

The discussion will be in the form of propositions put forward as hypotheses or questions raised to be explored. They should suggest the direction of research that might be undertaken. They are not exhaustive, but are illustrative of the range of inquiry that remains to be undertaken.

The Provision of a Minimum of Public Order

Where public order is taken for granted, as in most developed countries, it is like the air that is breathed. One is aware of its importance only when deprived of it. Where order is in jeopardy, men fear one another, the ordinary business of government and of private life cannot proceed, any future plans are overshadowed by the uncertainty of incipient violence, and the stakes of participating in politics rise sharply. Awareness of the importance of public order has been one of America's motivations for seeking to promote "stability" in many areas of the world.

Foreign assistance can encourage public order by improving police mobility and techniques. The police and military establishments are the principal instruments of "public order." The implicit intimidation that comes from the presence of effective police and/or military forces will prevent many disorders and challenges to a regime that otherwise might be faced with serious rebellions. Here police power and military power are closely interlinked in function. Ironically, however, where the police power becomes too highly developed, overbalancing the other elements of government, there is also unpredictability and fear, as the police become beyond the law. They may also become the instruments of a ruling elite seeking to perpetuate itself by police intimidation. Since military and police resources are essential, and since these are the elements of power most easily misused by outside powers, are there ways of utilizing international or regional organizations to maximize internal security capabilities while insulating the recipient country from great power pressures?

There are, of course, many other elements to adequate public order than mere police power, however important this may be in crisis situations or where organized infiltration and rebellion are supported from neighboring territories. Excluding these extreme though real contingencies, if there is a broad consensus on public policy and agreement on who has the legitimate right to rule, if there are accepted channels for the expression of group and mass demands and acknowledged ways of reaching decisions concerning public policy, there will be less need for police power than if these ingredients are missing. The thrust toward disorder may also be calmed by more extensive public services which are widely desired. Accordingly, there may be circumstances in which an effort to encourage any of these other aspects of a viable political society will contribute much more to public order than dealing with it by the more direct route of augmenting police power.

Manifest American efforts to improve police power may be to the political advantage or disadvantage of the United States, depending on its stake in the survival of a particular regime in the short run and on how that regime uses police power and other elements of government to develop its longer-run position. The prestige of the United States may be damaged in many countries by the misuse of police powers developed there with its assistance.

What have been American experiences with assisting the development of police facilities in new countries? Have American techniques been readily transferable? Can police technicians from abroad provide stiffening to local police forces which make them instruments of even-handed law-enforcement? Do not police forces often become almost exclusively the instruments of the ruling elite in suppressing opposition voices?

Do American police assistance programs seek to separate police activities from politics? Do they take account of the probable political setting in which the police the United States trains will have to function? How do Americans help others deal with this nontechnical but fundamental element in the application of police power?

The Provision of a Minimum of Essential Public Services

The level of discontent will be an important factor in determining the acceptance of or resistance to a particular regime. It will vary with the adequacy of public services as measured by local expectations, and with the way political opponents play up any inadequacies. What are considered indispensable public services will be very different in Vientiane, Calcutta, or New York. Postal service may count for much in London but little in Rangoon; sewage services are indispensable in New York but appear less important in Calcutta. In some countries government may be held responsible for flood control or food supplies in emergencies; in others these are outside the province of government.

By expanding some public services, assistance policy may help a regime to reduce discontent and thus strengthen its base of intermediary and mass support. Can American or other outside assistance make it possible for a regime to meet elite or mass demands more readily? Do improved train or bus services, purer water supplies, or less costly arrangements for food distribution affect the level of discontent and ease the pressures on a particular regime? Are there known instances where such improvements have eased a regime's problems or where deterioration of services has induced greater political instability?

Providing food supplies to governments may help them to make available a higher standard of consumption than their people could otherwise afford. Indeed, if investment rates for economic development are high, food supplies from abroad may be necessary to prevent a short-run real decline in living standards. Once started, however, such programs are very difficult to diminish or end without serious political consequences. This increases the government's dependence on assured foreign sources of supply. One consequence is that the United States and a particular regime become linked in close interdependence. This may or may not be to American advantage. Examples worthy of analysis are the 1952 food crisis in Ceylon and the price of rice as a political issue since then and the growing political importance of levels of food supply in many other countries. A regime's response to internal crises like famine, epidemics, or sudden depression may have much to do with the level of discontent, and prompt foreign aid in emergencies may be of political importance out of all proportion to the amounts involved.

Do programs of improved public services and government-sponsored food distribution win popular approval among different elites and masses? Do they undermine traditional sources of support for the government? Do they limit alternatives for the next government or for Americans? Do they identify Americans with a regime that is repugnant to competing elites and the people? Such service functions as these are usually performed by the public administration, although in certain countries the police, the army, cooperatives, elected district councils, and private groups such as churches assisted by the state, may also perform important public services.

Strengthening the internal rigor and operative effectiveness of the public administration is likely to have certain consequences: the hand of the central government is likely to be strengthened in dealing with dissident provinces, tribal or linguistic minority areas; government programs will be carried out with greater efficiency, and practice will be nearer to policy, reducing discontent directed against the government; the public service may be used less often as a source of sinecures and reward for political friends of the governing elite; corruption should therefore decline, fewer resources be "wasted," and public antagonism reduced; the public services (and police and army) may become a channel for opportunity for those less privileged but endowed with energy and talent, giving them ways to become identified with the problems of responsibility. A more effective and respected public administration may have certain liabilities, however.

A rapid conquest of the "area of insolence" by police and public administration may be indispensable for consolidating national unity. On the other hand, if the pace is too rapid, long standing tribal, ethnic, or regional loyalties may resist such intrusions, and hostility to the impatient central regime may weaken the central government's stance in the long run. This depends to an important extent on the way the police and administration go about their task and the degree to which new opportunities within the total national setting are available to the ambitious young men within these minorities.

Proponents of improved administration usually assume that government programs are desired by the populace but are impeded by bureaucratic inadequacy or by political intermediaries between the government and the people—landlords, village notables, small businessmen, and members of the political entourage of the regime. If, however, the proposed measures are considered harmful by the populace, a more effective administration may only accentuate popular hostility, thus weakening the central government. Effective police power may become all the more necessary to repress hostility for some time, but will prove to be an insufficient base of long-run political support.

An intractable difficulty is that the public service may become such a coveted career that the orientation of the whole educational system and the ambitions of all the educated are directed toward it. These services may drain off the best talent which is then not available for other crucial political or economic functions. And large numbers of young men who do not pass the entrance examination or for other reasons are not accepted into the services will not be fitted for much else by the education they have received. They become the articulate educated unemployed, a by-product of the educational system's orientation toward public service careers.

The role of sinecures and corruption in many new governments is of great importance. American urban politics of the nineteenth century provide a suggestive analogy. It was precisely by corruption, kickbacks, and the distribution of jobs that American urban bosses drew together large numbers of diverse ethnic, religious, and nationality groups into one political coalition of support. The distribution of "pork" to the known leaders of these diverse groups was an important method of aligning them all behind the one political boss. To find the right balance between indispensable and outrageous corruption is difficult, and some regimes are obviously being weakened by an over-addiction to manifest corruption. Others may be undermined because they fail to buy off leaders of groups that may defect from the regime unless they are given concrete inducements to win the support of their own political lieutenants.

One of the almost universal characteristics of emerging countries is the cultural and opportunity gap between the privileged, well-born few and the many. The police, public administration, and the army may provide opportunities for the less well-born but well-endowed to overcome their birthmark. *Le Rouge et Le Noir* has its counterpart in many developing countries. The openness of these channels depends on the educational requirements that are necessary for entry into the service and to the higher grades, and the accessibility of these educational prerequisites prior to entry. The public administration is less likely than the police and army to provide careers open to the talents available, since for the public services a higher level of education is usually required prior to entry or advancement.

But if these institutions are in fact open to the ambitious, and opportunities for advancement are available within them, they can be of great importance in reducing vocal discontent by absorbing those young men who otherwise would have no opportunities to identify with the problems of government.

Do American public administration training centers deal with the political consequences of changes in administrative practices and institutions? How can the United States contribute to raising the prestige and attractiveness of careers in politics in competition with the administration, police, and army in order that more highly qualified men will be drawn into responsible political activity? In some other countries, where there is already a surfeit of politicians, careers in technical, administrative, and production lines may be more urgently required.

American private organizations, like the Rockefeller Foundation, have been notably successful at assisting in the improvement of medical services. Missionary societies have often assisted in the development of medical and educational services. Are there other roles in the public services field for American nongovernmental organizations?

International organizations have made some beginnings in the field of improving public services. Could these be usefully expanded? In which services would there be the greatest increment or advantage over national or private assistance programs?

Further observations on public services and "bringing the government closer to the people" are to be found below.

Provide for the Common Defense and for
Dealings with Other Governments

American assistance concerned with providing for the common defense has been the province of military assistance. This is outside the scope of ICA programs, and only one aspect will be noted here.

Military measures and domestic politics. In the short run, military and police programs have assisted regimes to survive urgent external and internal crises. But the transition beyond the crisis to a broadened base of public support has been more difficult to achieve.

It is obvious that military forms of power are often required if a political order is to be established, particularly following invasion or other gross challenge to the civil order. But there are very real political problems inherent in the transition to an orderly, civilian, popularly supported, political society.

In crisis circumstances, when public order is near the point of breakdown or a regime must be constructed in a war torn country, the military and police functions are indispensable. However, it would appear as if the regimes so established are protected from coming to terms with the growing demands of their own people by the very strength of the police and military instruments which have been developed to meet the emergency. The officer corps is often as privileged as the regime. It may be more concerned with modernizing the country than was the ruling oligarchy, but quite often it is just as preoccupied with its own status and perquisites as were the civilian oligarchies. A revolt of young Turks in the military establishment may bring about a temporary "clean up." The Ataturk model is tempting, and much may be accomplished by the regime established by military take over.

On the other hand, once the web of legitimacy is torn by a *coup d'état,* it proves extraordinarily difficult to return to legitimate government, one which is capable of weathering temporary set-backs in part because it is widely believed to be the legitimate government. Without the aura of legitimacy, such a regime is always threatened by the next pretender. The succession of army leaders in Syria after Zaim's coup in 1949 is a classic example of this problem.

How have regimes that were established with strong military components in the midst of crisis been able to broaden the base of their political support? Where no *coup d'état* has occurred, what role have the military forces played in consolidating the regime? To what extent has genuine public discontent been ignored because the military forms of power were so firmly established? How have "young Turks" been able to accomplish the transition back to orderly, legitimate government after their *coups d'état*? In what ways have United States assistance programs contributed to any of these developments?

There may be other important by-products of military assistance programs. Young men may gain their first awareness of the nation in the army; they may learn mechanical or elementary reading and writing skills; the army may undertake public investment activities or public services. Foreign military training may bring in new conceptions of the military's role in nation-building and its proper stance toward politics, and most likely of all, military training may develop in the younger officers an impatience with the halting, often fumbling steps of the more traditionalist civilian leaders or higher officers in modernizing their countries. These have important long-run developmental and sometimes dramatic short-run political consequences. There are also severe limitations on military assistance as a means of institution-building. Here is a field for objective research as yet virtually untouched.

Assistance policy and skills of diplomacy. In dealing with other governments, the new states have difficulties in developing their own foreign services and evolving a view of their place in the state system that will provide them with maximum advantage without encroaching on their neighbors' legitimate rights. Making foreign policy in some new states tends to be highly emotional, often more concerned to exorcise the humiliations of the past than to grapple effectively with the problems of today and tomorrow. Slogans from the struggle for independence are carried forward as the only common political coin and limit the range of maneuver open to heads of state in foreign policy matters. Domestic political imperatives may seem to require xenophobic attacks on foreign enterprises which are desperately needed for economic and administrative development.

How has United States policy faced this problem? Have the limited in-service training programs in the State Department for beginning foreign diplomats been the best it could do? British experience in providing apprenticeships in the Commonwealth service is probably not relevant to American circumstances. And new nations are particularly sensitive to the implied infringement of their sovereignty which might come from efforts to provide technical assistance in the ways of diplomacy. American private ventures therefore may be peculiarly important here.

Could there be a program of in-service training in the more developed new countries such as India for those such as Nigeria which have come more recently to independence? Would they be likely to be helpful? Could we do more along the lines of the Johns Hopkins seminar program for young diplomats in Washington or the Fletcher School's training for Pakistani and other diplomatic students? Could there be an evaluation of what diplomatic training the United States has already undertaken? Might an international organization develop a training or apprenticeship program in the skills and practice of diplomacy and foreign policy-making?

Have Means for Resolving Conflicts Over Public Purposes

All political societies have conflicts over the purposes of government, the programs the government shall undertake, the ways in which scarce resources will be allocated. One of the characteristics of an emerging country is divergence of opinion concerning the ideal form of government and the underlying political values appropriate to that society. Views range from proponents of Jeffersonism to Leninism. Resolution of conflicts over public purposes is handled in many different ways. Narrow oligarchies need only reach truces among the oligarchs; two-party democracies resolve many, though by no means all, problems of public purposes through elections. Some regimes use liquidation of those protagonists whose views lose out in behind-the-scenes struggles for influence; others carry on interminable and heated debates which are never, in the end, settled one way or the other.

American foreign assistance programs may be able to affect this process, depending on the type of regime in question, the size of the aid mission and its resources, whether its contacts are largely at the ministerial level or more broadly based, whether mass communications are activated on behalf of the programs the United States sponsors, and whether the present leadership is under serious challenge by a political alternative.

The possible lines of influence can run to at least four distinguishable groups—to government officials, leading political figures, individuals who are intermediaries between the largely urban political system and the urban and rural masses, and, finally, the urban and rural masses. A few examples will suggest this line of inquiry.

Government officials. Aid missions can affect the relative importance government officials attach to different governmental activities. For example, do the aid mission's activities induce a greater interest in agricultural development and a lesser concern with heavy industrialization on the part of government officials? Do they affect those officials' view of the approximate balance between state enterprise and independent economic activity? Can it be demonstrated that a foreign assistance program can induce greater interest in official performance and less in official status than may have been the case before the aid began? Are officials more ready to seek out the wants of the people than before? Are they less responsive to the calls of family obligation and more rigorous in the application of governmental standards? Are officials more insistent on leading a life in the style set by their American counterparts than before the aid mission, and does this encourage corruption in order to keep up with the standards set by the aid mission personnel?

Political leaders. Assistance missions may have an influence on the issues that political leaders use in their political competition with one another. The skills that are brought in, the economic resources made available, or the policies that are promoted through the presence of the aid mission may bring to the fore issues that had not been part of political debate before. Indeed the United States and the policies it advocates are likely to become issues in the debate.

It may be important for the sake of economic development that economic issues be clarified in public debate, so long as this is based on a serious examination of alternative ways of dealing with local economic problems and is not merely an exchange of ideological slogans. This may speed the development of realistic policies and therefore contribute to a viable economy in the long run even if it may temporarily draw us into the controversy.

United States assistance policies may have an influence on the priorities politicians set for themselves and hold up before their country. Governments can set for themselves a broad range of purposes, stressing any one of the nine different purposes identified. One government may emphasize the external military threat and internal police powers; another may be more concerned with the politics of ethnic or regional groups; another with raising the gross national product. Each will set these purposes in a different order of priority.

Have United States aid missions had an effect on the priorities politicians have set themselves? It has been argued that the concern of the United States over military security has encouraged some political leaders to give greater stress to their military problems than they might otherwise have done. Conversely, this may have diminished their concern for other aspects of their internal political or economic development. Defense support may have contributed in fact more to economic growth than to the defense purposes it was alleged to serve. In countries where American economic assistance has been substantial, it seems probable that the United States has had considerable influence on development priorities. Since the United States has generally eschewed serious consideration of political forms and political practices, looking on these as the internal affairs of recipient countries, one would expect that it has had little effect on these matters.

Are such generalizations correct in fact? How has the United States affected the politicians' scheme of priorities? Have there been examples where the United States has had influence on the range of public debate? What have been the results, both locally and for United States policy?

Foreign aid missions may influence the manner in which political leaders deal with opponents and minorities. Can an aid mission affect the conception political leaders have of the appropriate attitude of their government toward popular demands as expressed by articulate interest groups? A government that knows it has outside support may be more ready to entertain demands from certain local groups than if it had to face them unassisted by outsiders. On the other hand, a government may also feel strengthened sufficiently by outside help to resist the pleas and pressures of certain groups it might otherwise have to placate if an aid mission were not backing it.

What examples are there of either trend and what have been the longer-run consequences of either effort on the part of the United States? Here, as in all these examples, the peculiar political context of each instance should be of great importance, and generalizations drawn from several places and times might not apply anywhere else without careful refinement.

Intermediaries between the urban political system and the rural masses. The next decades are likely to be marked by increasing political activity on the part of urban masses and the rural population. It will therefore become increasingly important for American assistance policy to be in effective relationship with the political intermediaries between the educated, usually wealthy, urban politicians and these mass groups. Identification of the intermediaries is not always easy. In many instances they will be local, land-based notables, tribal or religious leaders who still retain their following on the basis of traditional values. In others they will be semiprofessionals like school teachers, local doctors, elected or appointed village or town officials, or agricultural union leaders. In some, a growing group of small businessmen play an increasingly active role. In any one country, each of these groups may be affected differently by American technical and economic assistance.

Foreign assistance directed through central government ministries is likely to have little effect on the intermediaries between the largely urban political system and the rural masses. However, assistance involving local field operations may open greater opportunities. A basic hypothesis would be that few programs are designed with an eye to the impact they will have on the values and concerns of intermediary groups and what these will induce them to do politically. The influences would vary, depending on the types of programs being carried out, the political context of the program, the political and institutional setting in the specific country, whether or not central government policy is compatible with American field activities, and whether the United States is, in fact, working counter to central government activities.

Officials and political figures are usually based in cosmopolitan, urban centers and are so far away from the cultural, social, and economic reality of the rural areas that their grasp of rural political problems is often rudimentary. Urban groups—such as labor unions—outside the bureaucratic environment are almost as likely to be ignored. With notable exceptions, there may be few American representatives with the patience and the opportunity to grasp the subtle network of rural influences that have much to do with the political behavior of the rural masses. Even those who do gain such an understanding find that the central governments Americans must deal with are not themselves sensitive to these observations.

How do the intermediaries perceive the activities of the United States? How do its programs affect their interests, their sense of growing or narrowing opportunities, and their fears? How do the American people relate themselves to these different intermediary strata? Are they agents of desired or distrusted change, creatures of a disliked central government, collaborators with the central government in an admired common enterprise, or allies of the intermediaries against an oppressive distant regime?

The urban and rural masses. Similar questions could be raised concerning United States activities vis-à-vis the masses. On the other hand, in most emerging countries, as in developed countries, too, mass opinions are of less political relevance than the views of opinion leaders, organizational leaders, and the intermediaries. United States activities directed toward mass opinion, particularly extensive information programs, are likely to become hortatory and to awaken appetites rather than to induce fruitful local activity.

*Provide for the Expression of Public Demands and
Discontent without Political Disintegration*

This area of exploration concerns the relation between assistance policy and the ways in which public needs are voiced and political pressure on their behalf is organized. Research would focus on the political parties and interest groups which are the dynamic elements of politics in most countries—their relative and changing positions or power, their modes of organization, their political practices, and their policy demands. Does assistance policy as presently carried out affect these essentially political elements of a country's life?

Foreign assistance, hitherto, has had little impact on the nature of political parties and their organization. Political parties are fundamental to dealing with the problem of concentrating enough political power to give direction to government while broadening the base of political support to ensure governmental effectiveness and to accommodate change. Probably there have been instances where American assistance policy has sought to strengthen the position of a particular party or a particular set of leaders. Where crisis is imminent, military and police assistance may have had this end in view. But the United States has generally avoided concern over the organization and practices of political parties.

Can any connections be discerned between American assistance activities and the ways a party organizes a following or broadens its base of support, the issues which political parties attempt to use, or the ways in which they reach internal decisions, deal with dissidence, with recruitment to the parties, or their mode of campaigning? Since parties play such a crucial role in organizing political power for accomplishing the country's purposes, and in guiding the country's foreign policy, they deserve a good deal of careful attention from assistance personnel. There are, of course, inescapable inhibitions in the way of providing political parties with the type of manifest technical or financial assistance one can give to a public administration, for example, or even to military personnel. Too close association with outsiders can be used by opponents to make a party appear a tool of foreigners. Organizing political power is an art peculiarly dependent on a close knowledge of the temperament, aspirations, traditional style, and ways of the people being gathered together in the party.

Nevertheless, there are classic problems that all parties face—they must organize a following, they must be financed, they must have criteria for membership and must have ways of dealing with policy or personal differences that develop within the party. There must be ways of relating leaders to followers, of combining generalized principles and broad appeals to as large numbers as possible with specific and often very tangible rewards to the faithful or temporarily faithful,

if a following is to be built sufficient to accomplish necessary policy
objectives. Very often, new, nonauthoritarian parties lack stable organization in depth. Political leaders rarely have a ward and precinct
type of political organization developing a hard core of support that
can be counted on. Where such organization is lacking, political leaders may have to resort to rhetoric and slogans of highly emotional
kinds to enlist support from individuals who cannot otherwise identify
with the political leaders because they are often culturally alienated,
of a different ethnic group, from a different region, and often speaking
a different language. Rhetorical politics keeps the level of excitement
high but is unlikely to direct public energies toward necessary constructive activities. Trade union membership is often shifting and un-
reliable. This is a factor contributing to trade union extremism as competing union leaders appeal to drifting members by outbidding one
another.

Can assistance policy improve the ability and willingness of political
parties and interest groups to enlist support for the government's endeavors? In many types of political circumstances, the institutions for
voicing and organizing political demands are the same as those required to ensure governmental effectiveness. Political parties, trade
unions, ethnic groups, and many other organized elements in the society are the channels by which popular desires are voiced. They are
also essential means to the government's end of enlisting popular support for its programs, many of which may require effort and sacrifice.
Economic development, defense, even the moderation of communal
antagonism in the name of national unity or the finding of satisfaction
in the degree of respect already accorded to their own country—all
these essential elements of a viable political order can be promoted or
undermined by the organized groups in that society. More effective
organization can give a leader some assurance that he can retain his
following without having to pander to the most narrow feelings or
urgent demands of his organizational constituents. The goals of the
leaders of these parties and groups are important if they are to be responsible and constructive rather than merely critical and demanding.

How can assistance policy help to improve the organization of parties and interest groups? How can it encourage responsibility among
their leaders? What efforts have been made to share experiences of successful representative parties in one country with leaders or organizers
of similar parties in another country? What kinds of training programs,

seminars in third countries, in-service training in successful parties such as the Congress party in India and the Institutional Revolutionary party in Mexico, might be established? The political inventions in Colombia of an agreed transfer of power between parties or the limits on succession of Brazilian mayors may have wider application. Could anything applicable to American programs be learned from the experience of Communist parties? How could private organizations or international agencies be of assistance?

Questions to be examined in regard to the encouragement and development of political parties are legion. A comparison of the financing of the United National party in Ceylon with the Congress party in India might illuminate the advantages of the methods of the Congress party. How has the Institutional Revolutionary party as a single party, been able to accommodate such a broad spectrum of interests and adjust to the changing needs of Mexico for so many years? How could others follow a similar path? How do these or other parties resist the political fragmentation on personalist grounds which split so many parties in emerging countries? Does organization or do issues figure as central to the success of different parties?

In assessing the political results of leadership grants, it is as important to judge the career consequences of the grant as it is to discover whether the attitudes of grantees become more or less favorable to the United States as a result of their visit. Perhaps the grants have made little discernible difference in terms of their political futures, but they may have changed their opinions. For a rounded evaluation, an attempt should be made to explore the political consequences of inviting some leaders when, perforce, all cannot be invited. What of the attitudes and political success of those who are not invited? Are group visits by delegations of parliamentary or political leaders better than individual grants? Could the shared experience of a combined visit to the United States or to third countries help to reduce interparty frictions based on personal rivalries or do the strains of traveling together only sharpen personal antagonisms?

Assistance to professional or interest groups (doctors, teachers, small businessmen, trade unions) encourages the development of semiautonomous groups based on common professional or economic interests. Leadership grants, technical assistance to provide local facilities used by major groups, training programs designed to raise the level of skill in these activities—all such programs induce a greater desire for independence from traditional modes of organization. Kinship and ethnic exclusiveness are likely to decline as loyalties based on the new activities grow. Recognition by outsiders of the legitimacy and importance of this activity may be as important as the resources made available. Private and international organizations may have an important role to play.

The assumption that the national government alone is the source of all initiative is likely to decline if such groups as these gain some ability to take initiative to meet their own problems—and those of the community of which they are a part. Each country is likely to set its own balance wheel on this. If the association of any of these groups with outsiders is too close, they may become the victims of xenophobia and thus their real political influence will be reduced. If they come to gain so much autonomy that they are entirely free of governmental influence, there will be a serious political effort to limit this autonomy. Groups that developed quasi-autonomous status under the colonial regime will have that status progressively modified until they are more nearly equal to those groups that started recently.

United States assistance programs are likely to encourage greater membership participation within these organizations and to diminish the quasi-authoritarian practices of traditional modes of organization. Close association with specialists from the United States in any of these fields may diminish the role of kinship and traditional status; is likely to encourage those with initiative regardless of their origins; and may make issues of policy rather than of personality more important in internal decision-making. The political consequence may be that more groups would be willing and capable of challenging traditionalist authority and seeking a substitute mode of deciding major political issues. Would they also be more likely to resist authoritarian pretension from the extreme left as well? It would be useful to compare the development of such professional interest groups in, say, India and Pakistan, and in Ghana and Nigeria. The connections between these internal developments in interest group structure and process and their political environment might be of both theoretical and policy importance.

The mass media are likely to be affected by foreign assistance, because aid missions are likely to encourage more expectations than can be fulfilled. Aid missions have been less successful at encouraging responsible criticism and detailed, empirical reporting of government or private development efforts or other constructive activities and programs.

Almost inevitably, assistance missions are more likely to articulate the promise of a better future than they are to fulfill the promises that their efforts and their words imply. Their demonstrations of new methods, the equipment that comes to some and not to others, the goad of American or international agency opposite numbers are all bound to raise the level of impatience and are likely to accelerate and expand the revolution of rising expectations. The impulse of Americans to use mass media to dramatize their programs may so affect the content of the mass media as to increase political demands.

In many emerging countries, particularly in former British areas, the newspapers began as a relatively high level press for the resident westerners and the small, educated indigenous population. As circulations have grown, the quality of reporting and accuracy has declined, and a greater appeal is made to mass emotions. Reporters and rewrite men are grossly underpaid. Where the press is not rigorously controlled, destructive criticism is more common than responsible criticism. Reporting of foreign news is often vividly colored by gross oversimplifications. Highly doctrinaire solutions to local problems are often proposed on the basis of ideas learned abroad without a close understanding of the real and peculiar circumstances in their own country.

Has there been an analysis of the content of mass media to see what sort of images, simplifications, and themes are used in discussion of public policy issues? What sorts of exchange, seminar, study programs, and efforts to assist in the reorganization of the newspapers and mass media might be encouraged to ensure both the autonomy and responsibility of the press? Nongovernmental and international agency activities may be of especial utility.

Provide Orderly Means for Replacing those Who Rule in Ways that Bestow Legitimacy on Successors

Apart from accumulating power for governmental effectiveness, including awakening sufficient intermediary and popular support to ease the implementation of policy, perhaps the most difficult part of government is the orderly transition from one set of rulers to another. There are many factors that condition whether a transfer of power shall be easy or stormy, such as cultural and political traditions, attitudes toward authority and government responsibility, the opportunities for satisfying lives open to those who must step down, the presence or absence of institutions that provide ways of making orderly decisions about this without resort to gunfire, a certain core of fundamental continuity which persists despite changes in personnel of government.

In what circumstances has American policy sought to ease transitions, and when has it sought to retard transitions? When protests seem to be rising sharply, and a reasonably tolerable "next government" seems on the horizon, how has the United States reacted? In some instances it appears to have made it plain that it would welcome a change; in others it appears to have backed the regime in power. How has the United States decided that a potential "next government" deserved its support? Has there been policy consistency in this vital matter, or has the United States been responding in an *ad hoc* fashion to each situation according to the views of those on the spot? If so, by what criteria did they decide on the advice they gave to Washington? And by what criteria has Washington replied? These reflections call for a comparative study of transitions of power in those new countries where orderly procedures for transitions are lacking. Has the United States ever tried to encourage the establishment of institutions that would smooth this unavoidable political problem? Are there devices which it might explore other than its own form of elections? Has the United Nations experienced in the Saar, Korean elections, and the Congo any lessons on the possible role of international organizations in aiding political transition?

Meld Diversities so as to Consolidate National Unity
Without Provoking Additional Centrifugal Forces

Most emerging countries are divided by two fissures running in different directions. A horizontal division separates the few highly educated, relatively highly privileged, often culturally alienated elite from the illiterate, poverty-ridden, indigenous masses. If there is a middle class, it is usually so small and hard pressed that it plays only a minor role in mitigating conflict and encouraging moderate politics of compromise. A vertical fissure divides one ethnic or linguistic community from another in the "plural" society. The business, cultural, religious, and social life of members of each group rarely touch intimately on those in the other groups. If there is a middle class, its members are often the most acutely conscious of cultural or ethnic differences. Can foreign assistance policy contribute to an increased national unity?

As noted earlier, improved public administration may imperceptibly draw diverse groups into one common network of activity. Enhanced military and police capability may weaken attachment to local notables who traditionally provided security in return for absolute loyalty, but these intrusions may provoke profound hostilities. An educational system may draw the youth into a common universe of discourse and experience. But experience in Eastern Europe showed that efforts to force national assimilation do not work. Improved roads and other means of communication and a shift from barter to a market economy bring isolated people into closer touch with one another. Conscious efforts to combine diverse ethnic groups in one single work project, dam site, or training program may help to break down hostile stereotypes. Shared military experience or public administration service may bring at least one segment of the populace into a sense of common awareness, although jealousies over advancement and responsibilities are a constant invitation to antagonism along traditional lines.

If national unity is an urgent necessity in a fragmented, plural society that has not yet developed an overarching sense of national identity, foreign policy issues may be the most convenient way a leader can consolidate his country. Foreign policy issues, often anti-American or anti-Western in character, may be domestically essential if the nation's unity is to be consolidated. A dose of xenophobia may be indispensable to the development of a national sense. Are there examples of such a development? How have we responded?

More generally, foreign assistance resources channeled through national governments strengthen the central government in its relations to regional and parochial interests. Is it correct that in India, for example, the national Congress party has been strengthened in its efforts to deal with the centrifugal pulls of Indian diversity by the center's ability to grant or withhold scarce economic resources from the states? Has this been similarly true for the rulers of Iran, South Vietnam, or Turkey, to take but three examples? In what ways? What have been the specific linkages in this process? Does national economic planning carried out on presumably economic criteria independent of political judgments impede the central government from punishing those local leaders who press parochial demands and from rewarding those who work toward national unity? If the answer is yes, does planning not weaken the center's ability to allocate technical assistance and foreign aid in order to help it fulfill the fundamental political necessity of inducing national unity? Are there examples where the hand of the national government has been strengthened when large investment in areas of possible defection encourages leaders of these areas to co-operate with the national government? This is in some ways politically analogous to the rivers and harbors ploy in American politics.

Foreign assistance can contribute to diminishing the dramatic social, cultural, and psychological gap between those who man the institutions of national government and the rest of the population in transitional societies.

Can it be demonstrated that foreign assistance programs in fact have the result of "bringing the government closer to the people," as is often alleged? Where governments undertake social service programs such as improved medical care, food subsidies, or land distribution, all of which may be facilitated with assistance from the United States, one would expect the gap between ruler and ruled to be diminished and the rulers to be commensurately consolidated in their position.

The political consequences of any of these measures should be investigated. There are many other variables that may be as decisive as whether or not the program is undertaken. It is possible that opposition voices are sufficiently critical and well-organized so that no matter what is done is felt by the masses to be only half enough. The technical assistance undertaken may whet appetites faster than it assuages them. In order to achieve the economic and production changes the technicians see as necessary, new wants may be so rapidly awakened as to raise the amount of frustration directed against the government rather than to diminish it.

Community development programs in India are perhaps the most impressive example of a device designed to "bring the government to the people." For research purposes they have the virtue of being widely scattered in a country where there are good data on voting behavior, where there have been a series of free elections, and where relatively good data on social, religious, ethnic, and other variables also exist. An extensive research design could be devised which would compare electoral results in areas where there had been community development programs to results in areas where there was no such project. It might also be possible to compare voting behavior between districts where a large investment, such as a dam, had been introduced and where, by contrast, a more "balanced" program of community development had been carried out.[2]

Community development may produce a sense that the government now cares for the lot of the people as it never did before. If so, such programs diminish the gap between ruler and ruled. But community development may also induce a more rapid awakening of political consciousness and an awareness of unmet needs which will produce more political dissatisfaction than existed before. Whether this redounds to the advantage or disadvantage of the central government will depend perhaps as much on the political alternatives that seem available as on the nature of the community development program itself.

Have land reforms encouraged by American assistance been successful in winning mass rural support even though they may have alienated other centers of power in the entourage of a particular regime? Have the political consequences been helpful to the regime? Iran or Taiwan may be cases in point.

Road building may open areas hitherto inaccessible to markets and to contact with the outside. They may win approval of local leaders and bring city and country more closely together. Have road-building programs in fact strengthened the political following of a regime or contributed more to a disruption of the traditional relationships in the countryside on which a regime had previously depended for its assured support?

Promoting a network of private associations may help overcome national disunity. National unity may be more effectively encouraged if there develops a network of overlapping "voluntary" organizations which transcend in their membership and impact the limits of the particularistic communities or group structures of the traditional, plural society. These may deal with specific, relatively noncontroversial and nonpolitical problems of interest to large numbers of people. Women's associations, health clinics and societies, sports clubs, Red Cross or similar welfare societies, as well as the type of professional organization mentioned above are all examples. American and European private organizations, including professional organizations, cooperatives, and trade unions, could be helpful here.

[2] I am indebted to Myron Weiner, University of Chicago, for this suggestion.

Americans should be aware, however, that their tradition of pluralism, reflected in such a proliferation of autonomous and competing organizations, may in fact produce unity only where there is a broad consensus already. Where differences are as deep as in many emerging countries, such development may only serve to define additional lines of division. To work toward unity, therefore, such autonomous groups must cut across traditional differentiations and bring individuals from hitherto separated groups into working cooperation.

Although such voluntary associations are a fundamental part of the Anglo-Saxon tradition, they are very alien to the tradition of most emerging countries where colonial government or traditional social groups hitherto have provided the principal initiative for organization and activity. There have been some important developments, however, and case studies of the life history of such societies in different cultural settings are urgently required. There is considerable experience from among missionaries, foundations, and professional or business groups on which to draw for data.

Provide to the Elite and Prospective Elite a Sense of Recognition

A regime which is incapable of providing a sense of recognition and pride will not meet the subjective necessities of its elite, its intermediaries, and masses. Men do not live by bread or political order alone. Although these are vital, they are not sufficient. Particularly in new states that were previously colonies, the search for recognition and pride is profoundly important. Can American assistance policy contribute to this ingredient of a viable political system? This is often a matter of style as much as of substance.

Invitations to Latin American or Indian intellectuals to lecture in American universities about their own traditions, a sensitive reception to foreign visitors here, the way American diplomats or assistance personnel deal with local leaders and technicians, the way Americans live abroad, and the interest they feel in foreign tradition, art, or other creative expressions are all parts of this political imperative. The importance of the United Nations to political leaders in new countries is in part explicable by this imperative to prove to oneself that now, at last, "they"—the westerners, particularly, and not infrequently annoying neighbors—will pay attention to what "we" have to say. Here diplomacy in international organizations and assistance policy are closely linked in their role of inducing political viability.

Unfortunately, some American activities evoke little in the way of local pride and reassurance. Military aid programs designed to meet military contingencies or to contribute to local authority of the government may weaken pride of all but the military elite. Sometimes, however, the transfer of military equipment may have its principal use in bolstering pride, although other by-products may be less desirable.

Technical or economic assistance may be provided under such stringent conditions in order to meet audit or other domestic requirements within the United States that they are sources of friction and humiliation in the recipient country. Policy may seek so to publicize the American contribution to development programs that the United States appears to claim the credit rather than allowing full credit to reside where it will do the local regime—and perhaps Americans—the most good. Providing what they ask for, perhaps even stadia or large scale "impact" projects, may heighten local pride, or the dreams of glory of the leaders, but may not contribute to real economic growth. How has the United States balanced off these two contradictory criteria in practice? In what ways can the United States enhance pride and a sense of respect in the new countries? What have been the results in this respect in a variety of sample countries and programs? When conflict among criteria arises—as it is bound to—how does the United States deal with this matter of recognition and pride?

The Accumulation of Savings and Allocation of Resources to Increase Availability of Worldly Goods

There is a widespread assumption that an increase in standards of living will bring with it a political stability favorable to American interests. This is by no means assured. On the contrary, one can posit that rapid economic development will accelerate the social, psychological, and organizational changes that were necessary before economic development could get under way. This acceleration in itself will be disruptive, and these dislocations are bound to bring political disorder in varying degrees. The converse is also true, that if there is not economic change along lines desired by those who are either presently politically influential or are ready to grasp power should the present regimes falter, there will also be political disruption.

It is because there is bound to be rapid political change, generally disruptive, whether there is economic development or not, that the matter of political development is of such importance. Economic development in itself does not create a public order nor a viable political system.

A NOTE ON EDUCATION

The educational system is of great importance for developing values and practices of political behavior. It can contribute significantly to the conception political leaders and masses have of the good society, of where they themselves are moving and how best to reach their goal. The political values taught in the classrooms, the political convictions or argumentation of the teachers, the effect of the mode of teaching on the personalities of the children and their attitudes toward authority and dissent, and the practice provided in the schools and universities for experimenting with responsibility and the management of small controversies in a serious manner—all these and more elements in the educational experience are of importance to the socialization of young people into the modes and values of political life.

These aspects of the educational system go far beyond the technical education American assistance programs have tended to strengthen, although efforts to teach inventiveness and innovation in the technological line probably affect attitudes of students toward dealing with other aspects of life as well. Indeed, the more technological specialization, the more likely are students to become impatient with traditional social ways, but this in itself will not provide political skills or judgment for constructively changing these ways.

Research concerning the role of education in political development should draw on findings concerning the effects of differing educational experiences on personality growth and political attitudes. An effort should be made to apply these findings to the culture and existing educational systems in, say, Iran, India, Morocco, or Nigeria. The real impediments to changing an established educational system should not be overlooked. Foreign efforts to induce changes are bound to be marginal. Too rapid a change in the educational system may only further alienate the educated elite from its political following.

Nevertheless, there may be many ways in which the United States can, with tact and understanding, assist in curricular instruction and extracurricular activities. The aim should be to bring the educational system closer to the needs of the country; provide the type of skills which give young people real opportunities to exercise their talents in improving their own societies when they leave school or college; and encourage those values that lead to a sharing of power and responsibility, increased empathy toward other groups, broader participation in taking decisions, and easier collaboration with peers.

Comparative case studies of the effects of their experience on the political skills and values of students at the American University of Beirut, the Jaffna College in Ceylon, the Forman Christian College, Lahore, or other such colleges elsewhere, would be helpful. Comparison of personality and value development and opportunities open to students in technological and "liberal arts" curricula would give insight on the influences of different educational programs.

OBSERVATIONS ON THE LITERATURE ALREADY AVAILABLE

Thus far, students of politics have devoted relatively little systematic attention to the problems of emerging political societies. There are a variety of monographs on specific countries in which many useful insights can be discerned if they are analyzed with care. Many are more useful as provokers of hypotheses than as sources of data on questions relevant to American foreign policy or the development of viable political societies. This is because very few have approached the political problems of the country they have analyzed from the point of view of American foreign policy interests and the ways in which outside influences could usefully be brought to bear. Indeed, many describe with considerable acuity the impact of the colonial era on specific countries, but they tend to assume that with independence, such influences will be minimal. Alternatively, there is an assumption that the forces of world-wide modernization and industrialization will proceed virtually independently of human choice. The intervention of conscious policy in this process, particularly to favor or discourage alternative political consequences of this spontaneous process, is rarely considered.

Sample country monographs are those by James S. Coleman, *Nigeria, Background to Nationalism* (University of California Press, 1958), David Apter, *The Gold Coast in Transition* (Princeton University Press, 1955), George Kahin, *Nationalism and Revolution in Indonesia* (Cornell University Press, 1952), Howard Wriggins, *Ceylon: Dilemmas of a New Nation* (Princeton University Press, 1960). One directed particularly at the problems of minority political parties in India is Myron Weiner's *Party Politics in India, the Development of a Multi-Party System* (Princeton University Press, 1957). His forthcoming study of *The Politics of Scarcity* should be of considerable interest since he attempts to sketch a political strategy for the Indian Government in dealing with the political pressures that are bound to rise. Bert F. Hoselitz and Weiner have also speculated systematically on the political pressures that are mounting in India as a result of economic and social development. Selig Harrison's study of Indian national disunity, *India—The Most Dangerous Decades* (Princeton University Press, 1960) stresses the centrifugal pulls within India and the political difficulties of dealing with them. Lucian Pye examined the intractable problem of Communist guerilla tactics in his *Guerilla Communism in Malaya* (Princeton University Press, 1956).

Daniel Lerner in *The Passing of Traditional Society* (Free Press, 1958), stresses changes in the mass communication system in examining social and technological changes in the Middle East as they come to affect politics. Dankwart Rustow's essay on *Politics and Westernization in the Near East* (Princeton University, Center of International Studies, 1956), explored new ground on the effects of westernization on political ways.

In a pioneering effort to design a systematic structure for purposes of comparative political analysis in new countries, Gabriel Almond, James Coleman, and their collaborators have elaborated a scheme of political functions that encompasses more data than is ordinarily considered when examining western political institutions. As with all such schemes at first, terminological hurdles impede communication and there is some doubt whether the scheme is sufficiently dynamic to point up changing patterns and developmental trends rather than focusing on a very sophisticated analysis of political reality at any given moment. But the work of Almond and Coleman and their collaborators in *The Politics of the Developing Areas* (Princeton University Press, 1960) is an ambitious comparative analysis in depth of the political process in emerging countries, spanning Latin America, Africa, and non-Communist Asia. It is not directed toward an analysis of United States foreign policy problems. Edward Shils also undertook to present a systematic analysis of "Political Development in the New States" (available in *Comparative Studies in Society and History*, The Hague, Vol. 2, nos. 3 and 4) identifying types of regimes and sketching the dynamic developments of each type.

The studies prepared for the Senate Committee on Foreign Relations by the Massachusetts Institute of Technology, Center for International Studies, on "Economic, Social and Political Change in the Underdeveloped Countries and Its Implications for United States Policy" and by Syracuse University, Maxwell Graduate School, entitled "The Operational Aspects of United States Foreign Policy" are helpful contributions to different aspects of the problems raised here.[3]

George Liska's pioneering study on the use of foreign assistance as an instrument of foreign policy is by far the most sophisticated analysis of this problem publicly available. He deals with some of these issues of political growth and stability. His work assumes a rather completely Machiavellian state system and rationalistic statesmen of the enlightenment model. Foreign assistance is seen as fundamentally the search for control by the donor over the recipient. He may underemphasize the marginality of influence obtainable by foreign assistance and the depth of political analysis necessary to fully understand the political process in emerging countries. But his book *The New Statecraft* (University of Chicago Press, 1960) stands out above all others in the field.

Another important work is Charles Wolf, Jr., on *Foreign Aid: Theory and Practice in Southern Asia* (Princeton University Press, 1960). This empirical study by a member of the staff of the RAND Corporation analyzes in great detail the complicated and subtle choices underlying American assistance allocations over a period of years in South and Southeast Asia. His study is full of insights and identifies a multitude of the factors the United States has in fact attempted to

---

[3] Published in U.S. Senate Committee on Foreign Relations, *United States Foreign Policy, Compilation of Studies* (Government Printing Office, 1961).

take into account. His political assumptions, however, are overly simple, as he would be the first to admit.

Another type of literature concerns studies of political elites. These are peculiarly useful in emerging countries since the elites are narrow yet much more influential to the course of events than in more established, broadly based political systems. Edward Shils has done brilliant work on the Indian intelligentsia. Guy Pauker has studied the military elites of Southeast Asia. Lucian Pye has been exploring personality and other characteristics of Communist and non-Communist elites in Burma and other parts of Southeast Asia. Monroe Berger has written on the administrative and military elite in Egypt, and John Johnson has sought to delineate the characteristics of the increasingly important "middle sectors" in Latin America.

There is thus a growing body of literature from a variety of disciplines attempting to analyze significant aspects of the political development of emerging countries. Too little yet is directed toward answering the question: How can American foreign policy fruitfully assist in the process of political development?

THOUGHTS ON RESEARCH PROCEDURE

Research on political development should be promoted in a variety of ways.

Individual research scholars on leave from universities could be encouraged by foundation grants to undertake studies of specific aspects of this inclusive problem. The advantage would be their detachment from commitment to past policies; the serious liability would be that they are insufficiently attuned to the problems and limitations of policy.

Experienced research institutions like RAND, the Brookings Institution, the Center for International Studies at MIT, area centers such as Northwestern University, the University of Chicago, or institutions like the Institute for Defense Analyses (IDA) could more easily bring their guidance to bear on individual scholars working with them. This would make it more likely that the research undertaken would focus on United States policy and political development. Liska's study suggests that detailed empirical data from classified sources is not necessary for creative thought on this question. Highly qualified scholars with both policy experience and theoretical skill might be encouraged to concentrate on this problem in an environment such as RAND, IDA, or the Brookings Institution.

Within the United States government, useful research might also be undertaken, similar to ICA's current Study of Technical Assistance. Debriefings of returning administrators might lay greater stress on the political context of assistance programs and their political consequences. A group of experienced individuals, returned from countries where the United States has had extensive assistance missions, might be freed from administrative responsibilities for six months to examine their experience with skilled research personnel to guide the inquiry. The ICA training center at the Johns Hopkins School for Advanced International Studies might provide an ideal setting for such research. The post mortems would not seek to reflect on the man's operational skill but to use the benefit of his experience to enlighten a small research staff that would be seeking assumptions and generalizations drawn from experience.

If specific programs are to be examined, the following considerations might be helpful:

The assistance programs to be examined should have been operating for a considerable period of years.

Area specialists unconcerned with United States policy should be asked to define their conception of the secular trends within the society that bear on the aspects of assistance policy to be examined.

Program specialists should be interviewed in efforts to obtain their estimates of the political effects of their work.

Newspaper and official reporting from the field should provide a good deal of material.

The work of area specialists and program specialists should be compared to identify similarities, differences, and contradictions in the way trends and changes are perceived and explained.

Only then would field research be advisable to explore specific questions and hypotheses as they apply to specific countries.

Countries of particular interest would be Turkey, Iran, Pakistan, India, Vietnam, South Korea, Taiwan, Bolivia, Brazil, and Guatemala. Speculative projections of developments in Nigeria, Ghana, and Guinea based on similar variables would be of interest.

7

In Conclusion . . .

ROBERT E. ASHER*

ÉVERYONE CONCERNED WITH DEVELOPMENT PROGRAMS, I con-
clude, has to be a highly exceptional person. He must be cultured and
cross-cultured. He must be disciplined and interdisciplined. He must
be well stocked with empathy and antifreeze. He should be a model
himself, and he should know about model-building, institution-building, stadium-building, and body-building.

He should strive for results that are well-structured or require only
a minimum of re-structuring. He must view them in Technicolor, for
one of the first lessons learned by the would-be developer is that
nothing is all black or all white. Amidst population explosions, revolutions of rising expectations, and incipient imbalances of every kind,
he must remain serene and balanced, perennially poised for the long
run that follows every short run.

Unfortunately, even in the long run, mankind may not succeed in
creating the best of all possible worlds but—to borrow a felicitous phrase
from an earlier version of an essay in this collection—"we must maximize the opportunities for an optimal transformation."

Having now illustrated my familiarity with, if not my mastery of, the
jargon of development, I can turn to more important issues.

The foregoing essays constitute both more and less than an agenda
for research. They may, it seems to me, be considered from three
points of view: their contributions to a better understanding of the
process of development, their advice to the managers of foreign aid
programs, and their proposals for further research in their respective
fields. Taken together, the collection does not add up to a rounded

* Member, Senior Staff, Brookings Institution.

analysis of the problems of economic, social, and political development, and was not intended to do so.

The essays were not solicited with a view to providing a logical progression from one topic to another or a full catalog of research needs. The objective was a more modest one: to consider a group of problems that will demand serious attention from American policy makers during the 1960's. Broad areas such as natural resources development, the improvement of health, and the strengthening of public administration, were deliberately omitted despite their obvious importance, on the theory that research needs and research priorities in these fields were, by and large, better known than in the fields that were chosen.

Among the topics included, there is considerable overlap. Some of this is due to the fact that development problems simply do not lend themselves to treatment in watertight compartments. Some of it is inevitable in an era in which declarations of interdependence abound and the leading economists have become preoccupied with noneconomic factors in economic growth, while the lawyers and scientists devise policies to promote productivity, personal savings, and higher rates of capital formation.

Each of the essays offers some important new insights into the development process. It would be presumptuous of me to attempt to catalog these insights. The most that I dare do here is to recall a few points that I found interesting and significant.

UNDERSTANDING THE DEVELOPMENT PROCESS

Everyone now seems acutely aware of the pulls and cross-pulls among economic, social, and political forces, and of the difficulty of separating cause from effect. The breakdown of traditional attitudes and of the established social structure, scholars have learned, is not only a consequence of economic development, but also a necessary forerunner of economic growth. Modernization promotes urbanization, but urbanization also promotes modernization. Planning must proceed both from the top down and from the bottom up. The skills necessary to expedite agricultural development are chiefly those of farmers, but the solution of some of the most critical rural problems depends on administrators, politicians, and editors in the cities. Education is a consumer as well as a producer good—higher incomes lead to greater expenditures on education, and greater expenditures on education lead to higher incomes. In this wonderful world of feedback effects and circular causation, the cart looks just like the horse and must also be flogged if progress is to be made.

However, if cause and effect interact as vigorously as the experts say, must the conditions for more effective use of investment funds be established first, or will larger investments also speed the establishment of conditions for their effective use? Seven or eight years ago, it was widely recognized that the underdeveloped countries suffered from many ailments. But it was also fashionable to believe that sizable foreign grants and loans could help to mitigate at least some of these ailments. The public listened to the experts but remained unconvinced. Now, just as the public in the more developed countries is becoming prepared to bear the necessary financial burden, the experts consider it crude, boorish, and naive to stress the capital requirements of the less developed nations. They recommend little research specifically designed to improve estimated needs for capital, foreign or domestic. Have the lubricating effects of a generous injection of funds been downgraded unnecessarily in our search for more sophisticated prescriptions?

For the most part, the additional sophistication is clear gain. I found myself fascinated by Everett Hagen's description of the attitudes within individuals in all walks of life which constrain their own actions, make the activities necessary for economic change uninteresting or repugnant to them, or limit their creativity. This is not the first time that Mr. Hagen has stressed the role of the innovator in economic development and the shortage of creativity in traditional societies, but he has now thrown the whole problem into sharper focus than ever before.

Albert Hirschman's brilliant comments suggest some strategies for getting around alleged obstacles to development or finding new sequences for surmounting them. His catalog of the undulations and fluctuations in previous diagnoses of barriers to development, and his cautions against the wholesale swallowing of current clichés, deserve careful reading. His remarks are disconcerting, however, to those in quest of clearer criteria to govern eligibility for foreign aid. They would seem to lead to American involvement with the sinners and the unregenerated in the hope that, unwittingly, they will reform, and with the righteous because, wittingly, they have reformed.

The Colm-Geiger essay outlines the process of planning and programing development more lucidly than has yet been done. The authors advocate pragmatic planning that recognizes both the limits of mathematical methods and the role that qualitative judgment—and trial and error—must play. A country plan, they maintain, should be subjected to the democratic process of debate and final political action before it becomes official.

Arthur Mosher admittedly owes a great debt to his letter-writing legions, but his own wisdom and experience are plainly apparent in the rich research catalog he has assembled. I am especially impressed by his emphasis on research as something "much more than a staff activity preparatory to agricultural development or preliminary to developmental assistance." Inasmuch as technical advisers and local counterparts come from different cultures, he says, "the field experience of engaging together in systematic examination of local conditions and in joint searches for locally valid improved practices may be one of the easiest ways of establishing meaningful communication."

The same point is stressed by other contributors to this volume and by participants at the conference at which earlier versions of these essays were discussed. By first selecting research projects that are likely to be successful, a stimulus will be provided for further research and action. Gradually, respect for analytical methods may grow. The contributions of unencumbered emotionalism to the formulation of public policy should decline as research becomes respectable in the developing countries.

In his discussion of technological change, Richard Eckaus addresses himself with admirable directness and consistency to the subject assigned to him. He analyzes what is known and not known about the business of facilitating technological change—of finding new production methods suited to the resources and conditions in the emerging countries and introducing them into those areas. He suggests how one might go about learning some of the things that need to be known. He tries to indicate an order of priorities and to offer some guidelines for a division of labor between the universities and the government. He reports that the major deficiency today is the lack of integration of the rules of choice among technologies into an over-all programing framework. In the present state of knowledge, he says, the choice issue is usually analyzed for projects as if they could be considered separately from each other and independently of the over-all growth pattern of a country.

Bowman and Anderson provide a timely reminder that there is no magic in investment in human as against physical capital that guarantees its productivity irrespective of the kind of human capital created. They then seek to identify the critical factors that determine how far educational investments should be carried, and what kinds of educational investment promise high, low, or negative returns in given situations.

The special service that Howard Wriggins performs, it seems to me, is to provide a more orderly framework for thinking about political development in the emerging countries. He assumes that it is in the United States interest to assist newly independent states to become capable of orderly political growth and change at home, and capable of warding off threats to their independence from abroad. He singles out nine functions that governments must perform to exhibit and develop the necessary capabilities. He discusses these with perspicacity and awareness of the complex relationships among them. He cautions against overburdening assistance programs with too heavy a freight in political objectives.

In brief, each essay in this symposium contains some insights that should prove useful to both specialists and generalists. Most of them also contain handy hints of an operational nature—advice about the kinds of people needed to run an aid program and the tactics and devices they can employ.

PROGRAM MANAGEMENT

The handy hints relate largely to technical cooperation (formerly called technical assistance), in part because this is the most pervasive form of aid and the most demanding in terms of numbers of people and variety of skills. As I have already indicated, the techniques of mobilizing capital and applying it properly, or of finding growth-promoting price and wage policies, receive relatively little consideration in these essays. Moreover, the classic method of introducing new skills and fresh outlooks into established societies—immigration, followed by naturalization of the immigrants—is ignored completely. In this age, it is assumed that foreign specialists, like private foreign investments, should be repatriated.

Several years ago, I called attention to the fact that the payment of salaries and transportation for foreign experts represents only a minute fraction of the cost of a development program. I suggested that, after the value of this type of service had been demonstrated for another few years, steps should be taken to make the foreign experts more directly responsible to the governments of the host countries and less obviously the employees of the United States or the United Nations.[1]

The OPEX program of the United Nations, still operating on a very small scale, is an important step in this direction. Under this program, the United Nations, acting as a kind of employment service, finds operational and executive personnel needed by the developing countries—directors of central statistical services, deputy chiefs of planning, and so forth. The countries employ them, not as foreign advisers but as line officials of the government, and the United Nations supplements their salaries to enable them to accept the foreign post. They work in government offices, not in United Nations compounds; the government can fire them; and the bulk of the housekeeping and backstopping machinery that characterizes other technical assistance programs becomes superfluous. The United States has made some analagous arrangements, primarily by financing contracts between American specialists and foreign governments.

To enable as many of the foreign technical advisers as possible to become creatures of a governmental agency in the host country, Everett Hagen has suggested the creation of a trust fund out of which the host government could employ specialists who would not then be reporting to anyone in the American embassy. This might be a useful transitional measure. Although the fund would have to consist primarily of convertible currencies, the transfer to it of some American holdings of inconvertible foreign currencies could help meet the local expenses of experts while at the same time allaying foreign fears concerning American holdings of other currencies. Nevertheless, I hope that more of the emerging countries will recognize that they can already afford technical assistance without much subsidy from abroad.

Improving the climate within which the experts function is less important than improving the content and relevance of their advice. One cannot escape the conclusion that man's present understanding of the economics, politics, sociology, and psychology of development is fragmentary and grossly inadequate. If broadening and deepening existing knowledge—knitting the scattered fragments into a meaningful

---

[1] Robert E. Asher and Associates, *The United Nations and Promotion of the General Welfare* (Brookings Institution, 1957), p. 1051.

whole—is important for the survival and well-being of the free world, how expand most rapidly the extent of such knowledge?

The problem of getting on with the research that is needed may be approached from several directions: (1) the establishment of functional and geographic requirements and priorities—in other words, the consolidation and ranking of research projects previously segregated in separate categories as rural problems, urban problems, educational problems, health problems, and so forth; (2) the development of organizational arrangements designed to give the necessary status, prestige, leadership, and sense of urgency to research intended to improve development programs and operations; (3) the mobilization of man power for a more concerted attack on priority problems; (4) the financing of research.

Priorities, of course, can never be absolute. The fact that virtually every underdeveloped country has enormous agricultural problems, that most of them have serious transportation difficulties, and that relatively few have coal-mining or tin-mining problems does not mean that agricultural research as a functional category deserves a blanket priority. The first X per cent of research in some other field is likely to be more important than the last Y per cent of the agricultural projects. The problem is "to see that within the limits of the private and the public purse, urgent needs in one direction do not go unfulfilled while less urgent needs in another direction are in fact being satisfied."[2] Moreover, the value of research depends as much on who does it as on the topic selected. The explorer possessed of a sufficiently probing and speculative mind may discover gold where others were positive there was only gravel. It is not necessary to belabor these points, but it may be useful to have them in the record.

It is also obvious that research needs and research priorities differ according to whether they are looked at globally, by regions, or by countries. In this volume, the tendency has been to look at them globally, with frequent bows to the desirability of localized case studies. There might be real advantage in trying to assess require-

[2] Walter E. Heller, "Social Priorities and Economic Cost." Address at Annual Meeting of National Planning Association, Washington, D.C., October 27, 1961. "The notion of priorities," he said earlier in the same address, "suggests a linear ordering of goals, as if we take care of one problem first, and then move on to a second, and then shift over to a third. But in reality we do not and should not proceed that way. Every dollar of government or private spending has many alternative uses. The basic principle of government and private budgeting is to distribute the limited resources so that the last unmet need in each area is of approximately equal urgency."

ments regionally—for Africa, for Asia, and for Latin America—as the next order of business.

Discussions of organizational arrangements for the conduct of research are tiresome to some, but peculiarly fascinating to a multitude of others. Whether tedious or titillating, they should not be dismissed as irrelevant. They do have some effect on substance. The possibilities include the establishment of totally new institutions, the strengthening of existing centers, and the building of firmer links among established centers, public and private.

President Kennedy in an address in May 1961 to the Canadian Parliament proposed that the Organization for Economic Cooperation and Development "establish a Development Center, where citizens and officials, and students and professional men of the Atlantic area and the less-developed world can meet to study in common the problems of economic development."[3] The creation of an adequately endowed National Center for Research on the Problems of Emerging Areas might similarly serve not only to dramatize the government's interest in such problems, but to advance significantly its understanding of those problems. The national center could be a cooperative venture among a number of universities, comparable to the Institute for Defense Analyses, or an entity on the model of the RAND Corporation. The national center might embrace a group of institutes. One can also envisage a series of independent institutes, each carrying on a research program of its own but on occasion joining with others in cooperative projects. With the encouragement of the United States Department of State and the British Foreign Office, for example, the Brookings Institution in Washington and the Overseas Development Institute in London are planning some joint studies of development problems.

Arthur Mosher has suggested the establishment of an independent Institute of Agricultural Development to promote, finance, and conduct agricultural research. If the proposal is feasible with respect to agriculture, it is probably feasible also with respect to health research. Could an Institute of Technological Research help redress the imbalance to which Richard Eckaus calls attention? He notes that the amount of technological research directed specifically toward the problems of underdeveloped countries is negligible by comparison with

[3] White House Press Release, May 17, 1961.

the amount devoted to improving the lead already enjoyed by the more highly industrialized countries.

Is the real problem the lack of properly oriented, adequately financed institutes like the RAND Corporation or the National Institutes of Health, or is it an absolute shortage of man power qualified to undertake the research that is needed? Does the institute arrangement increase the availability of man power by freeing trained personnel from teaching and administrative responsibilities and by attracting a supporting cast who learn by association with outstanding experts? Or is it just as likely to reduce the future supply of experts by separating some of our best teachers from fruitful, classroom contacts with a rising generation of potential specialists?

Instead of, or in addition to, launching new centers, it is surely desirable to strengthen existing centers. More and more of the leading universities in the United States and abroad have established centers for the study of African, Asian, Middle Eastern, or Latin American problems, or for the study of problems common to several of these areas. This raises the question of the need, if any, for closer links among such institutions, for links between such institutions and the federal government, and links between the research centers and research firms here at home with those abroad. The object would be to enable all centers to keep better informed about research conducted elsewhere, to advise them of the current requirements of policy makers, and to provide financial support for needed studies that particular centers are qualified to undertake but would not otherwise tackle.

I am unable to muster much enthusiasm for coordinating committees and grand panjandrums to guide specialists in doing what comes naturally. However, the 1961 Act for International Development authorizes the President to use appropriated funds for research designed to make development assistance "of increasing value and benefit."[4] A major staff office in the new Agency for International Development (successor to the International Cooperation Administration) is in charge of stimulating, contracting for, and conducting research. If greater public financing of studies in the field of international development is to be a feature of the 1960's, it is probably important that the government have the advice of a representative group of nongovernmental experts. A National Advisory Committee

[4] Public Law 87-195, Sec. 241.

on Developmental Research, with adequate representation from the social as well as the physical sciences, could build on the foundations already laid by the Development Assistance Panel of the President's Science Advisory Committee. It could keep abreast of what is going on, initiate periodic appraisals thereof, identify problems most in need of study, and advise the government on procedural as well as substantive matters.

Those in touch with universities and private consulting firms that operated under contracts with the International Cooperation Administration heard an unending, and at times unfair, series of complaints about the contract system. With the help of a National Advisory Committee on Developmental Research, the AID might become more flexible than the ICA, without in any way abdicating its responsibility for ensuring that public funds are spent only for legitimate public purposes.

Committees beget subcommittees, which beget working parties, which beget smaller subsidiaries, and so on—*ad infinitum*. It is easy to over-organize. Some may feel that, by and large, social scientists with training and ideas are not being starved for funds or facilities and are attracting promising new recruits to their respective fields in sufficient numbers. Adherents to this view may prefer the status quo, allowing the situation to evolve in its own decentralized, uncoordinated, groping way.

RESEARCH NEEDS

Whatever the auspices may be, further research—basic and applied—must be undertaken to provide new, much-needed insights into the development process. The proposals for new research included in the preceding essays vary in relevance, specificity, and urgency. It is clear to me that the placement of a question mark at the end of a sentence indicates that what has preceded the question mark is not a simple declaration of fact. It is by no means equally clear to me that the mere posing of a question proves that research is required, or is feasible, in order to answer the question. I recognize, though, that asking the right questions is a necessary first step in the identification of research needs. Most of the right questions have now been asked by the authors.

It is evident that one of the biggest voids is systematic analysis and evaluation of aid projects and aid experience accumulated during the postwar period. This immense reservoir of practical knowledge remains virtually untapped as yet and can be tapped only if the United States Government itself participates in a professional way in the research process. Much of the work must be done abroad, but the feedback of results to research centers here and in third countries should be systematized and expedited. Each author bemoans the absence of accessible information on why specific undertakings are believed to have succeeded or failed. Some ingenious proposals are put forward for clearinghouse services, for case studies, for handbooks, and for integrating research with operations.

Clearinghouse proposals are fundamentally schemes to establish the "pre-conditions" for better research. The term "clearinghouse" is as loosely used as the term "research," however, and consequently not always limited to the provision of what are essentially library services. The Colm-Geiger reiteration of a proposal for a clearinghouse on economic programing information, for example, suggests that such a center might also prepare estimates of probable world demand for the more important exports of underdeveloped countries—in other words, that it might also perform a recognized research function.

The maintenance of any clearinghouse is likely to be a time-consuming and costly venture, requiring considerable cross-classification of data if the clearinghouse is to be truly useful. Central information on the location of major irrigation projects can doubtless be readily assembled. More valuable, however, would be data on the experience of each project with specific techniques of dam and canal construction, rate structure for water charges, education of farmers in shifting to more intensive forms of agriculture, and data on the apparent short- and long-term economic, social, and political effects of the project. Concurrently with the accumulation of data on projects throughout the world, the relevant literature ought to be combed and cataloged. Here again, it may not be too hard for a staff to maintain files on articles, books, reports, and speeches dealing specifically with irrigation. The difficult job will be to catalog reference material from fields such as anthropology, education, training, and communications, which could be helpful to the planners of irrigation projects in foreign countries.

As factual data are gathered by clearinghouses, the preparation of handbooks of various kinds should become easier. This would still represent a humdrum level of research, however helpful the handbooks might be in facilitating choices among alternative building materials or farm implements or technologies and in reducing time lags between the discovery and the use of information.

The point at which sophistication and higher-level professional competence become essential is in the design and execution of studies that will shed some direct light on the process of development. Dozens of proposals for such studies are contained in this volume and a recapitulation at this point is hardly necessary. There is heavy emphasis on case studies of all kinds and on comparative analyses, because of widespread conviction on the part of experts that what passes now for theory is too often based on insufficient empirical evidence.

Further research is urgently needed on the processes of individual and cultural change that are preconditions for rapid growth; on the common and the unique factors—political, economic, sociological—of the nations and regions in which development programs are being pursued; on the organization, procedures, and techniques by which foreign aid programs can be made most effective; on the kinds of people who are best qualified to carry out such programs, the methods of identifying them, and the training and orientation they require; on the ways in which scientific and technical knowledge can be adapted to the special needs of many differently endowed countries; and on the methods of measuring and evaluating results achieved.[5]

The accumulation of studies in depth, from which more valid generalizations about economic, social, and political development can be made, is an obvious necessity. It is encouraging to note that the importance of such research is recognized in the 1961 Act for International Development. However, it will be dangerous to oversell research as a way out of present dilemmas. The promotion of orderly change in a disorderly world will long remain as much an art as a science. The development process is incredibly complex and one cannot hope to close in short order the more serious gaps in understanding. Meanwhile, operations must continue—indeed, must be stepped up—with improvements introduced as rapidly as the state of knowledge and the skill of practitioners permit.

[5] In this paragraph, I have borrowed liberally from an unpublished memorandum written in May 1960 by John H. Ohly of the International Cooperation Administration.

Appendix

Conference on Research for the Improvement of Development Assistance Programs and Operations[1]

Charles Abrams
Massachusetts Institute of Technology

Gerald Alter
International Bank for Reconstruction and Development

C. Arnold Anderson
University of Chicago

Robert E. Asher
Brookings Institution

Vincent M. Barnett, Jr.
Williams College

Jack N. Behrman
Department of Commerce

Harold Betz
Pan-American Union

Karl F. Bode
International Cooperation Administration

Mary Jean Bowman
University of Chicago

Karl Brandt
Food Research Institute

Gerald Breese
Princeton University

Robert D. Calkins
Brookings Institution

Gerhard Colm
National Planning Association

Emile Despres
Williams College

Eleanor Dulles
Department of State

John T. Dunlop
Harvard University

Richard Eckaus
Brandeis University and Massachusetts Institute of Technology

Edward Fei
University of Wisconsin

Isaiah Frank
Department of State

Theodore Geiger
National Planning Association

Norton S. Ginsburg
University of Chicago

Richard Goode
Brookings Institution

Stanley Gordon
Ford Foundation

James P. Grant
International Cooperation Administration

Everett E. Hagen
Massachusetts Institute of Technology

Harold W. Hannah
University of Illinois

H. Field Haviland, Jr.
Brookings Institution

Samuel P. Hayes
University of Michigan

Albert O. Hirschman
Columbia University

Edward Hollander
Robert R. Nathan Associates

[1] Held at the Brookings Institution, Washington, D.C., May 25-27, 1961.

227

John B. Howard
Ford Foundation

Richard A. Humphrey
American Council on Education

Edward L. Keenan
Office of Civil and Defense
  Mobilization

Eric E. Lampard
University of Wisconsin

John P. Lewis
University of Indiana

Erven Long
International Cooperation
  Administration

James S. Maddox
North Carolina State College

Edward S. Mason
Harvard University

Karl Mathiasen, II
International Cooperation
  Administration

David Mayer
International Cooperation
  Administration

Walsh McDermott
Cornell University

George C. McGhee
Department of State

Raymond Mikesell
University of Oregon

Louis Miniclier
International Cooperation
  Administration

James M. Mitchell
Brookings Institution

Frederick T. Moore
RAND Corporation

Arthur T. Mosher
Council on Economic and Cultural
  Affairs

Robert Oliver
California Institute of Technology

Wilfred Owen
Brookings Institution

Nathan Pelcovits
Department of State

Harvey Perloff
Resources for the Future

Lucian Pye
Massachusetts Institute of
  Technology

James Quillen
Stanford University

Gustav Ranis
Yale University

Ralph Ruffner
International Cooperation
  Administration

Ruth B. Russell
Brookings Institution

Walter S. Salant
Rockefeller Foundation

Theodore W. Schultz
University of Chicago

Charles Shohan
Export-Import Bank

Eugene Skolnikoff
The White House

Joseph E. Slater
Department of State

Eugene Staley
Stanford Research Institute

Donald C. Stone
University of Pittsburgh

Irving Swerdlow
Syracuse University

Robert Thomas
Department of Labor

Kenneth W. Thompson
Rockefeller Foundation

Clarence Thurber
Ford Foundation

Raymond Vernon
Harvard University

Champion Ward
Ford Foundation

Ralph J. Watkins
Brookings Institution

Fletcher Wellemeyer
Consultant on Manpower Relations

Howard Wriggins
Library of Congress

Index

Abramowitz, M., 121

Act for International Development (1961), 223, 226

Administrative Sciences, International Institute of, 62n

Advertising program, effect on agricultural development, pilot project suggested, 104

Afghanistan, 2t

Africa:
  Correlation between political structure and economic development in countries of, 3, 6; table, 2
  Disintegration of colonial order in, effect on U.S. policy, 181
  Problems of rural development in, need for research, 108

Agency for International Development (AID), vi, 223, 224. *See also* International Cooperation Administration

Agricultural development (*see also* Rural problems):
  Africa, problems of, need for research, 108, 222
  Attitudes, values: importance of change in, 76; need for research on effect of, 96, 100-101
  Capital, role in, 82-84
  Circulating library in each country, need for, 112
  Community development, need for research, 89-95
  Culture, American, relevance to, need for research, 100-102
  Culture, national, impact on, need for research, 95-102
  Education, role in, need for research, 84-86, 91, 174, 179
  Experiment stations, need for, 107
  Extension. *See* Extension
  Factors triggering, need for research, 99-100
  Handbooks summarizing present knowledge, need for, 112, 225
  Importance of, 74
  Increases in production, role of extension and community development, and incentives for, need for research, 91, 99
  Legal, commercial, and social institutions involved in, need for research, 86-88
  Model farms for demonstration of techniques, 149
  Pilot projects in, suggestions for, 102-07, 116; table, 119

Political, economic, and legal framework for, 76

Public investment in, need for research, 89

Relationship of rural welfare to, 77-78

Requirements for, 75-77

Research in agriculture: extent of, 136; institutional arrangements for, and role of technical adviser, need for research, 87, 110-11

Roads, role and value of, need for research, 89

Services, facilities, and programs facilitating, listed, 75

Technological information, need for compilation, 141

Theories on, need for consolidated review, 113

Variations in rate of, 72-73

Agricultural Development, Institute of, proposed, 116, 222

Agricultural experiment stations, need for, 107

Agricultural production. *See* Agricultural development

Agriculture in low income regions, description of, 73-74

Aid, foreign. *See* Agricultural development; Development planning; Developmental assistance; Economic development; Education; Military assistance; Political development; Technological change

Åkerman, Johan, 156

Alliance for Progress, 45

Almond, G. A., 3n, 211-12

Anderson, C. Arnold, chapter on role of education in development, 153-80, 218-19

Angola, 28

Anthropologists, importance of consulting, 148-49

Argentina, 4t, 72

Ashby, A. W., 89

Asher, Robert E., summary chapter, 215-26

Asia:
  Disintegration of colonial order in, effect on U.S. policy, 181
  Governments in, relation of rural people to, 97
  Relation between political structure and economic development in countries of, 3, 6-8; table, 2

Aukrust, O., 156

Grants, Loans, and Local Currencies
Their Role in Foreign Aid

Robert E. Asher

This study is an attempt to explain the arrangements that have been used and can be used to finance American foreign aid. It traces the development of United States policy on foreign assistance since World War II—including the amount and kinds of aid given—and it proposes new procedures for evaluating the needs of emerging countries for "hard" loans, "soft" loans, and grants. A chapter analyzes the effects of the aid program on the United States balance of payments, on the balance of payments of the countries receiving aid, and on other countries. The objective is to clarify the issues for the citizen and the policy maker.

PAPER $1.50   CLOTH $2.50

The Foreign Leader Program
Operations in the United States

Robert E. Elder

What has this State Department program accomplished in its 13 years of operation? What changes in its procedures would enable it to accomplish more with its present appropriations? What might it accomplish if given larger appropriations for more reception centers in various regions, more staff, larger per diem for the foreign visitors?

This study, made in 1960 at the request of the Department of State, examines in considerable detail the procedures of selection of leaders to be invited, orientation abroad and in this country, the programming of tours, local sponsors and community participation, and other factors. It finds much to praise, but makes many specific suggestions for improvements in procedures. The program is currently bringing more than 900 foreign leaders to the United States annually.

PAPER $2.00

THE BROOKINGS INSTITUTION   WASHINGTON